SIBERIAN EDUCATION

'A compelling odyssey of revenge in an indelibly vivid memoir that has the certain trajectory of a bullet.' *Metro*

'[The] narrative is refreshingly devoid of the egotism and posturing of most gangster memoirs, and is replete with a genuine desire to find a higher truth . . . a delight to read.' *Guardian*

'Lilin is the last heir in a dynasty of criminals. His book is an autobiography which reads like a novel.' *GQ*

'Portrays an extreme kind of childhood where quarrels between children are settled with knives.' *Rolling Stone*

'Set to make the Anglophone world go "Woooah-Jesus-that-is-some-of-the-most-savagely-rugged-shit-that's-ever-gone-in-our-namby-pamby-eyeballs". . . an education, truly.' *Dazed and Confused*

'Astonishing . . . *Siberian Education* is terrifying. There are incidents and episodes which simply aren't quotable, not without serious disclaimers and some risk to stomach contents.' *Sunday Herald*

'*Siberian Education* paints a memorable world of anarchism, devotion, humor and respect. It is not one in which any sane-minded person would choose to live; but it is one that we could learn from.' *Wall Street Journal*

Nicolai Lilin was born in 1981 and grew up in the small republic of Transnistria, which declared its independence in 1990 but has never been recognised. Nicolai left home to fight in the Russian army against the Chechens. He later lived in Ireland, before moving to Italy, where he continues to work as a tattooist in Turin.

SIBERIAN
EDUCATION
NICOLAI LILIN

TRANSLATED FROM THE ITALIAN BY JONATHAN HUNT

CANONGATE
Edinburgh · London · New York · Melbourne

This paperback edition published by Canongate Books in 2011

1

Copyright © Nicolai Lilin, 2009
Translation copyright © Jonathan Hunt, 2010

The moral right of the author has been asserted

First published in Italy in 2009 as *Educazione siberiana* by
Giulio Einaudi editore s.p.a., Torino

First published in Great Britain in 2010 by Canongate Books Ltd,
14 High Street, Edinburgh EH1 1TE

www.canongate.tv

All the illustrations that accompany the text are details from original
tattoos executed by the author.

British Library Cataloguing-in-Publication Data
A catalogue record for this book is available on
request from the British Library

ISBN 978 1 84767 933 8

Typeset in Sabon by Cluny Sheeler, Edinburgh

Printed and bound in Great Britain by Clays Ltd, St Ives plc

SIBERIAN EDUCATION

'Some enjoy life, some suffer it; we fight it.'
Old saying of the Siberian Urkas

I know it shouldn't be done, but I'm tempted to start from the end.

For example, from the day we ran through the rooms of a ruined building, firing at the enemy from such close range we could almost touch them with our hands.

We were exhausted. The paratroopers worked in shifts, but we saboteurs hadn't slept for three days. We went on like the waves of the sea, so as not to give the enemy the chance to rest, carry out manoeuvres or organize their defences. We were always fighting, always.

That day I ended up on the top floor of the building with Shoe, trying to eliminate the last heavy machinegun. We threw two hand grenades.

In the dust that was falling from the roof we couldn't see a thing, and we found ourselves face to face with four enemies who like us were wandering like blind kittens through the grey, dirty cloud, which reeked of debris and burnt explosive.

I had never shot anyone at such close quarters in all my time in Chechnya.

Meanwhile, on the first floor our Captain had taken a prisoner and killed eight enemies, all by himself.

When I came out with Shoe I was completely dazed. Captain Nosov was asking Moscow to keep an eye on the Arab prisoner, while he, Ladle and Zenith went to check out the cellar.

I sat on the stairs next to Moscow, opposite the frightened prisoner, who kept trying to communicate something. Moscow wasn't listening to him, he was sleepy and tired, as we all were. As soon as the Captain turned his back, Moscow pulled out his pistol – an Austrian Glock, one of his trophies – and, with an arrogant leer, shot the prisoner in the head and chest.

The Captain turned round, and looked at him pityingly without saying a word.

Moscow closed his eyes as he sat down beside the dead man, overcome with exhaustion.

Looking at all of us as if he were meeting us for the first time, the Captain said:

'This is too much. Everyone into the cars! We're going for a rest, behind the lines.'

One after another, like zombies, we trooped off towards our vehicles. My head was so heavy I was sure that if I stopped it would explode.

We went back behind the lines, into the area controlled and defended by our infantry. We fell asleep instantly; I didn't even have time to take off my jacket and ammunition belt before I fell into the darkness, like a dead man.

Soon afterwards Moscow woke me by hammering the butt of his Kalashnikov on my jacket, at chest level. Slowly and reluctantly I opened my eyes and looked around; I struggled to remember where I was. I couldn't get things into focus.

Moscow's face looked tired; he was chewing a piece of bread. Outside it was dark; it was impossible to tell what time it was. I looked at my watch but couldn't see the digits; everything was hazy.

'What's happening? How long have we slept?' I asked Moscow in a weary voice.

'We haven't slept at all, brother . . . And I think we're going to have to stay awake quite a while longer.'

I clasped my face between my hands, trying to muster the strength to stand up and arrange my thoughts. I needed to sleep, I was exhausted. My trousers were dirty and wet, my jacket smelled of sweat and fresh earth. I was worn out.

Moscow went to wake the others:

'Come on, lads, we're leaving immediately . . . We're needed.'

They were all in despair; they didn't want to get up. But, grumbling and cursing, they struggled to their feet.

Captain Nosov was pacing around with the handset to his ear, and an infantryman was following him around like a pet dog, with the field radio in his rucksack. The Captain was angry; he kept repeating to somebody or other, over the radio, that it was the first break we'd taken in three days, and that we were at the end of our tether. It was all in vain, because eventually Nosov said, in a clipped tone:

'Yes, Comrade Colonel! Confirmed! Order received!'

They were sending us back to the front line.

I didn't even want to think about it.

I went over to a metal tank full of water. I dipped my hands into it: the water was very cool; it made me shiver slightly. I put my whole head into the drum, right under the water, and kept it there for a while, holding my breath.

I opened my eyes inside the tank and saw complete darkness. Alarmed, I jerked my head out, gasping for air.

The darkness I'd seen in the tank had shocked me. Death might be just like that, I thought: dark and airless.

I leaned over the tank and watched, shimmering on the water, the reflection of my face, and of my life up to that moment.

cried, expressing her milk with a breast pump to take to me in the incubator. It can't have been a happy time for her.

From my birth onwards, perhaps out of habit, I continued to be a source of worry and distress to my parents (or rather to my mother, because my father didn't really care about anything: he went on with his life as a criminal, robbing banks and spending a lot of time in prison). I've lost count of the number of scrapes I got into when I was small. But it was natural: I grew up in a rough district – the place where the criminals expelled from Siberia were re-settled in the 1930s. My life was there, in Bender, with the criminals, and the people of our villainous district were like one big family.

When I was small I didn't care about toys. What I liked doing when I was four or five was prowling round the house to see if my grandfather or my uncle were taking their weapons apart to clean them. They were constantly doing it, with the utmost care and devotion. My uncle used to say weapons were like women – if you didn't caress them enough they'd grow stiff and betray you.

The weapons in our house, as in all Siberian houses, were kept in particular places. The so-called 'personal' guns – the ones Siberian criminals carry around with them and use every day – are placed in the 'red corner', where the family icons hang on the walls, along with the photographs of relatives who have died or are serving prison sentences. Below the icons and the photographs there is a shelf, draped with a piece of red cloth, on which there are usually about a dozen Siberian crucifixes. Whenever a criminal enters the house he goes straight to the red corner, pulls out his gun and puts it on the shelf, then crosses himself and places a crucifix over the gun. This is an ancient tradition which ensures that weapons are never used in a Siberian house: if they were, the house could never be lived in again. The crucifix acts as a kind of seal, which can only be removed when the criminal leaves the house.

The personal guns, which are called 'lovers', 'aunts', 'trunks' or 'ropes', don't usually have any deeper meaning; they are seen as just weapons, nothing more. They are not cult objects, in the way that the 'pike', the traditional knife, is. The gun is simply a tool of the trade.

In addition to personal guns, there are other kinds of weapon that are kept around the house. The weapons of Siberian criminals fall into two broad categories: 'honest' ones and 'sinful' ones. The 'honest' weapons are those that are used only for hunting in the woods. According to Siberian morality, hunting is a purification ritual, which enables a person to return to the state of primal innocence in which God created man. Siberians never hunt for pleasure, but only to satisfy their hunger, and only when they go into the dense woods of their homeland, the Tayga. Never in places where food can be obtained without killing wild animals. If they are out in the woods for a week the Siberians will usually kill only one boar; for the rest of the time they just walk. In hunting there is no place for self-interest, only for survival. This doctrine influences the entire Siberian criminal law, forming a moral basis which prescribes humility and simplicity in the actions of each individual criminal, and respect for the freedom of every living thing.

The 'honest' weapons used for hunting are kept in a special area of the house, called the 'altar', along with the decorated hunting belts of the masters of the house and their forefathers. There are always hunting knives hanging from the belts, and bags containing various talismans and objects of pagan magic.

The 'sinful' weapons are those that are used for criminal purposes. These weapons are usually kept in the cellar and in various hiding places scattered around the yard. Every sinful weapon is engraved with the image of a cross or a patron saint, and has been 'baptized' in a Siberian church.

Kalashnikov assault rifles are the Siberians' favourites. In criminal slang each model has a name; no one uses abbreviations or numbers to indicate the model and calibre or the type of ammunition it requires. For example, the old 7.62 mm AK-47 is called a 'saw', and its ammunition 'heads'. The more recent 5.45 mm AKS with the folding butt is called a 'telescope', and its ammunition 'chips'. There are also names for the different types of cartridge: the bottom-heavy ones with black tips are called 'fat ones'; the armour-piercing ones with white tips, 'nails'; the explosive ones with red and white tips, 'sparks'.

The same goes for the other weapons: precision rifles are called 'fishing rods', or 'scythes'. If they have a built-in silencer on the barrel, they are called 'whips'. Silencers are called 'boots', 'terminals' or 'woodcocks'.

According to tradition, an honest weapon and a

sinful one cannot remain in the same room, otherwise the honest weapon is forever contaminated, and can never be used again, because its use would bring bad luck on the whole family. In this case the gun must be eliminated with a special ritual. It is buried in the ground, wrapped in a sheet on which a mother has given birth. According to Siberian beliefs, everything connected with childbirth is charged with positive energy, because every newborn child is pure and does not know sin. So the powers of purity are a kind of seal against misfortune. On the spot where a contaminated weapon has been buried it is usual to plant a tree, so that if the 'curse' strikes, it will destroy the tree and not spread to anything else.

In my parents' house there were weapons everywhere; my grandfather had a whole room full of honest weapons: rifles of various calibres and makes, numerous knives and various kinds of ammunition. I could only go into that room if I was accompanied by an adult, and when I did I tried to stay there as long as possible. I would hold the weapons, study their details, ask hundreds of questions, until they would stop me, saying:

'That's enough questions! Just wait a while. When you grow up you'll be able to try them out for yourself . . .'

Needless to say, I couldn't wait to grow up.

I would watch spellbound as my grandfather and my uncle handled the weapons, and when I touched them they seemed to me like living creatures.

Grandfather would often call me and sit me down in front of him; then he would lay on the table an old Tokarev – a handsome, powerful pistol, which seemed to me more fascinating than all the weapons in existence.

'Well? Do you see this?' he would say. 'This is no ordinary gun. It's magic. If a cop comes near, it'll shoot him of its own accord, without you pulling the trigger . . .'

I really believed in the powers of that pistol, and once, when the police arrived at our house to carry out a raid, I did a very stupid thing.

That day my father had returned from a long stay in central Russia, where he had robbed a number of security vans. After supper, to which my whole family and a few close friends had come, the men were sitting at the table, talking and discussing various criminal matters, and the women were in the kitchen, washing the dishes, singing Siberian songs and laughing together as they swapped stories from the past. I was sitting next to my grandfather on the bench, with a cup of hot tea in my hand, listening to what the grown-ups were saying. Unlike other communities, the Siberians respect children, and will talk freely about any subject in front of them, without creating an air of mystery or prohibition.

Suddenly I heard the women screaming, and then a lot of angry voices: within seconds the house was full of armed police, their faces covered, pointing Kalashnikovs at us. One of them came over to my grandfather, pushed the rifle in his face and shouted furiously, the tension in his voice unmistakable:

'What are you looking at, you old fool? I told you to keep your eyes on the floor!'

I wasn't in the least scared. None of those men frightened me – the fact of being with my whole family made me feel stronger. But the tone in which the man had addressed my grandfather had angered me. After a short pause, my grandfather, not looking the policeman in the eye but holding his head erect, called out to my grandmother:

'Svetlana! Svetlana! Come in here, darling! I want you to pass on a few words to this scum!'

According to the rules of criminal behaviour, Siberian men cannot communicate with policemen. It is forbidden to address them, answer their questions or establish any relationship with them. The criminal must behave as if the police were not there, and use the mediation of a female relative, or friend of the family, provided she is of Siberian origin. The criminal tells the woman what he wants to say to the policeman in the criminal language, and she repeats his words in Russian, even though the policeman can hear what he says perfectly well, since he is standing there in front of him. Then, when the policeman replies, the woman turns round and translates his words into the criminal language. The criminal must not look the policeman in the face, and if he refers to him in the course of his speech he must use derogatory words like 'filth', 'dog', 'rabbit', 'rat', 'bastard', 'abortion', etc.

That evening the oldest person in the room was my grandfather, so according to the rules of criminal behaviour the right to communicate was his; the others had to keep silent, and if they wanted to say anything they would have to ask his permission. My grandfather was well known for his skill in dealing with tense situations.

My grandmother came in from the kitchen, with a coloured duster in her hand. She was followed by my mother, who was looking extremely worried.

'My dear wife – God bless you – please tell this piece of filth that for as long as I'm alive no one is going to point weapons at my face or those of my friends in my house . . . Ask him what he wants, and tell him to order his men to lower their guns for the love of Christ before somebody gets hurt.'

My grandmother started repeating what my grandfather had said to the policeman, and although the man nodded to indicate that he had heard every word, she went on, following the tradition through to the end. There was something false, something theatrical about all this, but it was a scene that had to be acted out; it was a question of criminal dignity.

'Everyone on the floor, face down. We have a warrant for the arrest of . . .' The policeman didn't manage to finish his sentence, because my grandfather, with a broad and slightly malicious smile – which in fact was the way he always smiled – interrupted him, addressing my grandmother:

'By the passion of Our Lord Jesus Christ, who died and rose again for us sinners! Svetlana, my love, ask this stupid cop if she and her friends are from Japan.'

My grandfather was humiliating the police by speaking about them as if they were women. All the other criminals laughed. Meanwhile my grandfather went on:

'They don't look Japanese to me, so they can't be kamikazes . . . Why, then, do they come armed into the heart of Low River, into the home of an honest criminal, while he is sharing a few moments of happiness with other good people?'

My grandfather's speech was turning into what the criminals call 'song' – that extreme form of communication with policemen where a criminal speaks as if he were thinking out loud, talking to himself. He was merely expressing his own thoughts, not deigning to answer questions or establish any contact. That is the normal procedure when someone wants to indicate to policemen that what he is saying is the only truth, that there is no room for doubt.

'Why do I see all these dishonest people with covered faces? Why do they come here to dishonour my home and the good faith of my family and my guests? Here, in our land of simple, humble people, servants of Our Lord and of the Siberian Orthodox Mother Church, why do these gobs of Satan's spit come to afflict the hearts of our beloved women and our dear children?'

In the meantime another policeman had dashed into the room and addressed his superior:

'Comrade Captain, allow me to speak!'

'Go ahead,' replied a small, stocky man, in a voice that seemed to come from beyond the grave. His rifle was aimed at the back of my father's head. My father, with a sardonic smile, went on sipping his tea and crunching my mother's home-made walnut biscuits.

'There are crowds of armed men outside. They've blocked off all the roads and have taken hostage the patrol that was guarding the vehicles!'

Silence fell in the room – a long, heavy silence. Only two sounds could be heard: the crunch of my father's teeth on the biscuits and the wheezing of Uncle Vitaly's lungs.

I looked at the eyes of a policeman who was standing next to me; through the holes in his hood I could see he was sweaty and pale. His face reminded me of that of a corpse I had seen a few months earlier, after it had been fished out of the river by my friends: its skin was all white with black veins, its eyes like two deep, murky pits. There had also been a hole in the dead man's forehead where he had been shot. Well, this policeman didn't have a hole in his head, but I reckon both he and I were thinking exactly the same thing: that before very long he was going to have one.

Suddenly the front door opened and, pushing aside the policeman who had just delivered his chilling report, six armed men, friends of my father and my grandfather, entered the room, one after the other. The first was Uncle Plank, who was also the Guardian of our area; the others were his closest associates. My grandfather, completely ignoring the presence of the policemen, got to his feet and went over to Plank.

'By Holy Christ and all His blessed family!' said Plank, embracing my grandfather and shaking his hand warmly. 'Grandfather Boris, thank heaven no one has been hurt!'

'What is the world coming to, Plank? It seems we can't even sit quietly in our own homes!'

Plank started speaking to my grandfather as if he were summarizing what had happened, but his words were intended for the ears of the policemen:

'There's no need to despair, Grandfather Boris! We're all here with you, as we always are in times of happiness and trouble . . . As you know, my dear friend, nobody can enter or leave our houses without our permission, especially if he has dishonest intentions . . .'

Plank went over to the table and embraced all the criminals, one by one. As he did so he kissed them on the cheeks and gave the typical Siberian greeting:

'Peace and health to all brothers and honest men!'

They gave the reply that is prescribed by tradition:

'Death and damnation to all cops and informers!'

The policemen could only stand and watch this moving ceremony. By now their rifles were drooping as low as their heads.

Plank's assistants, communicating through the women present, told the policemen to get out.

'Now I hope all the cops present will leave this house and never come back again. We're holding their friends, whom we captured earlier; but once they're out of the district we'll let them leave in peace . . .' Plank spoke in a calm, quiet voice, and if it hadn't been for the content of his words, from his tone you might have thought he was telling a gentle, soothing story, like a fairy tale for children before they went to sleep.

Our friends formed a corridor with their bodies, along which the policemen began to file, one by one, hanging their heads.

I was elated; I wanted to dance, shout, sing and express some great emotion that I couldn't yet understand. I felt I was part of, belonged to, a strong world, and it seemed as if all the strength of that world was inside me.

I don't know how or why, but suddenly I jumped down from the bench and rushed into the main room, where the red corner was. On the shelf, lying on a red handkerchief with golden embroidery, were the guns of my father, my uncle, my grandfather and our guests. Without thinking, I picked up my grandfather's magical Tokarev and ran back to the policemen, pointing it at them. I don't know what was going through my head at that moment; all I felt was a kind of euphoria. The policemen were walking slowly towards the door. I stopped in front of one of them and stared at him: his eyes were tired and seemed bloodshot; his expression was sad and desolate. I remember for a moment feeling as if all his hatred was concentrated on me. I aimed at his face; I tried as hard as I could to pull the trigger, but couldn't move it a millimetre. My hand grew heavier and heavier and I couldn't hold the pistol up high enough. My father burst out laughing, and called out to me:

'Come here at once, you young rascal! It's forbidden to shoot in the house, don't you know that?'

The policemen left, and a group of criminals followed them, escorting them to the boundary of the district; and then, when the escort came back, the second car, containing the policemen who were being held hostage, started off towards the town. But it was preceded by a car belonging to Plank's friends, who drove slowly to prevent the policemen from speeding up, so that the locals could insult them at their leisure, accompanying them out of the district in a kind of victory ceremony. Before they started off, someone had tied a washing line onto the back of their car with various things hanging on it: underpants, bras, small towels, dishcloths, and even one of my T-shirts, my father's contribution to the work of denigration. Scores of people had come out of the houses to watch the sight of this washing line snaking its way along. The children ran along behind the car, trying to hit it with stones.

'Look at those thieving cops! They come to Low River to steal our underpants!' shouted one of the crowd, accompanying his comments with whistles and insults.

'What do they want with them? The top officials in the government must have stopped giving their dogs a bone. They haven't *got* any underpants!'

'Where's the harm, brothers, in being poor and not being able to afford a pair of underpants? If they come to us with honesty and like real men, with their faces uncovered, we'll give every one of them a nice pair of Siberian underpants!'

Grandfather Chestnut had even brought an accordion from his house, and he played and sang as he walked along behind the car. Some women started dancing, as he bellowed an old Siberian song at the top of his voice, raising his head, adorned by a traditional eight-triangled hat,[1] and closing his eyes like a blind man:

Speak to me, sister Lena, and you too, brother Amur![2]
I've travelled the length and breadth of my land,
Robbing trains and making my rifle sing.
Only the old Tayga knows how many cops I've killed!

---

1. For a description of this hat, see later in this chapter, p.43.
2. Lena and Amur are the names of two great Siberian rivers. Traditionally, criminal fortune is linked to these rivers: they are worshipped as deities, to whom you make offerings and whom you can ask for help in the course of your criminal activities. They are mentioned in many sayings, fairy tales, songs and poems. Of a fortunate criminal it is said that 'his destiny is borne on the current of Lena'.

And now that I'm in trouble, help me Jesus Christ,
Help me hold my gun!
Now that the cops are everywhere, Mother Siberia,
Mother Siberia, save my life!

I too ran along and sang, constantly pushing up the peak
of my own eight-triangled hat, which was too big for me
and kept slipping down over my eyes.

Next day, however, all my desire to sing melted away when
my father gave me a good beating with his heavy hand. I
had violated three sacred rules: I had picked up a weapon
without the permission of an adult; I had taken it from the
red corner, removing the cross that my grandfather had
laid on top of it (only the person who puts the cross on top
of a weapon can remove it); and lastly, I had tried to fire
it in the house.

After that spanking from my father, my bottom
and back were very sore, so, as always, I went to my
grandfather for consolation. My grandfather looked
serious, but the faint smile that flitted across his face told
me that my problems, perhaps, weren't quite as bad as
they seemed. He gave me a long lecture, the gist of which
was that I had done something very silly. And when I
asked him why the magic gun hadn't shot the policemen
of its own accord, he told me that the magic only worked
when the gun was used for an intelligent purpose, and
with permission. At this point I began to suspect that
my grandfather might not be telling me the whole truth,

because I wasn't convinced by this idea of a magic that only worked with adults' permission . . .

From that time on I stopped thinking about magic and started watching more closely the movements of my uncle's and my father's hands when they used their guns, and soon discovered the function of the safety catch.

In the Siberian community you learn to kill when you're very small. Our philosophy of life has a close relation to death; children are taught that taking someone else's life or dying are perfectly acceptable things, if there is a good reason. Teaching people how to die is impossible, because once you've died there is no coming back. But teaching people to live with the threat of death, to 'tempt' fate, is not difficult. Many Siberian fairy tales tell of the deadly clash between criminals and representatives of the government, of the risks people run every day with dignity and honesty, of the good fortune of those who in the end have got the loot and stayed alive, and of the 'good memory' that is preserved of those who have died without abandoning their friends in need. Through these fairy tales, the children perceive the values that give meaning to the Siberian criminals' lives: respect, courage, friendship, loyalty. By the time they are five or six, Siberian children show a determination and a seriousness that are enviable even to adults of other communities. It is on such solid foundations that the education to kill, to take physical action against another living being, is built.

THE EIGHT-TRIANGLED HAT AND THE FLICK-KNIFE

In Transnistria February is the coldest month of the year. The wind blows hard, the air becomes keen and stings your face. On the street people wrap themselves up like mummies; the children look like plump little dolls, bundled up in countless layers of clothes, with scarves up to their eyes.

It usually snows a lot; the days are short and darkness descends very early.

That was the month when I was born. Early, coming out feet first; I was so weak that in ancient Sparta I would undoubtedly have been left to die because of my physical condition. Instead they put me in an incubator.

A kindly nurse told my mother she would have to get used to the idea that I wouldn't live long. My mother

From a very early age children are shown by their fathers how animals are killed in the yard: chickens, geese and pigs. In this way the child grows accustomed to blood, to the *details* of killing. Later, at the age of six or seven, the child is given the chance to kill a small animal himself. In this educative process there is no place for wrong emotions, such as sadism or cowardice. The child must be trained to have a full awareness of his own actions, and above all of the reasons and the profound meanings that lie behind those actions.

When a larger animal, such as a pig, an ox or a cow, is killed, the child is often allowed to practise on the carcass, so that he learns the right way to strike with a knife. My father often used to take my brother and me to a big butcher's shop, and teach us how to handle the knife, using the bodies of the pigs that hung from the hooks. A hand soon becomes decisive and expert, with so much practice.

When he is about ten, the child is a full member of the clan of the youths, which actively cooperates with the criminals of the Siberian community. There he has the chance to face many different situations of the criminal life for the first time. The older kids teach the younger ones how to behave and through the fights and quarrels and the handling of relations with the youths of other communities, each boy is broken in.

By the age of thirteen or fourteen, Siberian boys often have a criminal record, and therefore some experience of juvenile prison. This experience is seen as important, indeed fundamental, to the formation of the individual's character and view of the world. By that age many

Siberians already have some black marketeering and one murder, or at least attempted murder, to their name. And they all know how to communicate within the criminal community, how to follow, hand down and safeguard the founding principles of Siberian criminal law.

One day my father called me into the garden:

'Come here, young rascal! And bring a knife with you!'

I picked up a kitchen knife, the one I generally used to kill geese and chickens, and ran out into the garden. My father, his friend, Uncle Aleksandr, known to everyone as 'Bone', and my Uncle Vitaly were sitting under a big old walnut tree. They were talking about pigeons, the passion of every Siberian criminal. Uncle Vitaly was holding a pigeon in his hands; he had opened its wing and was showing it to my father and Bone, explaining something.

'Nikolay, son, go and kill a chicken and take it to your mother. Tell her to clean it and make some soup for this evening, because Uncle Bone is going stay here for a chat.'

A 'chat' involves the males of the family sitting together drinking and eating all night long to the point of exhaustion, till they collapse in a heap, one after another. When the males are having a chat, no one disturbs them; everyone goes about their own business, pretending the meeting doesn't exist.

I dashed to the chicken run at the end of the garden and grabbed the first chicken I could find. It was a normal

chicken, reddish in colour, fairly plump and perfectly
calm. Holding it in both hands, I walked over to a nearby
stump of wood, which we used for cutting off the heads
of chickens like this one. It didn't try to escape and didn't
seem concerned; it just looked around as if it were being
taken on a guided tour. I grasped it around the neck and
placed it on the stump, but when I raised the knife in the
air to deliver the fatal blow, it started wriggling violently,
until it managed to free itself from my hold, and give me
a sharp peck on the head. I lost my balance and fell on
my backside: I'd been defeated by a chicken. Looking up,
I saw that my father and the others were watching the
show. Uncle Vitaly was laughing, and Bone had a smile on
his face too; but my father was more serious than ever –
he had got to his feet and was coming towards me.

    'Pick yourself up, killer! Give me that knife and I'll
show you how it's done!' He walked towards the chicken,
which in the meantime had started scratching a hole in
the ground a few metres away. Once he was close to the
chicken, my father arched his body, like a tiger poised to
spring on its prey; the chicken was quite calm, and went
on scratching at the earth for reasons known only to
itself. Suddenly my father made a quick grab at it, but the
chicken repeated its earlier action, and with a lightning-
fast movement eluded my father's grasp and pecked him
in the face, just under the eye.

    'Damn it! He got me in the eye!' shouted my father,
and my uncle and Bone got up from the bench under the
walnut tree and ran towards him. But first Uncle Vitaly
put the pigeon back in its cage, and then hung the cage up
a few metres off the ground, to keep it away from our cat,

Murka, which loved killing pigeons, and always stayed near Uncle Vitaly, since he messed about with them all day long.

The men started making lunges at the chicken, which remained perfectly calm and deftly succeeded in dodging them every time. After a quarter of an hour of fruitless attempts the three men were out of breath and looked at the chicken, which went on scratching the earth and going about its chickenish business with the same determination as before. My father smiled at me, and said:

'Let's let it live, this chicken. We'll never kill it; it can stay here, in the garden, free to do as it pleases.'

That evening I told my grandfather what had happened. He had a good laugh, then asked me if I agreed with my father's decision. I answered him with a question:

'Why free that chicken and not all the others?'

Grandfather looked at me with a smile and said:

'Only someone who really appreciates life and freedom, and fights to the end, deserves to live in freedom . . . Even if he's only a chicken.'

I thought about this for a while and then asked him:

'What if all chickens become like him one day?'

After a long pause grandfather said:

'Then we'll have to get used to supper without chicken soup . . .'

The concept of freedom is sacred for the Siberians.

When I was six my Uncle Vitaly took me to see a friend of his whom I had never met, because he had been in prison all my life. His name was Aleksandr, but my uncle called him 'Hedgehog'. The nickname, an affectionate term for a small, defenceless creature, had been coined when he was a baby and had stayed with him into adulthood.

Hedgehog had been released that very day, after fifteen years in prison. It was the custom among Siberians that the first people who went to visit a newly released prisoner should take children with them: it was a form of well-wishing, a lucky charm for his future life, free and criminal. The presence of children serves to demonstrate to people who have been excluded from society for a long time that their world still has a future, and that what they have done, their ideals and their criminal education, have not been, and never will be, forgotten. I, of course, understood nothing of this, and was simply curious to meet this character.

In our district there was always someone going to prison or coming out of it every day, so there was nothing strange to us children in seeing a man who had been in prison; we had been brought up to expect that we would go there ourselves sooner or later, and we were accustomed to talking about prison as something quite normal, just as other boys might talk about military service or what they're going to do when they grow up. But in some cases the characters of certain former prisoners took on a heroic stature in our stories – they became the models that we wanted to be like at all costs, we wanted to live their adventurous lives which shone with criminal glamour, those lives we heard the grown-ups discussing and which we then talked about among ourselves, often changing the details, making those stories similar to fairy tales or fantasy adventures. That was what Hedgehog was: a legend, one of those figures our young imaginations had been nourished on. It was said that he was still a teenager when he had been accepted as a robber into one of the most famous gangs of our community, made up of old Siberian Authorities[1] and run by another legendary figure, known to everyone as 'Tayga'.

Tayga was a perfect example of a pure Siberian criminal: the son of criminal parents, as a small boy he had robbed armoured trains and killed a large number of policemen. There were many fabulous tales about him, which portrayed him as a wise and powerful criminal who was expert in the conduct of illegal activities, and yet was also very humble and kind, and always ready to help the weak and to punish every kind of injustice.

Tayga was already an old man when he met Hedgehog, who was then an orphan child. He had helped in his own way, teaching him the criminal law and morality, and very soon Hedgehog had become like a grandson to him. And Hedgehog had earned his respect.

Once Hedgehog had been surrounded by the police, with five other criminals. There was no way out – all the members of his gang were of the old Siberian faith, and so would never let themselves be taken alive. They would fight on till victory or death. Feeling sorry for him, since he was so young, his companions had suggested that he slip away, offering him a certain escape route, but he, out of respect for them, had refused. They were sure they were all going to be killed – the police siege was unrelenting – but then

---

1. 'Authority' refers to a leading criminal figure in the community. The nearest equivalent in American criminal vocabulary is a 'made man'.

Hedgehog had done something crafty. He had hidden his submachine gun behind his back, and with cries of fear had run out towards the police, begging them to help him, as if he were just a victim who had nothing to do with the confrontation between the criminals and the police. The cops had let him pass round behind their backs, and as soon as he got there he had pulled out his gun and mown them down. Thanks to his quick thinking the old men had been saved, and Hedgehog had become a regular member of their gang, with all the rights of an adult criminal. To us kids he was an inspiration: a teenager who is accepted as an equal among adults is a very rare phenomenon.

Later, when he was about thirty, Hedgehog had been sent to prison after attempting to murder a policeman. There had been no proof or witnesses, but he had been convicted on the lesser charge of 'participation in a criminal group'; all that was needed to secure a conviction in this case was a couple of guns confiscated from his home and a few previous offences. By agreement with the police, the judge could hand down a sentence of as much as twenty-five years, with additional punitive conditions. Justice in the USSR was far from blind; in fact, at times it seemed to be examining us all through a microscope.

My uncle was a friend of Hedgehog's; in prison they had been members of the same 'family': since my uncle had been released earlier than him, one day he had gone to the home of old Tayga, who by now was close to death, bearing the good wishes of his adopted grandson. Before he died Tayga had blessed my uncle and told him that the first male child to be born in our family must bear the name of my great-grandfather, Nikolay, who had been his friend in his youth, and then had been shot by the police at the age of twenty-seven. The first male child to be born, five years later, was me.

Uncle Vitaly and I went on foot; it wasn't far – only half an hour's walk. Hedgehog had no home of his own; he was staying with an old criminal called 'Stew', who lived on the outskirts of our district, near the fields where the river made a wide bend and disappeared into the woods.

The gate was open. It was summer, and very hot; Stew and Hedgehog were sitting in the front yard, under a pergola of vines which provided pleasant shade. They were drinking kvas, a thirst-quenching drink made from black bread and yeast. The odour of kvas was very strong; you could smell it at once, on the still, warm air.

As soon as we entered, Hedgehog got up from his chair and hurried to meet my uncle: they embraced and kissed each other three times on the cheeks, as is the custom in our country.

'Well, you old wolf, can you still bite? Haven't the screws broken all your teeth?' Hedgehog asked, as if it were my uncle who had just been released from jail, not him.

But I knew why he had said it. My uncle had had a very nasty experience during his last year in prison. He had attacked a guard over a question of honour, to defend an old criminal who had been beaten up by a cop, and the guards had taken their revenge with some cruel tortures:

they had given him a long, severe beating, then drenched him with water and left him out in the open all night in the middle of winter. He had fallen ill. Fortunately he had survived, but his health had been permanently impaired – he had chronic asthma and one of his lungs was rotting away. My grandfather always used to joke that he had only retrieved half of his son from prison: the other half had stayed inside to rot forever.

'You're not so young yourself! What an ugly old sod you've turned out to be! Whatever happened to the best years of your life?' my uncle had replied, looking at him affectionately. It was clear the two men were good friends.

'Who's this young rascal? He's not Yuri's son, is he?' Hedgehog stared at me with a crooked smile.

'Yes, this is my nephew. We called him Nikolay, according to the wishes of old Tayga, may the earth lie as light as a feather upon him . . .'

Hedgehog bent over me, his face in front of mine. He looked closely into my eyes, and I looked at him. His eyes were very pale, almost white, with a faint trace of blue; they didn't seem human. They fascinated me, and I kept staring at them as if they might change colour at any moment.

Then Hedgehog put his hand on my head and ruffled my hair, and I smiled at him as if he were a member of my family.

'He's going to be a killer, this one. He's a true member of our race, may the Lord help him.'

'He's a clever lad . . .' said my uncle, with a strong note of pride in his voice. 'Kolima, boy, recite the poem about the drowned man to Uncle Hedgehog and Uncle Stew!'

It was Uncle Vitaly's favourite poem. Whenever he got drunk and wanted to go out and kill some cops, my grandparents, in order to stop him, would send me to recite that poem to him, as a kind of therapy. I would start to recite, and he would at once calm down, saying:

'All right, never mind, I'll kill those bastards tomorrow. Let's hear it again . . .' So I would recite the poem over and over again, till he fell asleep. Only then did my grandparents come into the room and take away his gun.

It was a poem by the legendary Pushkin. It's about a poor fisherman who finds the body of a drowned man caught in his nets. For fear of the consequences he throws the body back into the water, but the ghost of the drowned man starts visiting him every night. Until his body is buried in the ground below a cross, his spirit will never be able to rest in peace.

It was a wonderful story, but also a terrifying one. I don't know why my uncle liked it so much.

I wasn't shy about reciting poems in front of others, in fact I enjoyed it; it made me feel important, the centre of attention. So I filled my lungs and began to speak, trying to sound as impressive as possible, varying my tone and emphasizing my words with gestures:

'The children came into the house, and hurriedly called their father: "Father, Father! Our nets have caught a dead man!" "What are you talking about, you little devils?" replied the father. "Oh, these children! I'll give you "dead man" . . . Wife, bring me my coat, I'm going to see. Well, where is this dead man?" "There he is, Father!" And sure enough, there on the river bank, where the net had been laid out to dry, there was a corpse on the sand: a horrible, disfigured body, bluish and bloated . . .'

When I had finished, they applauded me. My uncle was the most delighted of all; he stroked my head, saying:

'What did I tell you? He's a genius.'

Old Stew asked us to sit down at the table under the pergola and went to fetch two glasses for us.

Hedgehog asked me:

'Tell me, Kolima, have you got a pike?'

At the word 'pike' my eyes started shining and I became as attentive as a tiger out hunting – I had never owned a pike, nor had any of my friends. Boys usually get one later, when they're ten or twelve years old.

The pike, as the traditional weapon of the Siberian criminals is called, is a flick-knife with a long, thin blade, and is connected with many old customs and ceremonies of our community.

A pike cannot be bought. It has to be earned.

Any young criminal can be given a pike by an adult criminal, as long as he is not a relative. Once it has been given, the pike becomes a kind of personal cult symbol, like the cross in the Christian community.

The pike also has magic powers, lots of them.

When someone is ill, and especially when he is suffering extreme pain, they put an open pike under his mattress, with the blade sticking out, so that, according to the beliefs, the blade cuts the pain and absorbs it like a sponge. What's more, when an enemy is struck by that blade, the pain collected inside it flows out into the wound, making him suffer even more.

The umbilical cord of newborn babies is cut with a pike, which must first have been left open overnight in a place where cats sleep.

To seal important pacts between two people – truces, friendships or brotherhoods – both criminals cut their hands with the same pike, which is then kept by a third person, who is a kind of witness to their pact: if either of them betrays the agreement he will be killed with that knife.

When a criminal dies, his pike is broken by one of his friends. One part, the blade, is put in his grave, usually under the dead man's head, while the haft is preserved by his closest relatives. When it is necessary to communicate with the dead man, to ask for advice or a miracle, the relatives take out the haft and put it in the red corner, below the icons. In this way the dead man becomes a kind of bridge between the living and God.

A pike keeps its powers only if it is in the hands of a Siberian criminal who uses it respecting the rules of the criminal community. If an unworthy person takes possession of a knife that does not belong to him, it will bring him bad luck – hence our idiom, 'to ruin something as a pike ruins a bad master'.

When a criminal is in danger, his pike can warn him in many ways: the blade may suddenly open of its own accord, or become hot, or vibrate. Some think it can even emit a whistle.

If a pike is broken, it means that somewhere there is a dead person who cannot find peace, so offerings are made to the icon, or dead relatives and friends are remembered in prayers, visits are made to graveyards, and the dead are remembered by talking about them in the family and telling stories about them, especially to children.

For all these reasons, at the word 'pike' my eyes lit up. To possess one is to be rewarded by adults, to have something that will bind you to their world forever.

The question Hedgehog had asked me was a clear sign that something incredible was about to happen to me – to me, a six-year-old boy. A legendary criminal was going to give me a pike, my first pike. I had never hoped, never even imagined anything like this, and yet suddenly, there before me was the chance to possess that sacred symbol, which for people who have received the Siberian criminal education is a part of the soul.

I tried to hide my excitement and look indifferent, but I don't think I was very successful, because all three of them were looking at me with smiles on their faces. No doubt they were thinking of their own first pike.

'No, I haven't,' I said in a very hard voice.

'Well, wait a minute and I'll be right back . . .' With these words Hedgehog went into the house. I was exploding with happiness; inside me a band was playing, fireworks were going off and billions of voices were shouting with joy.

Hedgehog came back straight away. He came over to me, took my hand and placed in it a pike. *The* pike.

'This is yours. May the Lord help you and your hand grow strong and sure . . .'

From the way he looked at me, it was clear that he was happy too.

I looked at my pike and couldn't believe it was real. It was heavier and bigger than I had imagined.

I released the safety catch by lowering a little lever, and then pressed the button. The sound of the knife opening was music to my ears; it was as if the metal had given voice. The blade flicked out sharply, in a split second, with immense force, and at once remained firm and straight, steady and fixed. It was shocking: this strange object, which when closed had seemed like some sort of writing implement from the turn of the century, was now a beautiful, graceful weapon, with a certain nobility and allure.

The haft was made of black bone – that's what we call the antlers of the red deer, which are dark brown, almost black – with an inlay of white bone, in the form of an Orthodox cross, in the middle. And it was so long I had to hold it with both hands, like the sword of the medieval knights. The blade, too, was very long, sharp on one side and polished till it gleamed. It was a fantastic weapon and I felt as if I were in heaven.

From that day on, my authority among my friends shot up. For a week I received visits from swarms of little boys who came from all over the district to see my pike; my house had become a kind of sacred shrine, and they were the pilgrims. My grandfather would let them into the yard and offer everyone cold drinks. My grandmother would hardly have time to make some kvas before it was all gone, so I spread the word that anyone who wanted to come

and see the first six-year-old boy to be the proud owner of
a *real* pike had to bring something to drink with him.

I was very flattered and proud of myself, but after
a while a strange form of depression came over me;
I was tired of telling the same story a hundred times a
day and showing the pike to everyone. So I went to see
Grandfather Kuzya, as I did whenever I had a problem or
felt depressed.

Grandfather Kuzya was an elderly criminal who
lived in our district in a small house by the river. He was
a very strong old man; he still had a full head of black
hair and was covered all over with tattoos, even on his
face. Usually he took me into the garden to show me the
river, and told me fairy tales and various stories about the
criminal community. He had a powerful voice, but spoke
in a quiet, languid way, so that his voice seemed to be
coming from far away, not from inside him. Down the left
side of his wrinkled face ran a long scar, a souvenir of his
criminal youth. But the most striking thing about him was
his eyes. They were blue, but a dirty, muddy blue, with a
hint of green; they seemed not to belong to his body, not
to be part of it. They were deep, and when he turned them
on you, calmly and without agitation, it was as if they
were X-raying you – there was something really hypnotic
about his gaze.

Well, I went to see him and told him the whole story,
making it clear that I was pleased to have the pike, but
that my friends treated me differently from before. Even
my good friend Mel, who was 'hewn with the same axe' as
me, as we say, behaved as if I were some kind of religious
icon.

Grandfather Kuzya laughed, but not unkindly, and told me I clearly wasn't cut out to be a celebrity. Then he gave me one of his long lectures. He advised me to do whatever came naturally. He told me that the fact of having a pike didn't make me different from the others, that I had simply been lucky to be in the right place at the right time, and that if Our Lord had so willed it I must be ready for the responsibility he had given me. After his talk, as always, I felt better.

Grandfather Kuzya taught me the old rules of criminal behaviour, which in recent times he had seen change before his very eyes. He was worried, because, he said, these things always began with small details which seemed to be trivial, but the end result was a total loss of identity. To help me understand this he often told me a Siberian fairy tale, a kind of metaphor, designed to show how men who lead the wrong kind of life because they are led astray end up losing their dignity.

The tale was about a pack of wolves who were in trouble because they had had nothing to eat for ages. The old wolf who was the leader of the pack tried to reassure his companions – he asked them to be patient and to wait, because sooner or later herds of wild boar or deer would come along, and then they would be able to hunt to their hearts' content and would at last fill their stomachs. One young wolf, however, was not prepared to wait, and started looking for a quick solution to the problem. He decided to leave the woods and go to ask men for food. The old wolf tried to stop him. He said that if he accepted food from men he would change and would no longer be a wolf. But the young wolf wouldn't listen. He replied bluntly that if you needed to fill your stomach it was pointless to follow strict rules – the important thing was to fill it. And off he went towards the village.

The men fed him on their leftovers whenever he asked. But every time the young wolf filled his stomach and thought of going back to the woods to join the others he would get drowsy. So he put off his return until eventually he completely forgot the life of the pack, the pleasure of the hunt and the excitement of sharing the prey with his companions.

He began to go hunting with the men, to help them, instead of the wolves with whom he had been born and raised. One day, during the hunt, a man shot an old wolf, which fell to the ground, wounded. The young wolf ran towards him to take him back to his master, and while he was trying to get hold of him with his teeth he realized that it was his old pack leader. He felt ashamed, and didn't know what to say. It was the old wolf who filled the silence with his last words:

'I have lived my life like a worthy wolf, I have hunted a lot and shared many prey with my brothers, so now I die happy. But you will live your life in shame, and alone, in a world to which you do not belong, for you have rejected the dignity of a free wolf to have a full stomach. You have become unworthy. Wherever you go, you will be treated with contempt; you belong neither to the world of wolves nor to that of men . . . This will teach you that hunger comes and goes, but dignity, once lost, never returns.'

That concluding speech was my favourite part of the story, because the old wolf's words were a true distillation of our criminal philosophy, and as Grandfather Kuzya spoke those words he reflected in them his own experience, his way of seeing and understanding the world.

The words returned to my mind a few years later, when a train was taking me to a juvenile prison. A guard decided to hand round some pieces of salami. We were hungry, and many threw themselves greedily on that salami to devour it. I refused it; a boy asked me why and I told him the story of the unworthy wolf. He didn't understand me, but when we reached our destination the guard who had distributed the salami announced in the main yard, in front of everyone, that before giving it to us he had dipped it in the toilet.

As a result, according to the criminal rule, all those who had eaten it had been 'tainted' and had therefore fallen to the lowest caste of the criminal community, and would automatically be despised by all, even before they got into the prison. This was one of the tricks the cops often played, to use the criminal rules as a weapon against the criminals themselves. These tricks were most successful with youngsters, who often didn't know that an honest criminal is not allowed to accept anything from a cop. As my late lamented uncle used to say:

'The only thing a worthy criminal takes from the cops is a beating, and even that he gives back, when the right moment comes.'

So, thanks to the sudden increase in my authority among my friends, I had begun to do a bit of advertising for the upbringing and education I'd received from Grandfather Kuzya. He was delighted, because this enabled him to influence all of us. And now we boys of the Low River district became known as 'Siberian Education' – a name that had been given to the Siberians in exile because of their loyalty to the criminal traditions and their extremely conservative spirit.

In our town every criminal community, especially if it was made up of young people, distinguished itself from the others by its clothes or how its members wore them. They also used symbols, which immediately identified you as belonging to a specific gang, district or national group. Many communities used to mark out their territory with drawings or slogans, but our elders had always forbidden us to write or draw anything on the walls, because they said it was shameful and ill-mannered. Grandfather Kuzya had once explained to me that our criminal community had no need to affirm its presence in any way: it simply existed, and people knew that, not because they saw graffiti on the walls of their homes, but because they felt our presence, and were sure they could always count on the help and sympathy of us criminals. The same went for an individual criminal: even if he were a legendary character, he should behave as the humblest of all.

In other districts it was completely different. The members of the gangs of Centre wore gold pendants of their own design. For example, members of the gang led by a young criminal nicknamed 'Pirate', who had built up a kind of personality cult around himself, distinguished themselves by wearing a pendant bearing the skull and crossbones of a pirates' flag. Another gang, from the Railway district, made all its members wear black, to emphasize their loyalty to the Black Seed caste. The Ukrainians of the Balka district, on the other hand, dressed in the American style, or more often like African-Americans. They sang songs which seemed meaningless, and they drew strange things all over the place with spray-cans. One of them had once drawn something in the Bank district on the wall of an elder, a former prisoner, and in revenge a young criminal, who was a neighbour of the old man, had shot him.

I remember commenting on this to Grandfather Kuzya. I said that in my opinion killing was unjust. You could demand compensation for the insult and the nuisance, and then you could always beat the guy up – a good thrashing will usually get a bit of sense into a guy's head. But Grandfather didn't agree with me and said I was too humane – too humane and too young. He explained to me that when boys went down a wrong road and wouldn't listen to their elders, in most cases they harmed themselves and those around them. The Ukrainian boys were putting at risk many youngsters of other districts, who would imitate them, because being ill-mannered was always easier and more attractive than following the road of good manners. Therefore it was necessary to treat them with cruelty and absolute severity, to make everyone understand where the path of disobedience to the traditions could lead. He added:

'Anyway, why do they pretend to be American blacks and not, say, North Koreans or Palestinians? I'll tell you why: this is filth that comes from the devil, through the television, the cinema, the newspapers and all the trash that a worthy and honest person never touches . . . America is a cursed, godforsaken country, and everything that emanates from it must be ignored. If these fools play at being Americans, soon they'll be whooping like monkeys instead of talking . . .'

Grandfather Kuzya hated everything American because, like all Siberian criminals, he opposed what represented power in the world. If he heard anyone talk about people who had fled to America, of many Jews who had made a mass exodus from the USSR in the 1980s, he would say in amazement:

'Why on earth does everyone go to America, saying they seek freedom? Our ancestors took refuge in the woods, in Siberia, they didn't go to America. And besides, why flee from the Soviet regime, only to end up in the American one? It would be like a bird that had escaped from its cage going voluntarily to live in another cage . . .'

For these reasons, in Low River it was forbidden to use anything American. The American cars which circulated freely all over town couldn't enter our district, and items of clothing, domestic appliances and all other objects that were 'made in the USA' were banned. For me personally this rule was rather painful, since I was very keen on jeans but I couldn't wear them. I secretly listened to American music – I liked blues, rock and heavy metal, but I was taking a big risk in keeping the records and cassettes in the house. And when my father carried out an inspection of my hiding places and finally found them, all hell would break loose. He would beat me and make me break all the records with my own hands in front of him and my grandfather, and then every evening for a week I would be made to play Russian tunes on the accordion for an hour and sing Russian folk or criminal songs.

I wasn't attracted by American politics, only by the music and by the books of some writers. Once, choosing the right moment, I tried to explain this to Grandfather Kuzya. I hoped that he would be able to intercede and give me permission to listen to the music and read American books without having to hide from my family. He looked at me as if I had betrayed him and said:

'Son, do you know why when there's an outbreak of the plague people burn everything that belonged to the victims?'

I shook my head. But I already imagined where this was leading.

He gave a sad sigh and concluded:

'The contagion, Nikolay, the contagion.'

And so, since everything American was forbidden, just as it was forbidden to flaunt wealth and power through material things, the people of our district dressed very humbly. We boys were in a terrible state as far as clothing was concerned, but we were proud of it. We wore like trophies our fathers' or elder brothers' old shoes, and their unfashionable clothes, which were meant to emphasize Siberian humility and simplicity.

We could have enjoyed life to the full. We were an ancient and very wealthy community, the houses in our area were huge, the people could have lived 'in grand style', as the phrase is in our country and in yours, but instead money was used in a strange way: no clothes, jewels, expensive cars, gambling. There were only two things the Siberians were happy to spend their money on: weapons and Orthodox icons. We all had an enormous quantity of weapons, and also of icons, which were very costly.

In all other respects we were humble – humble and in uniform. In winter we all wore quilted trousers – black or dark blue, very warm and comfortable. The jackets were of two kinds: either the classic quilted *fufayka,* which half the population wore in the days of the USSR, because it was the jacket that was given to workers, or the *tulup*, which had an enormous fur collar that you could pull right up to your eyes to protect yourself against the harshest cold. I wore the *fufayka*, because it was lighter and allowed me to move fairly freely. The shoes were heavy, and fur-lined, and there were also long woollen socks to ward off frostbite. On your head you'd wear a fur hat: I had a lovely one, made of white ermine – very warm, light and comfortable.

In summer we wore ordinary flannel trousers, always with a belt, in accordance with the Siberian rule. The belt is connected with the tradition of the hunters, for whom it was much more than a lucky charm: it was a request for help. If a hunter got lost in the woods, or had an accident, he would tie his belt round the neck of his dog and send it home. When the others saw the dog return, they would know he was in trouble. With the trousers we wore a shirt – usually white or grey, with a straight collar and with the buttons on the right – called *kosovorotka*, 'crooked collar'. Over the shirt we wore light jackets, grey or black, and very coarse, of military issue. The last item of our summer outfit was the legendary hat of the Siberian criminals, a kind of national symbol, known as 'eight triangles'. It consists of eight triangular segments of cloth sewn together to form a domed cap with a button on top; it also has a short peak. The colour must always be pale, or even white. In Russia this kind of hat is called a *kepka*, and there are many varieties. 'Eight triangles' is only the Siberian version. The real eight triangles of a bold and cunning criminal must have the peak bent well back, and rounded, not broken, so as to form a ridge in the middle. As a sign of contempt you break your enemy's peak, bending it till it goes out of shape.

My eight triangles had been a present from my uncle; it was an old hat and I liked it for that very reason.

The eight triangles was such an important hat that it generated stories and idioms. In criminal slang the phrase 'to wear eight triangles' means to commit a crime or to participate in the organizing of criminal activities. The phrase 'to keep eight triangles up' means to be on the alert, to be worried about some danger. 'To put eight triangles on the back of your head' means to behave aggressively, to prepare for an attack. 'To wear eight triangles askew' means to show calm, relaxed behaviour. 'To tip eight triangles over your eyes' means to announce the need to disappear, to hide. 'To fill eight triangles' means to take something in abundance.

Often I really did fill my hat, for example when we boys went to see Aunt Marta, a woman who lived alone on the river bank and was famous for her jams. We used to take her the apples we had stolen from the collective

farms on the other side of the river, and help her peel
them, so she could make the jam. She would bake the
pirozhki, little biscuits she filled with jam. We would all
sit in a circle on little stools in the yard in front of her
house, with the kitchen door wide open, through which
we could always see something boiling on the fire; we
would fish the apples out of the bags, peel them with our
knives and then throw them into a big pot with water in
it. When it was full, we would carry it into the house,
using two long planks of wood which we hooked onto
the pot like handles. Aunt Marta was very fond of us. She
gave us plenty to eat – we would always go home with full
stomachs and with *pirozhki* in our hands. I used to put
mine in my hat and eat them as I walked.

The eight-triangled hat is the subject of many proverbs,
poems and songs of the criminal tradition. Since I used to
spend a lot of time with the old criminals, listening to
them sing or recite poems, I knew many of them by heart.
One song, my favourite, went like this:

I remember I wore an eight-triangled hat,
Drank beer and smoked strong tobacco;
I was in love with my neighbour Nina
And together we'd go to the restaurant.
I wore a *shaber*[1] in my squeaking *kromachy*,[2]
Under my shirt a *telnyashka*,[3]
A gift from the thieves of Odessa . . .

1. A knife modelled on the military bayonet, used in attacking ships
on the rivers.
2. Literally 'polished ones': *kromachy* was our word for boots.
3. A sailor's vest, with blue and white stripes and long sleeves.

The eight triangles was at the centre of everything: it was constantly being mentioned, and people would bet on it in various situations. Often in conversations between criminals, both children and adults, you would hear the phrase: 'May my eight-triangled hat catch fire on my head if what I say is not true', or 'May my hat fly off my head', or the more gruesome variant, 'May my hat choke me to death'.

In our society swearing oaths was forbidden; it was considered a kind of weakness, an insult to yourself, because a person who swears implies that what he is saying is not true. But among us boys, when we talked, oaths would often slip out, and we would swear by our hats. You could never swear by your mother, your parents or relatives in general, by God or by the saints. Nor by your health, or even worse by your soul, for that was considered to be 'damaging God's property'. So the only thing left to take it out on was your hat.

Once my friend Mel swore by his hat that he would 'stuff his eight triangles up Amur's arse' (Amur was a dog that belonged to Uncle Plague, a neighbour of ours) if he didn't jump clean over the school gate from a standing position.

Even thinking about it today I've no idea how Mel thought he could jump over a gate over four metres high. But what worried me more at the time was how he would carry out the operation if he lost the bet, since Amur was the biggest and nastiest dog in our area. I was petrified by that monster; once I had seen him swim across the river and kill a goat, tearing it apart as if it were made of rags. He was a cross between a German shepherd and the breed which in our homeland, Siberia, is called Alabay, 'wolf-crusher'. Usually Amur roamed quietly around his owner's yard, but sometimes he became uncontrollable, especially if he heard the sound of a whistle. He had already been shot on two occasions, after attacking someone, but had survived because, as my father used to say, 'the more you shoot that dog, the stronger it gets'.

Well, Mel's idea seemed to me more than stupid. But once spoken, his word couldn't be taken back, and it only remained to witness that insane show, in which Mel, through his own pure idiocy, was both stage manager and actor.

So we headed for the school gate.

Mel made one attempt; he jumped half a metre, hitting his nose against the gate. Then, sitting on the ground, he drew his conclusions:

'Shit, it's really high! I'll never make it . . .'

I looked at him and couldn't believe how he could be so naive. Trying to save the situation, I said it had all been great fun and now we might as well go home. But Mel astounded me with his stupidity, saying that as a question of honour he had to keep his oath.

I felt like laughing and crying at the same time. But my other two friends, Besa and Gigit, were enthusiastic, and were already imagining all the ways in which Mel could most effectively creep up to the dog and carry out his devilish plan.

When we reached Plague's house, Mel climbed up onto the fence and jumped down into the yard. Plague wasn't at home; he had gone fishing – the net that was usually hung along the fence wasn't there.

Amur was lying by the gate with a slightly ironic expression on his horrendously ugly face.

Mel had brought a rope to tie the dog up, and he also had a tube of Vaseline which some friends had got from Aunt Natalia, the nurse. Mel approached him and Amur didn't move a muscle – he gazed at him with bored and indifferent eyes, as if he were looking straight through him. With every step Mel gained more courage until, when there were no more than a couple of metres between Mel and Amur, Gigit stuck two fingers in his mouth and gave a loud whistle, making such a piercing sound that it even startled me. A few seconds later I saw Mel fly magically over the fence, pass above my head and land on the pavement, hitting his forehead on the sun-softened asphalt. Immediately afterwards the gate jerked under the weight of Amur, who threw himself into it, making a strange noise that I had never before heard from any living creature. It was a kind of human cry mingled with a desperate and angry chorus of animal voices. As if an elephant, a lion, a wolf, a bear and a horse were competing to see who could make the loudest noise. If someone had asked me at that moment what the voice of the devil might sound like, I would have said like Amur.

The seat of Mel's pants was torn, and underneath you could see some bloody red weals, left by a blow from Amur's paw. Mel was terrified and still couldn't understand what had happened. Gigit and Besa were rolling about with laughter and kept whistling, to increase the fury of the dog, which from the other side of the gate kept spitting froth and uttering the sounds of his animal wrath.

And so in the end Mel lost his bet, but after the entertaining show he had provided we forgave him.

At the age of twelve I got into trouble. I was put on trial for 'threats in a public place', 'attempted murder with serious consequences' and, naturally, 'resistance to a representative of power in the pursuance of his duties of defending the public order'. It was my first criminal trial, and in view of the circumstances (I was a young boy and the victim was a previous offender a couple of years older than me) the judge decided to be lenient and give me a sentence which in slang is called a 'cuddle'. No prison and no obligation to follow any re-education programmes, after which most convicts usually become even nastier and angrier. All I had to do was observe a kind of personal curfew: stay at home from eight in the evening till eight in the morning, report to the juvenile office every week and attend school.

I would have to live like that for a year and a half, then I would be able to return to normal life. But if in the meantime I committed another crime I would land myself straight on the bunk beds of a juvenile prison, or at least in a re-education camp.

For a year everything went smoothly, I tried to keep as far as possible away from trouble. Certainly, I often went out at night, because I was sure I wouldn't be discovered, but the important thing, I told myself, was not to let myself get caught in a place far from home at the wrong time and above all not to be found mixed up in any serious crime.

But one afternoon Mel and three other friends came round to see me. We got together in the garden, on the bench under the tree, to discuss an incident that had occurred a week earlier with a group of boys from Tiraspol. We had a friend, a boy who had recently moved to our district. His family had been forced to leave St Petersburg because the father had got into trouble with the police. They were Jews, but in view of the special circumstances, and some business they had done together, the Siberians had guaranteed their protection.

Our friend was thirteen and was called Lyoza, an old Jewish name. He was a very quiet, weak boy: he had health problems, was almost deaf and wore enormous glasses, so in the Siberian community he was immediately treated with compassion and understanding, like all disabled people. My father, for example, never stopped reminding me to look after him and to get out my knife should anyone attack or insult him. Lyoza was very well-educated, had refined manners and always talked seriously – everything he said seemed convincing. So we had immediately given him an appropriate nickname: 'the Banker'.

Lyoza always went around with us. He never carried knives or other weapons and wasn't even capable of using his fists, but he knew everything, he was a kind of living enyclopaedia, he was always telling us the stories you find in books: how insects live and multiply, how the gills of fish are formed, why birds migrate, and things like that. I remember once he managed to do the impossible

– explain to Mel how hermaphrodite worms reproduce. It took him a long time, but in the end he succeeded; Mel wandered around in a daze, as if he'd seen Jesus, God the Father and the Madonna all at once.

'Wow, what a story! Worms don't have a family! They have no father and mother! They do everything on their own!' Getting my friend Mel to understand anything, even the tiniest thing, was proof of great human and intellectual qualities.

Mel and my other three friends, Besa, Gigit and Grave, told me that Lyoza had gone on his own to Tiraspol, to the second-hand market, to exchange some stamps, because he was a keen collector. During the return journey, on the coach, he had been attacked by a bunch of thugs who had hit him and stolen his stamp album. I was furious, so we arranged to meet the other kids of our district to make an expedition to Tiraspol.

Tiraspol is the capital of Transnistria; it is about twenty kilometres away, on the opposite side of the river. It is a much larger town than ours, and very different. The people of Tiraspol kept out of crime; there were a lot of munitions factories, military barracks and various offices, so the inhabitants were all workers or soldiers. We had a very bad relationship with the kids of that town; we called them 'mama's boys', 'billy goats' and 'ball-less wonders'. In Tiraspol the criminal rules of honesty and respect among people did not apply, and the youngsters behaved like real animals. So none of us was surprised at what had happened to Lyoza.

We went to Lyoza's house to see how he was and to ask him if he would come with us to help us identify the assailants. We explained to his father that we were going to Tiraspol to carry out an act of justice, to punish those who had attacked his son. His father gave him permission to go with us and wished us all good luck; he was very pleased that Lyoza had friends like us, because he profoundly respected the Siberian philosophy of loyalty to the group.

Lyoza said nothing; he fetched his jacket and came out with us. Together we returned to my house, where we planned everything.

At about eight in the evening thirty-odd friends gathered outside. My mother at once understood that we were planning some mischief.

'Perhaps it would be better if you kept calm. Can't you stay at home?'

What could I say in reply?

'Don't worry, mama, we're just going for a quick trip, then we'll come back . . .'

Poor Mama, she never dared to oppose my decisions, but suffered in silence.

We set out for a park on the outskirts, where all the thugs of the town gathered in the evening. It was called 'the Polygon'. There the kids used to ride around on scooters, barbecue meat and consume huge quantities of alcohol and drugs until late at night.

So as not to attract attention we arrived in town on the regular coach, and then, splitting up into groups of five, set off on foot towards the park.

My friend Mel showed me a five-shooter revolver, an old, small-bore weapon, which I called affectionately 'the prehistoric'.

'I'll let them see her this evening,' he said with a broad grin, and it was clear that he couldn't wait to do something nasty.

'Holy Christ, Mel, we're not going to war! Hide that thing, I don't even want to see it . . .' I really didn't like the idea of drawing our guns. Partly because according to our education a firearm is used only in extreme cases, but mainly because if word gets around that you reach for your pistol at the first opportunity, people start criticizing you. Ever since I was small I learned from my uncle that your gun is like your wallet: you only take it out to use it, all the rest is stupid.

But Mel tried to convince me that his behaviour made sense.

'But it's dangerous to go there without one; goodness knows how many guns they're carrying, they're prepared . . .'

'Yeah, I can just imagine how prepared they are, all high as kites, and with holes in their veins . . . By the Passion of Christ, Mel, they're all drunks or junkies, they shit themselves when they see their own shadows, aren't you ashamed to pull out your gun in front of them?'

'Oh all right, I won't use it, but I'll keep it ready, and if the situation gets out of hand . . .'

I looked at him as if he were mentally ill; it was impossible to explain anything to him. 'Mel, I swear to you, the only person who can make the situation get out of hand this evening is you, with your fucking pistol! If I see you use it, don't bother to try speaking to me ever again,' I snapped.

'All right, Kolima, don't be angry, I won't use it, if you don't want me to. But remember, everyone is free to do what he wants . . .' My friend was trying to teach me our law.

'Oh, sure, everyone's free to do what he wants when he's on his own, but when he's with the others he has to toe the line, so stop arguing . . .' I was always determined to have the last word, with Mel – that was my only hope of getting any sense into his head.

When we reached the park, the group assembled. The only 'principals' – that is, those who were responsible for the kids – were me and Yuri, known as 'Gagarin', who was three years older than me. We had to decide how to go about identifying Lyoza's assailants with precision, and how to get them to come out into the open.

'Let's take a couple of them – any two, at random – and threaten to kill them if the attackers don't show themselves!' proposed Besa, who in matters of strategy behaved like a tank, flattening everything in his path.

'And you know what would happen? In three seconds they'd all run away and we'd be left with two spaced-out idiots who had no connection with the problem . . .'

I had a plan to propose, but I wanted to do it delicately, because to my way of thinking, its success depended entirely on Lyoza.

'Listen, guys, I've got an idea that will definitely work, but it needs one person's courage. Yours, Lyoza. It needs you to show your balls.' I looked at him. He seemed exactly what he was: a kid who had nothing to do with our gang. With his perfectly buttoned jacket, his thick lenses that made him look like a monster and his hair cut in the manner of the actors of the 1950s, he looked completely out of place. Lyoza came closer to me, so as better to hear what I was about to say. 'You've got to go there on your own: that way those bastards will see you and show themselves. We'll surround the area and stand behind the trees, ready to act . . . As soon as you recognize them, all you have to do is shout or whistle, and we'll jump on them in a flash. The rest is already in the hands of the Lord . . .'

'Not bad, Kolima. Good plan, if Lyoza agrees,' said Gagarin, looking at Lyoza to see how he would react.

Lyoza adjusted his glasses on his nose, and in a resolute voice he said:

'Sure I agree. Only afterwards, when the fighting starts, I don't know what to do; I don't think I'll be able to hit anyone, I've never done it in my whole life . . .'

I was impressed by the dignity with which the boy told the truth about himself. He wasn't afraid at all, he was just explaining the facts, and my respect for him grew.

'When we jump out from the trees you hide behind them; Besa will keep close to you in case anyone tries to get at you.' Gagarin made a gesture to Besa, pointing two fingers at his eyes and then at Lyoza. 'Not one hair must fall from his head!'

We walked towards the centre of the park. We kept in the dark and avoided the main avenue. We reached the trees behind which there was an asphalted space with benches arranged in a circle, under the dirty yellow light from three lamp posts. The Polygon.

There was the sound of music; we could see the kids sitting on the benches, on the ground, on their scooters.

There were about fifty of them, including some girls. The atmosphere was very relaxed.

We split up into six groups and surrounded the area. At the right moment I nudged Lyoza with my shoulder:

'Go on, little brother, let's show them nobody messes around with the boys of Low River . . .'

He nodded and set off towards the enemy camp.

As soon as Lyoza came out into the open, there was a flurry of movement among those present. Some got up from the benches and peered at him curiously, others laughed, pointing at him. One girl screamed like a mad thing, laughing and sobbing at the same time. She was obviously drunk. Her voice immediately disgusted me. She sounded like an adult alcoholic, her voice ruined by smoking, very coarse and unfeminine:

'Look, Whisker! There's that fairy from the coach! He's returned to get his stamps!'

The girl couldn't pronounce her 'r's properly, so her speech sounded faintly comical.

We all listened attentively, ready to spring into action as soon as we identified the guy she'd spoken to. He didn't keep us waiting long. From a nearby bench, crammed with girls, a boy who had been strumming a guitar got up and, putting down the instrument, walked towards Lyoza with a light, theatrical step, throwing his arms apart as you might to welcome an old friend.

'Well, look who's here! You little bastard! Have you decided to commit suicide this evening? . . .' He didn't manage to say any more, because out of the darkness appeared the figure of Gigit, who leaped on him like a tiger and knocked him to the ground, giving him a rapid succession of violent kicks in the face. I too jumped out from the trees; in a second we were all on the square and surrounded our enemies.

Panic spread among them – some rushed first one way and then the other, trying to escape, but as soon as they came up against one of us they retreated. Then a group of more determined guys broke away from the rest and the fight really began.

I saw a lot of knives flash, and I too took out my pike. Gigit came close to me, and shoulder to shoulder we advanced, striking out in all directions and dodging the few attacks that came towards us.

A lot of them, seizing their chance, started running away. The girl who had screamed was so drunk she'd fallen down as she ran, and one of her friends trampled on her head – I heard her cry out and then saw the blood on her hair.

In the end we were left against about twenty of them and, as they say in our language, we 'gave them a good combing': none of them was left standing, they were all on the ground, many had cuts on their faces or their legs, some had their knee ligaments sliced through.

Mel marked the end of the fight with a flourish. Shouting like an enraged monster and making strange contortions with his hideous face, he picked up a scooter which was resting peacefully on its stand, raised it to the level of his chest and after running five or six metres threw it on top of a group of enemies, who were lying on the ground massaging their wounds.

The scooter landed with a crash, hitting one boy on the head, and others on various parts of their bodies. The ones who had been struck started screaming with pain all together, in chorus. For some reason Mel got even more angry because of those screams, and started hitting them with inexplicable violence. Finally he climbed on the scooter and cruelly jumped up and down on it (and on them). Those poor devils screamed desperately and begged him to stop.

'Hey, arseholes! We're from Low River! You beat up our brother, and you haven't finished paying for it yet!' Gagarin communicated his solemn message to all those who were lying on the ground. 'We've just taken our personal satisfaction, by beating you up and cutting you. But you still have to satisfy the criminal law, which you've shamefully violated! By next week five of you pansy bastards will report to our district with five thousand dollars, to be paid to our community for the trouble you've caused. If you don't do it, we'll repeat this massacre every week, until we've killed all of you, one by one, like mangy dogs! Goodbye and good night!'

We felt like unbeatable champions; we were so pleased with how things had gone that we set off for home singing our Siberian songs at the tops of our voices.

We crossed the park, breathing in the night air, and it seemed to us as if there would never be a happier moment than this in our whole lives.

When we came out of the park we found a dozen police cars in front of us: the cops were lined up behind the cars, with their guns trained on us. A searchlight flicked on, blinding us all, and a voice shouted:

'Weapons out of your pockets! If anyone tries anything stupid we'll fill him full of holes! Don't be fools, you're not at home now!'

We obeyed and all threw our weapons on the ground. In a few seconds a heap of knives, knuckledusters and pistols had formed.

They put us into the cars, hitting us with the butts of their rifles, and drove us all to the police station. I thought of my pike, that beloved knife that was so important to me, and which I would certainly never see again. That was the only thing I could think about. The idea that I might go to prison, because of my situation, didn't even cross my mind.

They kept us in the police station for two days. They beat us up and kept us in a cramped room without food or water. Now and then someone would be taken out of the room and brought back bruised and battered.

None of us gave our real names; the home addresses were false too. The only thing we didn't lie about was the fact that we belonged to the Siberian community. Under our law juveniles can communicate with the police – we exploited this possibility to trick them, and make their job more difficult.

Mel wouldn't calm down and tried to attack the police, who hit him very hard, striking him on the head with their pistol butts, giving him a nasty wound.

Finally they set us all free, saying that next time they would kill us. Hungry, exhausted and battered we set off for home.

Only then, as I dragged myself like a dying man through the streets of my district, did I suddenly realize that I'd been very lucky. If the police had identified me I would have had to spend at least five years on the wooden bunks of some juvenile prison.

It was a miracle, I said to myself, a real miracle, to be free after an experience like that. And yet I kept thinking about my pike: as if a black hole had formed inside me, or a member of my family had died.

I approached home staring at the tips of my shoes, eyes on the ground – under the ground if it had been possible, because I was ashamed; I felt as if the whole world was judging me because I hadn't been able to keep my pike.

When I arrived, I was like a ghost, transparent and lifeless. My Uncle Vitaly came out onto the veranda and said, smiling:

'Hey! Have they reopened Auschwitz? How come nobody told me about it?'

'Leave me alone, Uncle, I'm aching all over . . . I just want to sleep . . .'

'Well, young man, unfortunately it's not possible to give punches without taking them . . . It's the rule of life . . .'

For two days I did nothing but sleep and, occasionally, eat. I was covered with bruises, and every time I turned over on my side in bed I gritted my teeth. Now and then my father or my uncle would look in at the door of my bedroom and make fun of me:

'Really makes you feel good, doesn't it, a sound beating? Will you never learn?'

I didn't reply, I just sighed heavily, and they laughed.

On the third day the desire to return to normal life made me get up early. It was about six o'clock and everyone was still asleep, except Grandfather Boris, who was preparing to do his exercises. I felt a discomfort, a feeling very different from pain, but one which stiffens your body, so that every movement you make comes with effort; you're slow, like an old man who's afraid of losing his balance.

I washed, and examined my face in the bathroom mirror. The bruise wasn't as bad as I had expected, in fact it was barely visible. On my right hand, however, there were two very obvious black bruises, one unmistakably in the shape of a boot heel. While they were beating me up one cop must have crushed my hand: they often did this as a preventative measure, to give you irregular fractures which usually healed badly, so you would never be able to close your fist tightly or hold a weapon. Luckily they were only bruises – I had no fractures or torn ligaments. I had another big bruise between my legs, just below my male pride – it looked as though something black was stuck to my body, it looked very nasty, and above all it hurt when I emptied my bladder.

'Well, it could have been worse . . .' I concluded, and went to have breakfast. The warm milk with honey and a fresh egg put me back in the world.

I decided to go and check my boat on the river and mess about with the nets, and maybe go round the district to ask how my friends were doing.

Coming out of the house, I found my grandfather doing his exercises in the yard. Grandfather Boris was a rock – he didn't smoke and had no other vices, he was a total health fanatic. He did wrestling, judo and sambo, and transmitted these passions to all the rest of the family. When he was exercising he usually didn't stop for a second; so we only greeted each other with a look. I gestured to him, indicating that I was going out. He smiled at me and that was all.

I went down the street that led to the river. As I passed I saw on the corner, near Mel's front door, his massive figure. He was naked, except for his underpants, and was talking to a boy from our district, a friend of ours nicknamed 'the Polack'. He was showing him all his bruises and telling him what had happened, making a lot of gestures and punching imaginary enemies in the empty air.

I approached. He had a sewn-up wound on his head, a dozen stitches. His horrible face was lit up by a smile and eighty per cent of his body was various shades of blue, green and black. But despite his physical condition he was in a very good mood. The first thing he said to me was:

'Holy Christ, your poor mother! Look what a state you're in!'

I couldn't help laughing. Nor could the Polack: he bent double with laughter, tears were coming out of his eyes.

'You clown! Have you seen yourself in the mirror? And you say I'm in a bad way! Go and get dressed, come on, let's go down to the river . . .' I gave him a gentle shove with my shoulder and he let out a yell.

'Can't you be a bit more gentle with me? I took enough blows for all of you the other evening!' he said boastfully.

He hurried off to get dressed and we started towards the river. While we were walking he told me about the others: they were all okay – a little the worse for wear, but okay. The very next day after the fight Gagarin had gone to Caucasus, a district of our town, to settle a score with one of the locals. Lyoza and Besa, who had miraculously succeeded in hiding in the park and hadn't been caught by the police, were in the best state of all: they didn't have a scratch.

When I reached my boat I suggested to Mel that we go for a trip up the river. There was a cool wind – a pleasant morning breeze – the sun was rising and everything was bright and peaceful.

Mel jumped into the boat and lay down in the bow on his back, looking up at the cloudless sky – it was a yes.

I took one oar and with it pushed the boat away from the bank, then I rowed slowly, in a standing position: I had the wind on my face, it was wonderful and relaxing. Ten metres from the bank I felt the current of the river grow stronger and stronger, so I switched on the motor and, gradually increasing speed, I set off upstream towards the old bridge. I put on the jacket that I always kept in the boat. Mel was still lying down in the bow. He was hardly moving: his eyes were closed, and his foot was just faintly rocking to and fro.

When we reached the bridge I made a wide curve and turned back with the motor switched off, letting the current carry the boat, only occasionally rowing to correct the direction. As the boat floated slowly downstream, now and again we jumped into the river and swam around. In the water I felt protected, I let myself be carried by the current, holding onto the boat or keeping slightly away from it. It was the best medicine in the world, the water of the river; I could have stayed in it all day long.

When we touched the bank, Mel jumped down from the boat and said he wanted to go and see an old aunt of his who lived not far away and always complained that nobody went to visit her. I decided to go and see Grandfather Kuzya, to tell him about everything that had happened to us.

In the community of the Siberian Urkas the greatest importance is attached to the relationship between children and old people. As a result there are many customs and traditions which make it possible for elderly criminals with great experience to educate children, even if they have no blood relationship with them. Each adult criminal asks an old man, usually one who has no family and lives on his own, to help him in the education of his children. He often sends his children to him, to take him food or give him a hand about the house; in exchange the old man tells the children the stories of his life and teaches them the criminal tradition, the principles and rules of behaviour, the codes of the tattoos and everything that is in any way connected with criminal activity. This kind of relationship is called in the Siberian language 'carving'.

The word 'grandfather' in the Siberian criminal community has many meanings. The grandparents are naturally the relatives, the parents' parents, but also the highest Authorities in the criminal world – in this case the word 'Holy' or 'Blessed' is prefixed to 'grandfather', so that it is immediately clear that the person under discussion is an Authority. An elderly educator, too, is called grandfather, but never grandfather alone: his name or nickname must always be added.

My very personal and dearly loved educator was, as will have become clear by now, Grandfather Kuzya. As far back as I can remember, my father always took me to see him. Grandfather Kuzya was highly respected in the criminal community, and he had earned this respect partly through the sorrows and sacrifices he had undergone for the sake of the community.

Grandfather Kuzya was ageless. His mother had died when he was very small and his father had been shot not long afterwards, and the family that had adopted him never knew exactly how old he was.

As a young man Grandfather Kuzya had belonged to a gang of Urkas led by a famous criminal called 'Cross', a man of the old Siberian faith who had opposed first the power of the tsar and later that of the communists. In Siberia, Grandfather Kuzya explained to me, no criminal ever supported a political force; everybody lived only following their own laws and fighting any government power. Siberia has always been coveted by the Russians because it is a land that is very rich in natural resources. Besides the fur-bearing animals, which in Russia are considered a national treasure, Siberia had large amounts of gold, diamonds and coal; later oil and gas were discovered too. All governments have tried to exploit the region as much as possible – of course without the slightest regard for the population. The Russians would arrive, said Grandfather Kuzya, build their towns in the middle of the woods, dig up the land, and carry off its treasures on their trains and ships.

The Siberian criminals, expert robbers whose ancestors had for centuries attacked the mercantile caravans coming from China and India, had had no difficulty in attacking the Russian ones too.

In those days the Urkas had a particular philosophy, a world-view, which they called the 'Great Pact'. It was a plan which made it possible to maintain a concerted resistance against the government. According to the old criminal law, each individual gang could carry out no more than one robbery every six months: in this way the quality of criminal activity was kept at a high level, because it is clear that if a group has only one chance to rob a caravan, it must prepare well and take no risks, avoiding any false moves. People were keen to organize the job well, otherwise they would have to go half a year without eating. The Great Pact eliminated this rule, allowing the gangs to carry out robberies continually, because the aim was not that of self-enrichment, but of driving the Russian invaders out of Siberia. Old criminals joined forces with the new ones, forming very large gangs. The most famous were those of Angel, Tiger and Tayga.

Cross had a smaller gang, comprising about fifty men. They robbed trains and the small ships that plied from the diamond mines on the River Lena to southern Siberia, and to the region called Altay. One day they made the mistake of coming out of the woods, and ran into the forces of the communist army. They tried to resist but in the end were outnumbered by the communists:

they were surrounded, and almost all of them died in battle.

The Urkas never surrendered; to them it was unworthy to be captured, so if they saw that the situation was hopeless they would say their farewells, wish each other good fortune and plunge into the fray, until the enemy killed them. The only possibility of surviving was to be captured because of your wounds: to be wounded and taken prisoner was not considered unworthy.

In that battle three young Urkas were captured. One of them was Kuzya; he had taken a blow to the head and passed out. The communists, to show all the Siberians how those who opposed the government were treated, immediately ordered an exemplary 'people's' trial for the prisoners in the town of Tagil, where the population had surrendered to the Russians, who had set up military barracks and police stations everywhere.

Many people attended the trial, because many Siberians sympathized with the Urkas and supported their struggle against the communists.

The judge and his 'jury', made up of 'representatives' of the people, and naturally all communists, sentenced all three to death. The sentence was to be carried out the following day by firing squad, in front of the walls of the old railway station.

Next day the place was full of people. Many had brought icons and put crosses outside their shirts, to emphasize their aversion to the communist regime. The women wept and asked for a pardon, the men prayed to the Lord to welcome those three slaves of His who were about to be killed unjustly. The atmosphere was very tense, and reinforcements had been sent from the police station with orders to go into action should the people become dangerous.

At last the criminals were driven up, taken out of the car and made to stand up, in chains. They were led before the judge and the public prosecutor, who read out to them all the charges which the Soviet government had brought against them. Then the judge read out the sentence and authorized the police to carry it out at once.

The three were placed with their backs turned and their faces against the wall, but none of them wanted to stand in that position, so they turned around to face the firing squad. Some of the crowd threw crucifixes onto the ground near the criminals' feet, praying to the Lord to make the authorities pardon them.

The commander of the firing squad gave a series of orders to his men, who prepared their rifles, took aim at their targets and fired. Two of the condemned men fell dead on the ground, but the third, the one in the middle, continued to stand up and look at the people. His shirt was soaked with blood and he had eight wounds in his body, but he didn't fall; he stood motionless, breathing in the cold morning air deeply. It was Kuzya, the young Siberian Urka.

According to the rules of the Soviet state the death sentence could only be carried out once; if the condemned person survived he must be set free. For this reason, years later the communists took to shooting the condemned prisoners from half a metre away and straight in the head – to remove all possible doubt.

The people went wild with joy; to them Kuzya became a symbol, living proof of the existence of God, who had heard their prayers and shown His powers. From that day on every Siberian knew the story of Kuzya and referred to him as 'the Marked One'.

Partly because of this miraculous event, Kuzya was considered an Authority among the criminals. His advice was listened to by many good, honest criminals of different castes, and since he was wise and intelligent and had no personal interests – because his life, as he was fond of saying, belonged totally to the community – he succeeded in winning everyone's cooperation and friendship.

He had been in many Russian prisons, had sanctioned many alliances with various criminal societies and mediated the resolution of conflicts between gangs. Thanks to his intervention many criminals had signed truces among themselves, agreeing to live in peace to their mutual benefit, thus enhancing the prosperity of the whole community.

If in any part of Russia two criminal powers clashed over a certain question, he would set off on his travels and, using his authority, would force people to negotiate, to find the ways towards a peaceable solution. When I asked him questions about this role of his as a 'man of peace', he would reply that the people who made war were those who didn't follow the true principles, who had no dignity. There was nothing in this world that could not be shared in such a way as to make everyone happy.

'He who wants too much is a madman, because a man cannot possess more than his heart is able to love.

Everyone wants to do business, to see his family happy and bring up his children in goodness and peace. This is just. Only in this way can we share the world that Our Lord created for us.'

Grandfather Kuzya dedicated his whole life to keeping peace in the criminal community; as a result everyone was fond of him and he had no enemies. My father told me that once, when Grandfather Kuzya was in a maximum security prison, a group of young criminals from St Petersburg – people of the 'new style', who didn't respect the old rules – had broken a truce that had been agreed some time earlier between various communities thanks to his assistance. They had killed a lot of people, gaining control of a large area of business, after which they had tried to prove to others, the people who followed the old criminal rules, that those rules were no longer valid and had no real power behind them. To do this they needed to strike at some great Authority, and they chose the figure of Grandfather Kuzya, because he represented the highest power in the Siberian community. They devised a simple and very offensive plan, sending to him in prison a letter of invitation to a meeting that was to be held in St Petersburg, informing him that if he did not attend they would no longer consider him to be an active criminal.

This kind of blackmail is a very serious matter for a criminal, far more serious than the murder of a relative or a personal insult, because it affects the prestige that is accorded an individual by the entire community, so the insult extends to the whole community and its representatives.

Well, Grandfather Kuzya forced the prison admin-
istrators to grant a week's release to him and five other
Siberian Authorities who were being held in different
prisons in Russia, by threatening a mass suicide, which
none of them would have hesitated to carry out.

In the middle of the meeting, when the young St
Petersburg criminals were already planning in minute detail
how to compel all the supporters of the old Authorities to
hand over control of the area to them, taking it for granted
that none of them would attend, Grandfather Kuzya and
the other five prisoners arrived.

After that encounter the young men disappeared,
they just vanished into thin air: many thought of the old
Siberian ritual which involves the bodies of enemies being
minced up to the point of complete disintegration and
then mixed in with the soil of the woods.

According to the Siberian criminal law, every active
criminal can give up his post and retire – become a kind
of 'pensioner'. Once he has done this he no longer has the
right to use his name or express his opinion on questions
connected with criminal affairs or the resolution of
conflicts. The criminal community supports him by giving
him enough money to live on, and in exchange he takes
on the responsibility of educating the young. He becomes,
as has already been mentioned, a 'grandfather': a name
that is given as a mark of great respect. People who are
so called are regarded by the rest of the community
as wise men able to give essential advice to younger

criminals, and usually criminal meetings are organized at their homes.

Grandfather Kuzya had retired from business – or, as we say, 'tied the knot' – in the early 1980s, when I was born. His retirement had caused considerable tension in the criminal community: many feared that without him a lot of old truces would be broken and there would be war.

Grandfather Kuzya said that with or without him things were bound to change, because it was the times and the individuals that were different. When he discussed the matter with me, he explained it like this:

'The young want easy money, they want to take without giving anything in exchange, they want to fly without first having learned how to walk. They'll end up killing each other. Then they'll come to terms with the cops, and when that happens, I hope for your sake, my dear, that you'll be far away from here, because this place will become a graveyard of the good and honest.'

Naturally I considered everything Grandfather Kuzya said to be the highest expression of human intelligence and criminal experience.

We talked about the future, about what our life would be like and how things would be organized. He was very pessimistic, but he never feared that I would disappoint him; he considered me to be different from the other youngsters of our community.

After 1992, when the military forces of Moldova tried to occupy the territory of Transnistria, our town was abandoned by everybody; we were left to fend for ourselves, as in fact we always had done. All the armed criminals resisted the Moldovan soldiers, and after three months of battles they drove them out.

When the danger of an all-out conflict had passed, Mother Russia sent us her so-called 'help': the Fourteenth Army, led by the charismatic general Lebed. When they arrived in our town, which had already been free for several days, they applied the policy of military administration: curfew, house-to-house searches, the arrest and elimination of undesirable elements. During that period the river often brought to the bank the bodies of the people who had been shot, their hands tied behind their backs with wire and signs of torture on their bodies. I myself fished out four corpses of people who had been executed, so I can confirm with all my youthful authority that shootings by the Russian military were very common in Transnistria.

The Russians tried to exploit the circumstances to install among us, in the land of criminals, their government representatives, who would have the job of administering what had previously been solely in our hands. Many Siberian criminals during that period ran a serious risk of being killed; my father, for example, was the target of three attacks, but he miraculously escaped and, not wanting to wait for a fourth, left Transnistria and moved to Greece, where he had friends as a result of some old trading connections.

The criminals of the town tried to join forces to fight the Russian military, but many members of the communities were frightened and in the event proved willing to collaborate with the new regime. The Siberians renounced all contact with the rest of society, and by 1998 were completely isolated; they didn't collaborate with anyone and didn't support anyone. Other communities reached a compromise with the regime, which had proposed one of its own men as president of the country and political watchdog over all business. Very soon new government forces eliminated the people involved in those terms, taking over the administration of affairs.

Grandfather Kuzya told me everything he knew:

'Our law says that we mustn't talk to the cops: do you know why it says that? Not just out of caprice. It says this because the cops are the government's dogs, the tools the government uses against us. My son, they shot me when I was twenty-three years old, and ever since then I have lived my whole life in humility, without possessing anything – no family, no children, no house: all my life has been spent in prison, suffering, and sharing my sufferings with others. That's why I have power, because many people know me and know that when I cross my arms on the table I don't speak in my own private interest, but for the good of everyone. That, my boy, is why in our world everyone trusts me. And now tell me why we should trust those who have spent their whole lives killing our brothers, locking us up in prison, torturing us and treating us as if we didn't belong to the human race? How is it possible, tell me, to trust those who live thanks to our deaths? Cops are different from the rest of humanity, because they have an innate desire to serve, to have an employer. They don't understand anything about freedom, and they're scared of free men. Their bread is our sorrow, my son; how is it possible to reach an agreement with these people?'

Everything Grandfather Kuzya told me helped me to cope with reality, not to become the slave of a mistaken idea or a never-realized dream. I knew with certainty that I was witnessing the death of our society and so I tried to survive, passing through this great vortex of souls, human stories, from which I was drifting further and further away.

Every time I went to see Grandfather Kuzya, my mother would give me a bag of home-cooked food. My mother was an excellent cook; in our district she was renowned for her red soup, her wels catfish stuffed with rice, vegetables and apples, her pâté of caviare and butter, her country-style fish soup and, especially, her cakes. Grandfather Kuzya called her 'little mother': that's how the criminals express the greatest respect and admiration for women. Whenever I took him something made by my mother, he would say:

'Lilya, Lilya, my sweet little mother! What else can we do but kiss your hands all the time?'

Outside Grandfather Kuzya's house there was an old wooden bench. He would often sit there and watch the river. I would settle down next to him and we would sit there all day like that, sometimes till evening. He would recount to me the adventures of his own life, or the stories of the Siberian Urkas, which I loved. We sang songs. He was very good at singing, and knew a lot of criminal songs by heart. I had a good memory; I only had to hear a song a couple of times and I'd remember it instantly. Grandfather

Kuzya was very pleased about this, and he would always ask me before he sang:

'Do you remember this one?'

'I certainly do! It's my favourite!'

'Well done, young rascal! Sing along with me, then!' And we'd sing together, often arriving late for supper.

What I liked most of all was when Grandfather Kuzya told me about Siberia: the stories of the Urkas, of how they had opposed the regime of the tsar and that of the communists. It was wonderful, because in those stories you felt the thread that held my family together, and connected the people of the past with those of the present. Thanks to this thread everything seemed much more believable, real.

While he was narrating, he would almost always emphasize the link between the characters and the people we met every day in the street, to make me understand that although times had changed, the values had remained the same.

Grandfather Kuzya had been one of the first Siberians to arrive in Transnistria. He told the story of that move with sorrow, and it was clear that he had many dark feelings inside him, connected with that time.

'The soldiers arrived in the village at night. There were lots of them, all armed, with bayonets fixed, as if they were going to war . . . I was only small, about ten years old; my parents had died a long time ago, and I lived with some good people who had raised me as if I were their own son. The men were all away, in the Tayga; there was no one in the village but the old men, and the women with the children. I remember they entered the house without knocking and without taking their boots off. There was a man dressed in a black leather jacket and trousers. I remember the smell of that leather; it was sickening, unbearable. He looked at us and asked Pelagea, the lady of the house:

'"Do you have any news of your husband? Do you know where he is?"

'"He's gone hunting in the Tayga. I don't know when he'll be back . . ."

'"I thought as much. Right, put on some warm clothes, take only the most essential things, go outside and line up with the others." This man was a commander; he had the air of someone who knew he had power in his hands.

'"But what's happening? Why do we have to get dressed and go outside? It's night; the children are asleep . . ." Pelagea was agitated and her lips trembled as she spoke.

'The man stopped for a moment, looked carefully round the room and went over to the red corner, where the icons were: he picked one up and hurled it against the wall. The icon broke in two. He picked up some other icons, put them in the stove and said:

'"In ten minutes we're going to set fire to the village. If you want to stay here and be burnt alive, please yourselves."

'Pelagea had five children; the youngest was four, the eldest thirteen. In addition she looked after me and a fourteen-year-old girl, Varya, who had also lost her parents. She was a good woman, and very brave. Calmly she explained to us children that there was nothing to be afraid of, that everything was in the hands of the Lord. She made us dress in warm clothes, fetched the gold she kept in a safe place and hid it in our clothes. She took some ash from the stove and dirtied Varya's face; she did this deliberately, to make her ugly, because she was afraid the soldiers would rape her.

'"If they ask you anything, don't speak, don't look them in the face, let me do the talking. Everything will be all right."

'She took a big bag full of bread and dried meat and we went out.

'Outside there were a lot of people; the soldiers were looting the houses, breaking doors and windows and carrying off various objects, especially the golden frames of the icons. They had made a bonfire in the middle of the road, onto which they threw icons and crucifixes. Everyone was standing outside their houses, helplessly watching this disaster.

'An officer went along the lined-up people with a soldier, and whenever he saw an old person he ordered the soldier:

'"This one, out!" and immediately the person he had picked out was run through with a bayonet. They were eliminating anyone who might slow down the trek.

'A young woman, the mother of three children, was taken by a group of soldiers into a house, where they raped her. Suddenly she rushed out naked, screaming in despair, and from the window of the house a soldier shot her in the back: she fell down on the snow, dead. One of her children, the eldest, ran towards her, crying out; a nearby soldier hit him on the head with the butt of his rifle, and the boy fell to the ground unconscious.

'Then an officer shouted angrily:

'"Who fired that shot? Who was it?"

'The soldier who had fired out of the window emerged, looking sheepish.

'"It was me, comrade!"

'"Are you out of your mind? The order was only to fire in an emergency! Use your bayonet – I don't want to hear any gunfire! If those in the woods hear us, we'll never make it to the train!" He was agitated, and immediately afterwards he ordered an NCO: "Hurry up! Set fire to the houses and get the people lined up, start the march!"

'The soldiers pushed everyone into the middle of the road, forming a column, then they ordered us to walk. We went away, full of hatred and fear; now and then we looked back and saw our houses burning in the darkness like little paper boxes.

'We walked all night, till we reached the railway in the middle of the woods; waiting for us there was a train with wooden wagons, without windows. They ordered us to get on, and when we did so we realized that the train was already full of people from various other villages. They told their story, which was a duplicate of our own. Someone said he'd heard the train was bound for a distant region, in the south of Russia; it would travel across Siberia for another week, collecting people from the various burnt-out villages.

'They distributed firewood to burn in the little stoves that the wagons were equipped with, and a little bread and ice-cold water. The train left, and after a terrible journey lasting a month we reached our destination, here, in the region called Transnistria, which some also called Bessarabia.

'When the train stopped we realized that the soldiers were no longer on it, only the drivers and a few railwaymen.

'We didn't know anyone here; we only had a bit of gold with us; a lot of people had managed to bring their weapons too.

'We went to live by the river: we'd grown up on the Siberian rivers and were good at fishing and sailing; and that was the origin of our district, Low River.'

In present-day Russia hardly anyone knows about the deportation of the Siberians to Transnistria; some remember the times of communist collectivization, when the country was criss-crossed by trains full of poor people being moved from one region to another for reasons known only to the government.

Grandfather Kuzya used to say the communists had planned to separate the Urkas from their families so as to make our community die, but that instead, by an irony of fate, they had probably saved it.

From Transnistria many young men went to Siberia, to participate in the war against the communists: they robbed trains, ships and military stores and created a lot of difficulties for the communists. At regular intervals they returned to Transnistria to lick their wounds, or to spend time with their family and friends. Despite everything, this land has become a second home, to which the Siberian criminals have bound their lives.

Grandfather Kuzya didn't educate me by giving lessons, but by talking, telling his stories and listening to my opinions. Thanks to him I learned many things which have enabled me to survive. His way of seeing and understanding the world was very humble; he didn't talk about life from the position of one who observes from above, but from that of a man who stands on the earth and endeavours to stay there as long as possible.

'Many people desperately seek what they are not able to keep and understand, and consequently are full of hatred and feel bad all their lives.'

I liked his way of thinking, because it was very easy to understand. I didn't have to put myself in someone else's shoes, I just had to listen to him, remaining myself, to understand that everything that came out of his lips was true. He had a wisdom that came from deep down, it didn't even seem human, but as if derived from something greater and stronger than man.

'Look what a state we're in, son . . . Men are born happy, yet they convince themselves that happiness is something they have to find in life . . . And what are we? A herd of animals without instinct, which follow mistaken ideas, searching for what they already have . . .'

Once, while we were fishing, we were discussing happiness. At one point he asked me:

'Look at the animals: do you think they know anything about happiness?'

'Well, I think they feel happy or sad now and then, only they can't express their feelings . . .' I replied.

He looked at me in silence and then said:

'Do you know why God gave man a longer life than that of the animals?'

'No, I've never thought about it . . .'

'Because animals base their lives on instinct and don't make mistakes. Man bases his life on reason, so he needs part of his life for making mistakes, another part for understanding his mistakes, and a third for trying to live without making any more.'

I often went to visit Grandfather Kuzya, especially when I was a bit depressed or worried about something, because he understood me instantly and managed to make all my unpleasant thoughts disappear.

That morning, after I'd been beaten up by the police, I felt such a weight in my soul that it almost hurt me to breathe. When I thought about what had happened to me I was close to tears, I swear it – tears of despair and humiliation. The boat trip with Mel had done me good, but now I really needed Grandfather Kuzya and his warm words. I walked towards his house like a sleepwalker who doesn't know where he's going; it was a kind of instinct that guided me at that moment.

Grandfather Kuzya always woke up very early, so as soon as I reached the gate of his sister's house, where he lived, I found him already on the roof, launching the first pigeons into the air. He saw me and beckoned to me to come up. I got an old, twisted ladder with two rungs missing, rested it against the roof and started to climb. Grandfather Kuzya in the meantime was watching a female pigeon fly off into the sky; she was already quite high. Then he looked down at me and said:

'Do you want to fly this one?' showing me a male pigeon which he was holding in his right hand.

'Yes, I'll try . . .' I replied. I knew very well how to launch pigeons – we had a lot of them in my family. My Grandfather Boris was famous for his pigeons – he travelled all over Russia looking for new breeds, then crossed them and selected the strongest ones.

Grandfather Kuzya didn't have many pigeons – no more than fifty or so – but they were all exceptional specimens, because the many people who came to see him from all over the country brought him the finest pigeons they had, as gifts.

The pigeon Grandfather Kuzya was holding in his hand was of an Asiatic breed. He came from Tajikistan. He was very strong and handsome, one of the most expensive on the market. I picked him up and was about to launch him, but Grandfather Kuzya stopped me:

'Wait, let her get up a bit higher . . .'

To wait was to risk losing her – if they fly too high, many female pigeons drop down dead. They're used to being in a pair, together with the male: without the male to help them descend they can't return to the ground; they have to be guided. So it's essential to launch the male at the right moment: he rises, and the female, hearing him beat his wings and turn somersaults in the air, starts flying down towards him. But our female was already a long way off.

'Now, Kolima, let him go!' said Grandfather Kuzya, and at once, with a vigorous sweep of my arms I launched the pigeon.

'Well done! Good boy! May Jesus Christ bless you!' Grandfather Kuzya was pleased; he watched the pigeons approach one another in the air. Together we witnessed that spectacular union: the male did more than twenty somersaults, and the female flew in ever tighter circles around him, almost touching him with her wings. They were a beautiful couple.

Eventually the two joined together in the air, and one beside the other they began to descend lower and lower, in wide circles. Grandfather Kuzya looked at my face, pointing at my bruise.

'Come on, let's make some chifir . . .' We got down from the roof and went into the kitchen. Grandfather Kuzya put the water for the chifir on the fire.

Chifir is a very strong tea which is made and drunk according to an ancient ritual. It has a powerful stimulant effect: drinking one cup is like drinking half a litre of coffee all in one go. It is prepared in a small saucepan, the *chifirbak*, which is not used for any other purpose and is never washed with detergent, only rinsed in cold water. If the *chifirbak* is black – dirty with the residue of tea – it is more highly prized, because the chifir will come out better. When the water boils, you extinguish the fire and add black tea, which must be of whole leaves, not crumbled, and must only come from Irkutsk, in Siberia: there they grow a particular tea, the strongest and tastiest of them all, and beloved of criminals all over the country. Very different from the famous tea of Krasnodar, which is highly popular with housewives: a weak tea, widespread especially in Moscow and in southern Russia, and good for breakfast. For a proper chifir you use up to half a kilo of tea leaves. The leaves have to be left to brew for no more than ten minutes, otherwise the chifir becomes acidic and unpleasant. You put a lid on the saucepan so that the steam doesn't escape; it's advisable to wrap the whole thing in a towel, to maintain the temperature. The chifir is ready when there are no more leaves floating on the surface: hence we say the chifir has 'fallen' to indicate that it's ready. It is filtered through a strainer: the tea leaves are not thrown away, they are put on a dish and left there to dry; they will be used later for making ordinary tea, which can be drunk with sugar and lemon, while eating cake.

Chifir must be drunk in a large mug made of iron or silver, which can hold more than a litre of tea. You drink it in a group, passing round this mug, called *bodyaga*, which in the old Siberian criminal language means 'flask'. You pass it to your companion in a clockwise direction, never anticlockwise; each time you must drink three sips, no more, no less. While drinking you must not speak, smoke, eat or do anything else. It is forbidden to blow into the mug: that is considered bad manners. The first person to drink is the one who has made the chifir, then the mug passes to the others, and the one who finishes it must get up, wash it and put it back in its place. Once that has been done you can talk, smoke, or eat something sweet.

These rules are not the same in all communities: for example, in central Russia they don't take three sips but only two, and blowing into the mug is considered an act of kindness to the others, because you are cooling the boiling drink for them. In any case, offering a chifir to someone is a sign of respect, of friendship.

The best chifir is that made over a burning wood fire. Consequently in many criminals' houses the fireplaces have a special structure for making chifir; otherwise we use a stove, but never one heated by gas.

In Siberia, once it has been made, the chifir must be drunk straight away: if it gets cold it is not warmed up again, but thrown away. In other places, especially in prison, the chifir can be warmed up, but not more than once. And warmed-up chifir is no longer called chifir, but chifirok – a diminutive, in all senses.

We drank the chifir in silence, as the tradition requires, and only when we had finished did Grandfather Kuzya start talking:

'Well, how are you, young rascal?'

'I'm fine, Grandfather Kuzya, except that a few days ago we got into some trouble, in Tiraspol, and we were roughed up a bit by the cops . . .' I wanted to be honest, but at the same time I didn't want to exaggerate. With someone like Grandfather Kuzya there was no need to boast or to moan about what happened in your life, because he had certainly been through worse.

'I know all about it, Kolima . . . But you're alive, they didn't kill you. So why are you in such a bad mood?'

'They took my pike, the one Uncle Hedgehog gave me . . .' When I uttered these words I felt as if I were attending my own funeral. What had happened became even more terrible, and broke my heart, as I described it.

When I think of what I must have looked like at that moment I feel like laughing, which is exactly what Grandfather Kuzya did:

'All this gloom just because the cops took your pike! You know that everything that happens is in the hands of God and forms part of His great plan. Think about it: our pikes are powerful because they contain the force that Our Lord puts in them. And when someone takes our pike and uses it without honesty, the pike will lead him to ruin, because the force of the Lord will destroy the enemy. So what have you got to cry about? A good thing has happened: your pike will bring many misfortunes to a cop, and eventually kill him. Then another will take it, and another, and your pike will kill them all . . .'

Grandfather Kuzya's explanation gave me some relief, but although I was pleased that my pike would harm the police, I still missed it.

I didn't want to disappoint him and whine in front of him, so I put a lilt in my voice, making it sound as cheerful as possible:

'Okay, I'm happy, then . . .'

Grandfather Kuzya smiled.

'Good boy! That's the way: always hold your chest like a wheel and your pecker like a pistol . . .'

A week later I went round to Grandfather Kuzya's again to take him a jar of caviare pâté and butter. He called me into the living room and stood me in front of the red corner of the icons. There, on the shelf, was a beautiful open pike, with a very thin blade and a bone handle. I gazed at it spellbound.

'I had it sent all the way from Siberia, our brothers brought it for a young friend of mine . . .' He picked it up and put it in my hand. 'Take it, Kolima, and remember: the things that matter are the ones inside you.'

I was again the happy owner of a pike and I felt as if I'd been given a second life.

In the evening I wrote in big letters on a sheet of paper the words Grandfather Kuzya had said to me, and hung the paper in my bedroom, near the icons. My uncle, when he saw it, looked at me with a question-mark in his eyes. I made a gesture with my hands, as if to say: 'That's how it is.' He smiled at me and said:

'Hey, we've got a philosopher in the family!'

WHEN THE SKIN SPEAKS

When I was small I loved drawing. I carried a little exercise book around with me and drew everything I saw. I liked to see how the subjects transferred onto paper, and I loved the process of drawing. It was like being inside a bubble, enclosed in a world of my own, and God only knows what happened in my head during those moments.

We children all wanted to be like the grown-ups, so we imitated them in everything we did: our speech, the way we dressed, and also our tattoos. The adult criminals – our fathers, grandfathers, uncles and neighbours – were covered in tattoos.

In the Russian criminal communities there is a strong culture of tattoos, and each tattoo has a meaning. The tattoo is a kind of identity card which places you within the criminal society – displaying your particular criminal 'trade', and other kinds of information about your personal life and prison experiences.

Each community has its own tradition of tattooing, symbology and different patterns, according to which the signs are positioned on the body and eventually read and translated. The oldest tattooing culture is that of Siberia; it had been the forebears of the Siberian criminals who had created the tradition of tattooing symbols in a codified, secret manner. Later this culture was copied by other communities and spread throughout prisons all over Russia, transforming the principal meanings of the tattoos and the ways in which they were executed and translated.

The tattoos of the most powerful criminal caste in Russia, which is called Black Seed, are all copied from the Urka tradition, but have different meanings. The images may be the same, but only a person who is able to read a body can analyse their hidden meaning and explain why they are different.

Unlike the other communities, Siberians tattoo only by hand, using various kinds of small needle. Tattoos done with electrical tattoo machines or similar devices are not considered worthy.

In the tradition of the Siberian Urkas the process of tattooing continues throughout the life of a criminal. The first few signs are tattooed when he is twelve years old. Then, over the years, other details are added, gradually building up a narrative. Each experience he has in his life is encoded and concealed within this single large tattoo, which becomes increasingly complete as time goes on. It has the structure of a spiral, starting from the extremities

– the hands and feet – and ending at the centre of the body. The last parts of the body to be tattooed are the back and chest; this is done when the criminal is about forty or fifty years old. You will never see young people with large, complete tattoos in the Siberian criminal community, as you do in other communities.

To be able to read bodies decorated with such complex tattoos you need a lot of experience and you have to know the tattooing tradition perfectly. As a result the figure of the tattooist has a special place within the Siberian criminal community: he is like a priest, trusted by everyone to act on their behalf.

As a child I was intrigued by this tradition, but I didn't know much about it – only what my grandfather, my father and my uncle had told me. I was interested in the idea of being able to read everything that was written on their bodies.

So I spent a long time copying the tattoos which I saw around me, and the more I copied them the more I despaired, because I couldn't find one tattoo that was the same as another. The main subjects recurred, but the details changed. After a while I understood that the secret must lie in the details, so I began to analyse them: but it was like trying to learn a foreign language without having anyone to teach you. I had noticed that certain images were placed on some parts of the body but not on others. I tried to make connections between the images, venturing hypotheses, but the details felt elusive, like sand that slipped through my fingers.

When I was about ten I began to do fake tattoos on my friends' arms, recreating with a biro the images I had seen on grown-up criminals. Later, neighbours started asking me to do specific drawings for them, which they would then go and have tattooed on their bodies. They would explain to me how they wanted it to look and I would reproduce it on paper. Many paid me – not much, ten roubles a time, but to me the mere fact that they paid me at all was amazing.

In this way, without intending to, I became quite well known in the district, and the old tattooist who did all the tattoos based on the drawings that I prepared – Grandfather Lyosha – sent me his regards and his compliments now and then, through different people. I was pleased: it made me feel important.

On my twelfth birthday, my father had a serious talk with me: he told me I was old enough and must think about what I wanted to do with my life, so that I could break away from my parents and become independent. Many of my friends had already done a bit of smuggling under the guidance of the adults, and I too had made a number of trips with my Uncle Sergey, crossing the border repeatedly with gold in my rucksack.

I replied that I wanted to learn the tattooist's trade.

A few days later my father sent me to Grandfather Lyosha's house to ask him if he would take me on as his apprentice. Grandfather Lyosha gave me a warm welcome, offered me some tea, leafed through my drawing-book and examined the tattoos that I'd done on myself.

'Congratulations! You've got a "cold hand",' he commented. 'Why do you want to be a tattooist?'

'I like drawing, and I want to learn our tradition; I want to understand how to read tattoos . . .'

He laughed, then he got up and went out of the room. When he came back he was holding a tattooing needle in his hands.

'Look at this carefully: this is what I tattoo honest people with. It's this needle that has won me the respect of many and earned me my humble bread. It's because of this needle that I have spent half my life in prison, tormented by the cops; throughout my life I have never succeeded in possessing anything except this needle. Go home and think about it. If you really want to lead this life, come back to me: I'll teach you all I know about the trade.'

I thought about it all night. I didn't like the idea of spending half my life in prison and being tortured by the cops, but given that the alternatives that lay ahead promised more or less the same, I decided to give it a try.

Next day I was back at the door of his house. Grandfather Lyosha explained to me first of all what it meant to 'learn' to be a tattooist. I would have to help him with the housework – doing the cleaning, going shopping, gathering firewood – so that he would have time to devote to me.

And that was how it turned out. Little by little Grandfather Lyosha taught me everything. How to prepare a work-station for the tattooing, how to do a drawing, how best to transfer it onto the skin. He gave me homework, too: for example, I would have to invent ways in which images could intertwine, while still remaining faithful to the criminal tradition. He taught me the meanings of the images and their positions on the body, explaining the origin of each one, and how it had evolved in the Siberian tradition.

After a year and a half he allowed me to retouch a faded tattoo for a client, a criminal who had just been released from prison. All I had to do was go over the lines. The tattoo was a rather poorly executed image of a wolf – I remember that it was out of proportion – so I suggested that I should also alter it slightly from the 'artistic' point of view. I drew a new image, which I could easily use to cover the old one, and showed it to my master and his client. They agreed. So I did the tattoo, which came out well: the criminal was happy and thanked me profusely.

From that moment my master allowed me to fix all the old and faded tattoos, and when I had become more expert, with his permission I began to do new jobs, on virgin skin.

I started to create images for the tattoos using the symbology of the Siberian criminal tradition with ever greater confidence. Now, whenever Grandfather Lyosha gave me a new assignment, he no longer showed me how to draw the image; he simply told me the meaning that had to be encoded in it. I used the symbols, which I knew by now, to create the image, as a writer uses the letters of the alphabet to build up a story.

Sometimes I met people with unusual tattoos, which had interesting stories behind them. Many of them came to see my master, and he would show me their tattoos, explaining their meaning to me. These were what the criminals call 'signatures': tattoos that have a final meaning which incorporates a symbol, or even the name, of some elderly, powerful Authority. They work like a passport, and often prevent a person being given a hostile reception in some place far from his home. Usually these tattoos are executed in a highly individual style. It is possible to make them unique, without directly linking their meanings with the name or nickname of the person who wears them: you have to exploit the characteristics and peculiarities of the body and connect them with the meanings of the other tattoos. I saw signatures on various people, and each time I discovered different ways of combining the subjects to create unique images.

Once when I was at home a boy came to call me, saying that Grandfather Lyosha wanted to see me, to show me something. I went with him.

There were some people in my master's house – about ten in all. Some were from our district, others I had never seen before. They were criminals who had come all the way from Siberia. They were sitting round a table and talking among themselves. My master introduced me:

'This young rascal is studying to become a *kolshik*.[1] I teach him well; hopefully one day, with the help of Our Lord, he really will become one.'

A sturdy man got up from the table. He had a long beard and a number of tattoos on his face which I read

---

1. In the criminal language this means 'he who stings', i.e. the tattooist.

instantly – he was a man who had been condemned to death but pardoned at the last moment.

'So you're Yury's son?'

'Yes, I'm Nikolay "Kolima", son of Yury "The Rootless",' I replied in a firm voice.

The criminal smiled, and laid his gigantic hand on my head:

'I'll come round to see your father later. We're old friends, in our youth we belonged to the same family in a juvenile prison . . .'

My master patted me on the back:

'Now I'm going to show you something that you must be able to recognize, if you want to become a good tattooist . . .'

We crossed the room and went out into the back yard, where there was a small orchard with a few fruit trees. We entered a little toolshed made of wood and rusty corrugated iron. My master lit a lamp which hung down from the ceiling, dangling at the level of my face.

On the floor lay a large object which had been covered with a sheet of coarse cloth. My master removed the sheet: underneath was a dead man. He was naked, and there were no signs of knife wounds or blood, only a big black bruise on the neck.

Strangled, I thought.

The skin was very white, almost like paper; he must have been dead for several hours. The face was relaxed, the mouth slightly open, the lips purple.

'Look here, Kolima, look closely.' Bending down and turning towards me Grandfather Lyosha pointed to a tattoo on the dead man's right arm.

'Well, what do you say? What is this tattoo?'

He asked me this with a kind of mystery in his voice, as if the time had come for me to show what I had learned from him.

Without really meaning to, I began to analyse the tattoo and express my conclusions out loud. Grandfather Lyosha listened to me very patiently, keeping the corpse turned towards me.

'It's the signature of a Siberian Authority nicknamed "Tungus". It was done in Special Prison no. 36, in the year 1989, in the town of Ilin, in Siberia. There is also the blessing for the reader, a clear sign that the tattooist who did it is a Siberian Urka . . .'

'Is that all? Don't you see anything else?' my master asked me suspiciously.

'Well, it's fine, as a tattoo: it's well executed, perfectly legible, has a classic combination of images and is very clear . . . But . . .'

Yes, there was a but.

'It's the only tattoo on the body,' I continued, 'and yet in the image there are references to other tattoos, which are missing here . . . It was done in 1989, but it seems to have healed only a few months ago: it's still too black, the pigment hasn't faded . . . Also, this signature is in a strange position. Usually the arm is where you draw "seeds" or "wings",[1] whereas signatures act as a kind of bridge between two tattoos. They can be done on the inside of the forearm, or more rarely just above the foot, on the ankle . . .'

---

1. The tattoos so called do not represent seeds or wings: they contain various images which allude to the criminal's personal characteristics, the promises he has made and any romantic attachments he might have.

'And why are they done there?' my master interrupted me.

'Because it's important for the tattoo to be in a place where it can be easily displayed in any situation. Whereas this one has been put in an inconvenient place.'

I stopped for a moment. I made some calculations and deductions in my poor head, then finally gazed at my master wide-eyed:

'I don't believe it! Don't tell me, Grandfather Lyosha . . . He can't be a . . .' I stopped again, because I couldn't utter the word.

'Yes, my boy, this man is a cop. Look at him closely, because who knows? Some time in your life you may come across another who tries to pass himself off as one of us, and then you won't have time to think, you'll have to be a hundred per cent sure and recognize him straight away. This guy somehow found out that one of us wore a signature, and he copied it exactly, without knowing what a signature really is, how it's made and how it's read and translated . . . He got himself killed because he was too stupid.'

I wasn't shocked, either by the body of the strangled policeman or by the story of the tattoo copied from a criminal. The only thing that seemed strange, unnatural and alien at that moment was the cop's empty, tattooless body. It seemed to me an impossible thing, almost like a disease. Ever since I was a baby I had always been surrounded by tattooed people, and to me this was completely normal. Seeing a body with nothing tattooed on it had a strange effect on me – a physical suffering, a kind of pity.

My own body, too, seemed strange to me – I found it too empty.

According to the rule, tattoos are made in particular phases of life; you can't have all the tattoos that you like done immediately, there is a particular sequence.

If a criminal has a tattoo done on his body which doesn't convey any real information about him, or has a tattoo done prematurely, he is severely punished, and his tattoo must be removed.

After having a particular experience, you describe it through the tattoo, like in a kind of diary. But since the criminal life is hard, tattoos are not said to be 'done', but 'suffered'.

'Look! I've suffered another tattoo.' The expression doesn't refer to the physical pain felt during the process of tattooing, but to the meaning of that particular tattoo and the difficult life that lies behind it.

Once I met a boy called Igor. He was always getting into trouble, and a lot of people regarded him as a hothead. He was the son of a Moldovan woman who worked in a factory and had no connection with the criminal life. She had been married to a Ukrainian criminal who had gambled and owed money to half the town. Then one day he had been killed – someone had cut his hands off and thrown him into the river, where he'd drowned. There was only one thing left of him: his son Igor.

His son was a lot like him in some respects – he stole money from his mother and then went and squandered it playing cards; he did dirty little jobs for certain criminals of the Centre district, who used him in small-scale scams. Once he was caught at the market trying to steal the handbag of my friend Mel's mother. In revenge Mel had permanently disfigured and crippled him.

Anyway, this boy was eventually caught by the policemen of a Ukrainian town trying to rob an old woman by threatening her with violence. Since he was scared of going to prison for this kind of crime, which is despised by the criminal community, he made up an incredible story: that he was an important member of the Siberian community, the police were out to frame him and the old woman was in league with them. To lend his story added credibility, the idiot gave himself some tattoos while he was in a cell at the police station. Using a piece of wire and the ink from a biro, he scored some Siberian images on his fingers and hands, without even knowing their meaning.

When he got to prison he told his story, hoping his cellmates would believe him. But since the jails are usually full of experienced people who are capable of understanding the psychology of other human beings, they immediately became suspicious of him. They contacted the Siberian community, asking if anyone knew Igor and knew anything about his tattoos. The answer was negative. So they killed him, throttling him with a towel in his sleep.

Usurping someone else's tattoo is, for the Siberian tradition, one of the biggest mistakes you can make, and is punishable by death. But this is only true of an existing tattoo, which someone already has on them and which represents codified personal information. By contrast, using the tradition to create tattoos for strangers is like giving them a lucky charm. Many people who do business with people who belong to the Siberian criminal community – friends and supporters – may wear traditional tattoos, provided that the person who tattooed them and prepared the design is a Siberian tattooist and an expert.

The relationship between the tattooist and his client is a complex one, and requires a separate explanation.

As well as being able to tattoo, create designs and read them on the body, the tattooist must know how to behave and how to follow certain rules. The process of requesting a job is a very long one. Before 'suffering' a tattoo, the criminal must be introduced to the tattooist by a friend who vouches for him – only if these conditions are met may the tattooist accept the job.

The tattooist may only refuse a client if he has grounds for being suspicious of him. In this case, he has the right to ask the criminal to contact a well-known Authority in Siberian society who can give him formal permission to be tattooed. The tattooist must, however, behave politely, so as not to offend anyone. He cannot talk about his suspicions, he must simply ask his prospective client to do him a favour – that of 'taking some news' to an old Authority. And even when the criminal reaches this Authority, he must never say straight out 'I want permission to have a tattoo', but only 'Tattooist x requests permission to send you his greetings through me.' In response, the Authority gives him a letter or sends one of his men to accompany him.

At this point, the tattooist, according to the criminal rule, may only refuse a job in the event of bereavement or serious illness. The criminal, for his part, cannot compel the tattooist to meet a deadline imposed by him – consequently, a large tattoo often has to wait for several years.

The methods of payment, too, follow a ritual. Honest criminals, as a matter of dignity, never speak of money. In the Siberian community all material goods, and particularly money, are despised, so they are never even mentioned. If the Siberians speak of money, they call it 'that', or 'rubbish', 'cauliflower', or 'lemons', or they simply specify the figures, pronounce the numbers. The Siberians do not keep money in the house because it is said to bring bad luck into the family – it destroys happiness and 'scares off' good fortune. They keep it near the house, in the garden, for example, in a special hiding place, such as an animal hutch.

So before beginning a tattoo they never mention a fixed price – they don't mention anything connected with money. Only afterwards, when the work is finished, does the client ask the tattooist 'What do I owe you?' and the tattooist replies, 'Give me what is right.' This is the answer that is considered most honest, and is therefore most frequently used by the Siberian tattooists.

Free criminals pay well for the tattooist's work: in money, weapons, icons, cars, and even property. In prison it's different. There the tattooist will settle for a few cigarettes, a packet of tea or a jar of jam, a cigarette lighter or a box of matches, and occasionally a little money.

Among tattooists there is complete cooperation and a sense of brotherhood. When they are not in prison they go and visit each other and exchange the latest techniques.

In prison tattooists often share clients, because one may like doing one type of image, another a different type. Generally the older tattooist supervises the younger, coaches him a little and teaches him what he has learned in life. Many tattoos are done by more than one tattooist because criminals often change prison or cell. So the work begun by one tattooist may be continued by a second and finished by a third, but tradition requires that each subsequent tattooist ask the permission of the one who began it. And the process of asking is complicated. In the Siberian criminal community nobody ever asks for anything directly: there is a form of communication which satisfies people and takes the place of explicit requests. For example, if a new criminal with an unfinished tattoo arrives in a prison where a tattooist works, the tattooist asks him the name of the master who began that work. The new tattooist writes a letter in the criminal language, which finds its way, via the prisoners' secret postal system, known as the 'road', to the first tattooist. The letter appears to be extremely polite and full of compliments, but in fact it is very formulaic: it follows the principles of Siberian education. If this letter were read by a person who did not belong to the criminal world it would seem to him a jumble of incoherent words.

I've often written this kind of letter myself, both in prison and outside. I remember one particular case: I was serving my third sentence, by now an adult, when a Siberian criminal arrived in our cell who had a beautiful tattoo on his back that needed finishing. It had been begun by a famous old tattooist, Afanasy 'Fog'. I had heard a lot about this legendary man. Apparently he had taken up tattooing quite late in life, at the age of about forty; previously he had been an ordinary criminal, a train robber. During a gunfight he had been shot in the head and left deaf and dumb. Suddenly he had started doing drawings which were considered far more than beautiful – they were perfect – and then he had learned how to tattoo. In a diary that he kept he explained it like this: he said he was constantly hearing in his head the voices of God and the angels suggesting to him iconographical subjects connected with Siberian Orthodox religion. This diary was very well-known in our community – people passed it around and copied it out by hand, as is customary in the criminal society with any document or testimony written by a person who is considered to be 'marked' by God. I had read it myself when I was a boy, my master had lent it to me and I had copied it out into an exercise book, and as I did so I felt I learned many things.

I had only seen examples of his work on two occasions and had been struck by how full of suffering those images were. He had an unusual technique. It wasn't very refined, in fact I'd say it was downright coarse, but he succeeded in creating forms and subjects which fed the imagination. They were different from all others. When you looked at them you didn't feel as if you were seeing a body with a tattoo on it; it was the tattoo itself that was a living thing, with a body underneath it. It was stunning – more powerful than any other thing I had ever seen on human skin.

I had long yearned to meet Fog, and I dreamed of finding a way of telling him about myself, and about my work.

The criminal who had come to our cell had a tattoo on his back called 'The Mother'; it was very complex and full of hidden meanings. Like all large tattoos, the Mother is the centre of a galaxy; within the design the meanings of the smaller images intersect and sometimes overlap, whirling around in a spiral until they enter the principal image and disappear at the very moment when the study of the details focuses the observer's attention on a single subject.

When the criminal asked me to finish the tattoo I couldn't believe it: to follow the lines traced by Fog would be an honour. At once I wrote a letter to him using all my knowledge of the rules that regulated relations between criminal tattooists:

> Dear Brother Afanasy Fog,
>
> The writer of this letter is Nikolay Kolima, with the help of the Lord and all the Saints a humble *kolshik*.
>
> Praying to the icons, I hope all of us will continue to enjoy the blessing of the Lord.
>
> Into the house which, thanks to Our Lord, I share with honest people, there has descended and, with the help of God, taken up residence an honest, orphan vagabond, Brother Z . . .
>
> He holds, with the grace of the Lord, The Mother, which sings your miraculous hand, guided by God himself.

Through the love of Our Saviour Jesus Christ,
The Mother is illuminated; not much is lacking to the
completion of her splendour.

With brotherly love and affection, in the grace of
Our Almighty Lord, I wish you good health and many
years of love and faith in the Marvellous Siberian
Cross.

Nikolay Kolima

I was simply asking him for permission to finish his work,
but in order to do this I was using codified phrases which
formed a kind of poetry with hidden meanings. Let me
explain.

If a criminal calls another man *brother*, he does so not
out of politeness, but to make him understand that he is
not merely a member of the criminal society like him, but
a colleague of his.

It is very important in the law of criminal communication to introduce yourself immediately – name,
nickname and trade – otherwise the words that precede
and follow have no importance.

Humble kolshik – that is, humble 'stinger' – is another
way of describing the tattooist's trade. The word *kolshik*
is slang and ancient, and must always be accompanied by
an adjective such as 'humble' or 'poor', which emphasizes
the unambitious position, devoid of the least vanity, that
is characteristic of those who carry on that trade.

After the official introduction comes a bridge-sentence,
which doesn't convey any concrete message with respect
to the meaning of the letter. It is written in obedience to
an ancient tradition – in any form of communication, the

important information must never be given immediately, but only after a short, 'transparent' passage which deals not with criminal affairs but with ordinary, mundane, obvious things. This section is used to express the state of mind of the person who is making the request, because any open display of emotion is not tolerated between criminals – even in the most difficult situations you must maintain your self-control, and keep, as they say, a cool head. In this case I wrote a sentence which conveyed a hint of religious hope, which is never a bad thing in letters, or indeed in any kind of communication between criminals.

After this you come to the point.

I say that in my cell, which is called a *house*, there has arrived – *descended* – a criminal, who *has taken up residence*, that is, has been accepted by the other criminals, *honest people*. Which means that the new arrival has a letter, safe-conduct or tattoo, the signature of an Authority.

I call the new arrival an *honest vagabond*, to indicate that he is an unambitious, humble person who knows how to behave.

Orphan is a word which in slang can have many meanings: in this case I was alluding to the fact that he had been forced to leave his previous prison. It was important to stress this in the letter, because criminals do not respect those who ask to be transferred – they call them 'mad horses', and say 'as soon as anything happens, these guys jump at the door like mad horses'.

After this I wrote that the new arrival *holds with the grace of the Lord*, which simply means that he has a tattoo. Among criminals it is not usual to say 'I have a tattoo', you say 'I hold with the grace of the Lord', and then you specify which tattoo in particular you have; if you are referring to all the tattoos together you call them 'the honest seeds', 'the tears of the Lord', or 'His seals'. In this case *The Mother*, because that was the specific tattoo that the criminal had on his back.

The Mother sings your miraculous hand is a compliment to Fog. If a tattoo has been executed well, it sings the hand of the tattooist.

Then comes another, more significant compliment: Fog's hand is *guided by God Himself*. This is not to be taken in a literal sense – God in this case means the criminal law. The tattoo, that is, has been executed according to the rules of the criminal tradition, in a very professional manner.

The letter culminated in the words, *The Mother is illuminated*. This means that the tattoo, though unfinished, works perfectly. 'To illuminate' means to put hidden information into the tattoo itself, so I was saying that this element of the work was complete and there was no need to add or change anything; it was sufficient to put the finishing touches to it, to strengthen a line here and there, fill it out with nuances of colour, etc.

The phrase *not much is lacking to the completion of her splendour* is an indirect request for permission to continue the work.

Then come the traditional greetings and good wishes, and lastly the signature. In the Siberian tradition the surname is never used, only the first name and nickname, because belonging to a family is considered to be a private matter.

When I had finished the letter I was very pleased – it felt like a turning point in my life. I gave the letter to the people who organized the circulation of mail in our cell. They were obliged to stay at the window all the time and wait for a signal. The letters passed along strings from one window to another – if they were addressed to someone in that cell, they were delivered to the addressee, otherwise they continued to move on from cell to cell, and if necessary from prison to prison. The prison mail was far more reliable and speedy than the normal mail, which indeed nobody used. In the space of two weeks the letters would reach any prison in the region, and to travel right across the country it would take less than a month. The prison to which I was sending my letter was a long way away, so it would take time.

I waited anxiously for the reply. After two months and a few days, a boy broke away from the team of 'postmen', holding in his hand a small letter written on a leaf from a lined exercise book:

'Kolima, it's for you, from Afanasy Fog.'

I took the letter from his hands and opened it excitedly. Written on it, in a very rough, cramped hand, were the words:

Greetings, dear brother Nikolay Kolima, and long years in the glory of Our Lord!

I, Afanasy Fog, thanks to Jesus Christ a humble *kolshik*, will remember in my prayers you and all the honest vagabonds who live in this blessed Land.

In the glory of the Lord one breathes well, enjoying peace and His love.

> The news of Brother Z . . . gives me immense
> joy, may the Lord bless him and send him long years,
> strength and health.
> The Mother, who with the help of the Saviour
> Jesus Christ is illuminated, with his same help will be
> continued.
> An embrace of brotherhood and affection to you;
> may Christ be with you and your family, and may He
> and all the Saints protect your blessed hand.
> Afanasy Fog

I read it and re-read it again and again, as if searching for
something else that might appear between the lines.

I was very proud that Fog had replied to me with such
respect and love, as if we were friends and had known
each other all our lives.

Many in the cell knew who Fog was, and as word got
around my authority increased.

It took me four months to finish Fog's tattoo. One
day my work happened to be seen by an old tattooist of
the Black Seed caste called Uncle Kesya, who occasionally
came out of the special security block to be given the
medication he needed at the infirmary. Using his authority,
Uncle Kesya sent me a parcel, containing a packet of tea,
cigarettes, sugar and a jar of honey. In the accompanying
letter he paid me a lot of compliments and said he was
pleased to see a job executed by a young man who hadn't
abandoned the needles and the traditional techniques for
the electric devices, which he called 'gobs of the devil'.

After that, many inmates, intrigued and moved by
the respect the old man had shown me, started asking me

to tattoo them according to the old Siberian principles – even people who were remote from our tradition and who belonged to different castes. It was delightful to see how men whom I had previously thought profoundly different from me, and with whom I would never have imagined I could have any relationship, except a business one, became very friendly. They wanted to know about Siberian history and the system of tattoos, and this created a bridge between us, a connection founded solely on curiosity about another culture, without any sordid interest connected with criminal affairs.

During those days I told them a lot of the stories that I had heard as a child from my grandfather and from other old men. Many of my cellmates were simple men, who had been sent to prison for ordinary crimes – men with no underlying criminal philosophy. One of them, a strapping young man called Shura, was serving a five-year sentence for killing someone in obscure circumstances. He didn't like talking about it, but it was clear that jealousy had something to do with it – it was a story of love and betrayal.

Shura was a strong man and as such he was sought after by several criminal groups – in prison the Authorities of the castes or families always try to make alliances with people who are strong and intelligent, so that they can dominate the others. But he kept to himself, didn't take anyone's side and lived his sad life like a hermit. Now and then some member of the Siberian family would invite him to drink tea or chifir, and he would come willingly because, he said, we were the only ones who didn't invite him to play cards in order to cheat him and then use him as a hitman. He spoke very little; usually he listened to the others reading their letters from home and sometimes, when somebody sang, he would sing too.

After the story of Fog's tattoo and my sudden fame, he took to spending more time with the Siberians; nearly every evening he would come to our bunks and ask if he could stay with us for a while. Once he arrived with a photograph which he showed to everyone. It was an old picture of an elderly man with a long beard, holding a rifle. He wore the typical Siberian hunting belt, hanging from which was the knife and the bag containing the lucky charms and the magic talismans. On the back of the photo was a note:

'*Brother Fyodot, lost in Siberia, a good and generous soul, an eternal dreamer and a great believer*', and a date: '*1922*'.

'That's my grandfather; he was Siberian . . . May I be part of the Siberian family, since my grandfather was one of you?' He seemed very serious, and his question was entirely devoid of vanity or any other negative feeling. It was a genuine request for help. Shura, it seemed, must be tired of living on his own.

We told him we would examine the photograph and ask some questions at home, to see if any of the old folk remembered him.

We didn't send the photo anywhere and we didn't ask anyone; during those years in Siberia lives were swallowed up in a great maelstrom of human history. We decided to wait a while and then take the giant Shura into our family – after all, he was quiet, he had already served two years without creating any problems, and we didn't see any reason for preventing a human being from enjoying some company and brotherhood, if he deserved it.

A week later we told him he could enter the family, provided that he promised to respect our rules and laws, and we gave him back the photo, saying that unfortunately no one had recognized his grandfather. He thought about this for a while and then confessed, in a trembling voice, that the photo wasn't really his – he had got it from his sister who worked in some historical archive in a university. He apologized to us for deceiving us; he said he really liked us as people, and that that was why he was so keen on entering our family. I felt sorry for him. I understood that as well as being simple, he had a kindly soul, and there was nothing bad in him. In prison people like him usually died after a few months; the luckiest ones were used as puppets by one of the more experienced criminals.

We took pity on him.

'Shura has become one of us,' we announced that same evening, and everyone in the cell was very surprised. We allowed him to live with us, in the family, even though he wasn't a true Siberian, forgiving him because he had confessed his error.

He soon learned our rules; I explained everything to him as you might to a child, and he discovered them as children do, not concealing his astonishment.

When the time came for me to be released, he bade me an affectionate farewell and said that if it hadn't been for the story of the tattoo he would never have decided to join the Siberians, and would never have discovered our rules, which he considered just and honest.

'Perhaps my humble trade has saved his life,' I thought. 'Without the family in prison he would have died in some brawl.'

To me tattooing was a very serious matter. To many of my young friends it was a game – they only had to see a few scrawls on their skin and they were satisfied. Others took it a little more seriously, but not very.

Conversations on the subject would go something like this:

'My father's got a big owl with a skull in its claws . . .'

'An owl means a robber, I assure you . . .'

'And what does a skull mean?'

'It depends.'

'I know. An owl with a skull means a robber and a murderer, I swear it does!'

'Don't talk rubbish! A robber and a murderer is a tiger's face with oak leaves – my uncle's got one!'

In short, everyone fired out theories at random.

For me, however, it was a very different affair, a complicated business. I liked subjects which left a trace of the hand that had made them. So I asked my father, my uncles and their friends to tell me about the tattooists they had known. I would study their tattoos, trying to understand what techniques they had used to create different effects. Then I would talk about them with my master, Grandfather Lyosha, who helped me to understand the techniques of others better and taught me to adapt them to my own way of seeing the subjects, drawing them and tattooing them on the skin.

He was pleased, because he saw that I was interested in the subjects not just because of their links with the criminal tradition, but because of their artistic qualities.

Even during the preparatory phase of the drawings, I began to wonder, and to ask him, why each tattoo couldn't be understood exclusively as a work of art, irrespective of its size. My master used to reply that true art was a form of protest, so every work of art must create contradictions and provoke debate. According to his philosophy, the criminal tattoo was the purest form of art in the world. People, he would say, hate criminals, but love their tattoos.

I suggested it might be possible to establish a connection between high-quality art and the profound meaning – the philosophy – of the Siberian tradition. He would reply to me, with great confidence in his voice:

'If we ever reach the point where everybody wants to be tattooed with the symbols of our tradition, you'll be right . . . But I don't think that will happen, because people hate us and everything connected with our way of life.'

BORIS THE ENGINE DRIVER

In the mid-1950s the Soviet government declared it illegal to keep mentally ill people at home, thus forcing their relatives to send them to special institutions. This sad state of affairs compelled many parents who didn't want to be separated from their children to move to places which the long arm of the law could not reach. So in the space of ten years Transnistria was filled with families who had come from all over the USSR because they knew that in the Siberian criminal tradition both mentally and physically handicapped people were considered sacred messengers of God and described as 'God-willed'.

I grew up among these people, the God-willed, and many of them became my friends. To me they didn't *seem* normal, they *were* normal, like everyone else.

They are not capable of hatred – all they can do is love and be themselves. And if ever they are violent, their violence is never driven by the force of hatred.

Boris was born a normal child in Siberia and lived in our district with his mother, Aunt Tatyana. One night the cops arrived at his parents' house – his father was a criminal, and had robbed an armoured train, getting away with a lot of diamonds. The cops wanted to know where he had hidden the diamonds and who else had been involved in the train robbery. The man refused to talk, so the cops took little Boris, who was six years old, and clubbed him on the head with a rifle butt to make his father talk. His father didn't talk, and eventually they shot him.

Boris, having suffered severe brain damage, remained forever a six-year-old.

His mother moved to Transnistria with him. They lived nearby and he was always in our house. My grandfather was very fond of him, and so was I. We flew pigeons together, went down to the river, stole apples from the Moldovans' orchards, fished with our nets during the summer nights and played by the railway line.

Boris had a fixation: he thought he was an engine driver. In the town, some distance from our area, near the railway, there was an old steam train displayed like a monument, motionless on its sawn-off rails. Boris used to get into it and pretend to be the chief engineer. It was his game. We used to go with him. We would all get into the cabin and he would get angry if we entered with our shoes on, because Boris went barefoot in his train. He even had a broom to sweep up with, and kept the place as clean as if it were his own house.

The train drivers at the station liked him; they had even given him a real train-driver's hat – it was like those worn by naval officers, white on top, with a green edge and a black plastic peak. It also bore the railway's golden badge, which shone in the sun so brightly you could see it from a long way off. He was very proud of that present; when he put on his hat he would immediately become serious and start addressing us like a railway official talking to passengers, saying things like 'Respectable comrades', or 'Citizens, please, I request your attention'. The transformation was hilarious.

My father had once given Boris a T-shirt which he had brought home at the end of a prison sentence he had served in Germany. This T-shirt was emblazoned with two doves: behind one was the German flag, behind the other the Russian one, and it bore the words 'Peace, friendship, cooperation', in both languages. Boris had taken it and stood stock still for half an hour, gazing at it. He was astonished by the colours, because there were no coloured clothes in our country in those days, everything was more or less grey, in the Soviet fashion. That garment, however, shone with bright colours, and immediately became Boris's favourite item of clothing. He always wore that T-shirt – sometimes he would stop abruptly, pull it up with his hands and look at the picture, smiling and whispering to himself.

Boris was a very communicative boy – he wasn't shy at all and could talk for hours, even with strangers. He was direct; he said whatever came into his head. When he talked he looked you straight in the eye, and his gaze was strong but at the same time relaxed, not tense. He could read; he had been taught by the widow Nina, a woman who lived on her own and whom we boys often went to visit. We used to help her do the heavy jobs in her vegetable garden, and she would give us something good to eat in return. She was a cultured woman. She had been a teacher of Russian language and literature. And so, with the consent of Aunt Tatyana, she had taught Boris to read and write.

Around this time, in 1992, there was a war in Transnistria. After the fall of the USSR, Transnistria stayed outside the Russian Federation and no longer belonged to anybody. The neighbouring countries, Moldova and Ukraine, had designs on it. But the Ukrainians already had difficulties of their own, because of the massive corruption in the government and the ruling administration. The Moldovans, meanwhile, despite the catastrophic situation in their country – the predominantly rural population lived in abject poverty, not so say squalor – made a pact with the Romanians, and tried to occupy Transnistrian territory by military force. According to the agreement with the Romanians, Transnistria would be divided up in a special way: the Moldovan government would control the land, leaving the Romanian industrialists the job of running the numerous munitions factories, which had been built by the Russians in the days of the USSR and afterwards had remained completely under the control of the criminals, who had turned the Transnistrian territory into a kind of weapons supermarket.

Without any warning the Moldovan military swung into action. On 22nd June a division of Moldovan tanks, accompanying ten military brigades, including one of infantry, one of special infantry and two of Romanian soldiers, reached Bender, our town on the right bank of the River Dniester, on the Moldovan border. In response, the inhabitants of Bender formed defence squads – after all, they were not short of weapons. A brief but very bloody war broke out, which lasted one summer, and ended with the criminals of Transnistria driving the Moldovan soldiers out of their land. Then they began to occupy Moldovan territory. At that point Ukraine, fearing that the criminals, if they won the war, would bring turmoil to their territory too, asked the Russians to intervene. Russia, recognizing the inhabitants of Transnistria as its own citizens, arrived with an army to 'assist the peace process'. This army set up a military regime, reinforced the police stations and declared Transnistria an 'area of extreme danger'.

Russian soldiers patrolled the streets in armoured vehicles and imposed a curfew from eight in the evening to seven in the morning. Many people began to disappear without trace; the bodies of the tortured dead were found in the river. This period, which my grandfather called a 'return to the Thirties', lasted a long time. My Uncle Sergey was killed in prison by his guards: many people, to save themselves, were forced to abandon their land and take refuge in various other parts of the world.

Boris didn't know anything about this situation. His brain couldn't grasp reality, much less a normal reality made up of brutal violence and politico-military logic. All he wanted to do was drive his train, and he did so even at night, because, like other trains all over the world, his train sometimes had night schedules too . . .

One evening, as he was walking towards the railway, the soldiers, like cowards, shot him in the back, without even getting out of their armoured car, and left him dead on the road.

When I heard the news I suddenly felt grown-up.

It was a watershed – something inside me died forever. I felt it quite distinctly; it was an almost physical sensation, like when you sense that certain ideas, fantasies or modes of behaviour are things you will never experience again, because of some burden that has fallen on your shoulders.

My grandfather turned pale and shook with rage; he wasn't as upset even when they killed my uncle, his son. He kept repeating that these people were cursed, that Russia was becoming like hell, because the cops were killing the angels.

My father and other men from our district went to the cops' area, and at dead of night, when the lights went out in their huts, they poured a torrent of lead into the buildings. It was an expression of blind and total rage, a desperate cry of sorrow. They killed a few cops and wounded many others, but in so doing unfortunately they only proved to the whole of Russia that the presence of the police in our country was truly necessary.

Nobody knew what was really going on in Transnistria; the television news presented things in such a way that after watching their crap even I began to wonder whether everything I knew was unreal.

I remember Boris's body after they retrieved it from the road and brought it home. It was the saddest thing I had ever seen.

An expression of fear and pain was etched on his face which I had never seen there before. His T-shirt with the doves was riddled with bullet-holes and soaked in blood. He was still clutching his engine-driver's hat tightly in his hands. The position of the body was shocking: as he died he had curled up like a newborn baby, with his knees tight to his chest. You could tell that during his last moments he must have felt intense pain. His eyes were wide open and cold and they still expressed a desperate question: 'Why do I feel so much pain?'

We buried him in the cemetery of our district.

Everyone went to his funeral, people from all over Transnistria. From his home to the cemetery a long procession formed, and in accordance with an old Siberian tradition his coffin was passed from hand to hand among the people until it reached the grave. Everyone kissed his cross; many wept and angrily demanded justice. His poor mother watched everything and everyone with crazed eyes.

A year later the situation deteriorated. The cops started eliminating criminals in the light of day, shooting in the streets. I got my second juvenile sentence, and when I was eventually released I no longer recognized the place where I'd been born. Since then many things have happened to me, but through all these experiences I have continued to think that the Siberian law was right: no political force, no power imposed with a flag, is worth as much as the natural freedom of a single person. The natural freedom of Boris.

MY BIRTHDAY

We boys of Low River, as I mentioned before, really lived in accordance with the Siberian criminal laws; we had a strict Orthodox religious upbringing, with a strong pagan influence, and the rest of the town called us 'Siberian Education' because of the way we behaved. We didn't use swear-words, we never took the name of God or the mother in vain, we never talked disrespectfully about any elderly person, pregnant woman, small child or orphan, or anyone disabled. We were well integrated, and to tell the truth we didn't need swear-words to make us feel grown-up, as the kids of our age in other districts did, because we were treated as if we were genuinely part of the criminal community; we were a real gang, made up of juveniles, with responsibilities and the same hierarchy as the adult criminal community.

Our job was to act as look-outs. We would walk round our area, spend a lot of time on the borders with other districts and inform the adults about any unusual movement. If any suspicious character passed through – a policeman, an informer, or a criminal from another district – we'd make sure our adult Authorities knew about it within a few minutes.

When the police arrived, we usually blocked their path: we'd sit or lie down in front of their cars, forcing them to stop. They'd get out and move us with a kick up the backside or by pulling us by the ears, and we would fight back. We usually singled out the youngest one and jumped on him as a group – someone would hit him, someone else would grab his arm and bite it, someone else would cling on to his back and snatch off his hat, yet another would rip the buttons off his uniform or take his pistol out of his holster. We'd go on like this till the cop couldn't stand any more, or till his colleagues started hitting us really hard.

The unluckiest of us got hit on the head with a truncheon, lost some blood and ran away.

Once a friend of mine tried to steal a policeman's gun from his holster: the cop grabbed his hand in time, but he gripped it so hard that my friend squeezed the trigger and involuntarily shot him in the leg. As soon as we heard the shot we scattered in all directions, and as we fled those idiots started shooting at us. Luckily they didn't hit any of us, but while we ran we heard the bullets whistling past us. One went into the pavement, chipping off a piece of cement which hit me in the face. The wound was a minor one and not very deep – they didn't even give me a single stitch afterwards – but for some strange reason a lot of blood came out of that hole, and when we got to my friend Mel's home his mother, Auntie Irina, picked me up in her arms and rushed off towards my parents' house, screaming out to the whole district that the police had shot me in the head. I tried in vain to calm her down, but she was too taken up with the effort of running, and finally, a few metres from home, through the blood that covered my eyes, I saw my mother go as white as death, already looking prepared for my funeral. When Auntie Irina stopped in front of her, I writhed like a snake to get free and jumped out of her arms, landing on my feet.

My mother examined my wound and told me to go indoors and then gave Auntie Irina a sedative, to soothe her agitation.

They sat down together on the bench in the yard, drinking valerian tea and crying. I was nine years old at the time.

On another occasion the policemen got out of their cars to clear us out of the way quickly. They picked us up by the legs or the arms and dumped us at the side of the road; we jumped up and again went back into the middle, and the cops started all over again. To us it was a never-ending game.

One of my friends took advantage of a cop's momentary abstraction and released the hand-brake of his car. We were at the top of a hill, on a road that led down to the river, so the car shot off like a rocket and the policemen, rooted to the spot but scowling with rage, watched it run all the way down the hill, hit the water and – *glug* – disappear like a submarine. At that point we too disappeared hurriedly.

As well as acting as look-outs we also carried messages.

Since people in the Siberian community don't use the phone, which they regard as unsafe, and as a contemptible symbol of the modern world, they often use the so-called 'road' – communication by means of a mixture of messages passed on orally, written in letters or encoded in the shapes of certain objects.

A verbal message is called a 'puff'. When an adult criminal wants to make a puff he calls a boy, perhaps one of his own children, and tells him the content of the message in the criminal language *fenya*, which derives from the old language of the forebears of the Siberian criminals, the Efey. Oral messages are always short and have a firm meaning. They are used for relatively straightforward, everyday matters.

Whenever my father called me to give me an oral message to take to someone, he would say: 'Come here, I've got to give you a puff.' Then he would tell me the content, for example: 'Go to Uncle Venya and tell him the dust here is like a pole', which was an urgent request to come and discuss an important matter. I had to set off at once on my bike, greet Uncle Venya properly, say a few conventional things which had nothing to do with the message, in accordance with Siberian tradition, such

as inquiring about his health, and only then would I get
to the point: 'I bring you a puff from my father.' Then I
had to wait for him to give me permission to pass it on to
him; he would give that permission, but without saying
so directly. Humbly, so as not to convey the least hint of
arrogance, he would reply: 'God bless you, then, my son',
or 'May the Spirit of Jesus Christ be with you', indicating
to me that he was ready to listen. I would deliver the
message and wait for his answer. I couldn't leave without
an answer; even if Uncle Venya or whoever it was had
nothing to say, he had to think of something. 'Tell your
father that I'll sharpen my heels, go with God', he would
say to me, indicating that he accepted the invitation and
would come as soon as possible. If he didn't want to say
anything, he would say: 'As music is to the soul, so is
a good puff to me. Go home with God, may he bestow
health and long life on your whole family.' Then I too
would take my leave of him in the conventional way and
return home as quickly as possible. The faster you were,
the more highly you were appreciated as a messenger,
and the better your pay. Sometimes I'd get as much as a
twenty-rouble banknote (in those days a bicycle cost fifty
roubles), on other occasions a cake or a bottle of fizzy
drink.

We also had our own small part to play in the delivery
of letters.

Letters could be of three types: the *ksiva* (which in the
criminal language means document), the *malyava* (little
one) and *rospiska* (signature).

The *ksiva* was a long, important letter in the criminal
language. It was very rarely written, and then only by

elderly Authorities, usually in order to take orders into a prison, to influence the policy of the administration of prisons, foment revolts or persuade someone to resolve a difficult situation in a particular way. A letter of this kind would be passed from hand to hand, and from jail to jail, and because of its importance was never entrusted to an ordinary messenger, only to people very close to the criminal Authorities. We boys never carried letters of that type.

The *malyava*, on the other hand, was the typical letter that we almost always carried, backwards and forwards. Usually it was sent from jail to communicate with the criminal world outside, avoiding the checks of the prison system. It was a small, concise letter, always written in the criminal language. On a particular day, every second Tuesday in the month, we would go and stand outside Tiraspol prison. That was the day when the prisoners 'launched the flares': that is, using the elastic from their underpants, they catapulted their letters over the prison wall, for us to pick up. Each letter had a coded address – a word or a number.

These letters were written by almost all prisoners and used the 'road' of the prison, that system of communication from cell to cell which I have already mentioned. During the night prisoners 'sent the horses' – various parcels, messages, letters and suchlike – along strings that ran from one window to another. All the letters were then collected by a team of inmates in the blocks nearest to the wall, where the windows didn't have thick metal sheets over them but only the standard iron bars. From there, people called 'missilists' fired the letters one after another over the wall. They were paid to do this by the criminal community and had no other task in prison; they practised their skills every day by firing scraps of cloth over the wall.

To launch a *malyava* you first made a 'missile', a small tube of paper with a long, soft tail, usually made of paper handkerchiefs (which are very difficult to get hold of in prison). This tube was folded over on one side, forming a kind of hook which was fixed to one end of the elastic; then you gripped it between your fingers and pulled. Meanwhile another person lit the soft paper tail, and when it caught fire the little tube was fired off.

The burning tail enabled us to locate the letter when it fell on the ground. You had to run as fast as possible, to put out the fire and not let the little tube with the precious letter inside it get burnt. There were nearly always at least ten of us, and in half an hour we would manage to collect more than a hundred letters. Returning home, we would distribute them to the families and friends of the prisoners. We were paid for this work.

Each criminal community had its own special day on which to fire the letters, once a month. In some cases, if there was a very urgent letter, it was customary for criminals to help each other, even if they belonged to different communities. So sometimes the letters of members of other communities ended up with the letters of our own criminals, but we would still take them to the addressee. Or rather, the rule was that the person who delivered it must be the one who had picked it up off the ground, which served to prevent quarrels among us.

In cases like these we were not paid, but they usually gave us something. We would take the letters to the house of the Guardian of the area, and one of his helpers would take them and put them in a safe: later people would go to see him and say a word or a number in code, and he, if he found a letter marked with the same code, would hand it over to the addressee. This service was not paid for but was one of the Guardian's responsibilities; if there was any trouble with the post, if a letter disappeared or none of us went to collect it under the prison, the Guardian could be severely punished, even killed.

The *rospiska*, or 'signature', was a type of letter that circulated both inside prison and outside it. It might be a kind of safe conduct provided by an Authority, who guaranteed a peaceful stay and a brotherly welcome for a criminal in places where he didn't know anybody, for example in prisons far from his region or in towns where he went on business trips. As I have already mentioned, the signature was tattooed directly on the skin.

In other cases the *rospiska* was used to spread important information, for example about a forthcoming meeting of criminal Authorities, or to send openly and without any risk an order addressed to several people. Thanks to the coded language, even if the signature fell into the hands of the police it didn't matter.

I delivered letters of this kind a couple of times: they were normal, and always open. The Authorities never seal their letters, not only because they're in code, but particularly because the content must never throw any shadow over them; usually it has a demonstrative purpose, to exhibit the powers of the laws and spread a kind of criminal charisma.

Once I delivered a signature with an order originating from the prisons of Siberia and addressed to the prisons of Ukraine. It instructed Ukrainian criminals to respect certain rules in prison; for example homosexual acts were forbidden, as was the punishment of individual prisoners by physical humiliation or sexual abuse. At the end of this letter were the signatures of thirty-six Siberian Authorities. The signature which came into my hands was one of the many copies of the document, which was intended to be reproduced and disseminated among all the criminals in prison or at liberty throughout the USSR.

Another form of communication, called the 'throw', came about through the delivery of certain objects. In this case, an object which had a particular meaning in the criminal community was given to any messenger, even a child. The messenger's task was to take it to the addressee, saying who had sent it; there was no need to wait for an answer.

A broken knife meant the death of some member of the gang, or someone close to you, and was a very bad sign. An apple cut in half was an invitation to divide up the loot. A piece of dry bread inside a cloth handkerchief was a precise warning: 'Watch out, the police are nearby, there's been an important development in that case in which you're involved.' A knife wrapped in a handkerchief was a call to action, for a hired killing. A piece of rope with a knot tied in the middle meant: 'I'm not responsible for what you know.' A bit of earth in a handkerchief meant: 'I promise I'll keep the secret.'

There were simpler meanings and more complex ones, 'good' ones – intended, for example, for protection – and 'bad' ones – insults or threats of death.

If it was suspected that a person had relations which compromised his criminal dignity – relations with the police, say, or with other criminal communities (without the permission of his own) – he would receive a little cross with a nail, or in extreme cases a dead rat, sometimes with a coin or a banknote in its mouth, an unequivocal promise of the harshest possible punishment. This was the 'bad throw', the worst one, and it meant certain death.

If, on the other hand, you wanted to invite a friend to party, to have fun, to drink and enjoy yourselves, you would send him an empty glass. That was a 'good throw'.

I often carried messages of this kind, never any bad ones. They were mostly administrative communications, invitations or promises.

Another of our duties was to organize ourselves in a decent manner so as to carry forward the glorious name of our district: in simple words, we had to be able to sow chaos among the boys of the other districts.

This had to be done in the right way, because our tradition requires that violence must always have a reason, even though the final result is the same, since a head broken for a good reason is still a broken head.

We worked with the elders – old criminals who had retired and who lived thanks to the support of the younger ones. Like eccentric pensioners, they took care of us youngsters and our criminal identity.

There were many of them in the district, and they all belonged to the caste of the Siberian Urkas: they obeyed the old law, which was despised by the other criminal communities because it obliged you to follow a humble and worthy life, full of sacrifices, where pride of place was given to ideals such as morality and religious feeling, respect for nature and for ordinary people, workers and all those who were used or exploited by the government and the rich.

Our word for the rich was *upiri*, an old Siberian term for creatures of pagan mythology who live in marshes and dense woodland and feed on human blood: a kind of Siberian vampire.

Our tradition forbade us to commit crimes that involved negotiating with the victim, because it was considered unworthy to communicate with the rich or government officials, who could only be assaulted or killed, but never threatened or forced to accept terms. So crimes like extortion, or protection rackets, or the control of illegal activities through secret agreements with the police and the KGB, were utterly despised. We only carried out robberies and burglaries, and in our criminal activities we never made agreements with anyone, but organized everything ourselves.

The other communities didn't think like this. The younger generations, in particular, behaved in the European and American way – they had no morality, respected only money and endeavoured to create a pyramidal criminal system, a kind of criminal monarchy, something quite different from our system, which might be compared to a network, where everyone was interconnected and no one had personal power and everyone played his part in the common interest.

Already when I was a boy, in many criminal communities the individual members had to earn the right to speak, otherwise they were treated as if they didn't exist. In our community, by contrast, everyone had the right to speak, even women, children, the disabled and the old.

The difference between the education we had received and the education (or lack of it) received by members of the other communities created an immense gap between us. Consequently, even if we weren't aware of it, we felt the need to assert our principles and our laws, and to force others to respect them, sometimes by violence.

In town we were always causing trouble; when we went into another district it would often end in a fight, with blood on the ground, beatings and knifings on both sides. We had a fearsome reputation; everyone was scared of us, and this very fear had often led to our being attacked, because there's always someone who wants to go against his natural instincts, to try his luck and attempt to overcome his fear by attacking the thing that causes it.

A fight wasn't always inevitable; sometimes by diplomacy we managed to persuade someone to change his mind, and there would only be a few punches thrown on both sides, after which we would start talking. It was nice when it ended like that. But more often it ended in bloodshed, and in a chain of ruined relations with an entire district, relations which once they had been ruined it was very hard to revive.

Our elders had taught us well.

First of all, you had to respect all living creatures – a category which did not include policemen, people connected with the government, bankers, loan sharks and all those who had the power of money in their hands and exploited ordinary people.

Secondly, you had to believe in God and in his Son, Jesus Christ, and love and respect the other ways of believing in God which were different from our own. But the Church and religion must never be seen as a structure. My grandfather used to say that God didn't create priests, but only free men; there were some good priests, and in such cases it was not sinful to go to the places where they carried out their activities, but it definitely was a sin to think that in the eyes of God priests had more power than other men.

Lastly, we must not do to others what we wouldn't want to be done to us: and if one day we were obliged to do it nonetheless, there must be a good reason.

One of the elders with whom I often discussed these Siberian philosophies used to say that in his opinion our world was full of people who went down wrong roads, and who after taking one false step went further and

further away from the straight path. He argued that in
many cases there was no point in trying to persuade them
to return to the right road, because they were too far
away, and the only thing that remained to do was to end
their existence, 'remove them from the road'.

'A man who is rich and powerful,' the old man would
say, 'in walking along his wrong road will ruin many lives;
he will cause trouble for many people who in some way
depend on him. The only way of putting everything right
is to kill him, and thereby to destroy the power that he has
built upon money.'

I would object:

'But what if the murder of this person were also a false
step? Wouldn't it be better to avoid having any contact
with him, and leave it at that?'

The old man would look at me in amazement, and
reply with such conviction that it made my head spin:

'Who do you think you are, boy – Jesus Christ? Only
He can work miracles; we must only serve Our Lord . . .
And what better service could we do than to remove from
the face of the world the children of Satan?'

He was too good, that old man.

Anyway, because of our elders we were certain that we
were in the right. 'Woe betide those who wish us ill,' we
thought, 'because God is with us': we had thousands of
ways of justifying our violence and our behaviour.

On my thirteenth birthday, however, something
happened which gave me a few doubts.

It all began like this: on the morning of that freezing cold February day, my friend Mel came round to my house and asked me to go with him to the other side of town, to the Railway district, where the Guardian of our area had ordered him to take a message to a criminal.

The Guardian had told him he could take only one person with him, no more, because it was ill-mannered to take messages in a group: it was considered to be a display of violence, almost a threat. And Mel, unfortunately, had chosen me.

I had no desire to go all that way in the cold, especially on my birthday: I had already arranged with the whole gang to have a party at my uncle's house, which was empty because he was in jail. He had left his house to me, and I could do what I liked there, as long as I kept it clean, fed his cats and watered his flowers.

That morning I wanted to get things ready for the party, and when Mel asked me to accompany him I was really disappointed, but I couldn't refuse. I knew he was too disorganized, and that if he went on his own he was bound to get into trouble. So I got dressed, then we had breakfast together and set off for the Railway district. The snow was too deep to cycle, so we walked. My friends and I never went by bus because you always had to wait too long for one to come; it was quicker on foot. As we walked we usually talked about all kinds of things – what was happening in the district or elsewhere in the town. But with Mel it was very hard to talk, because Mother Nature had made him incapable of constructing comprehensible sentences.

So our conversations took the form of a dialogue conducted entirely by me, with brief interjections of 'Da', 'A-ha', 'M-m-m', and other minimal expressions which Mel could emit without too much effort.

Every now and then he would stop dead, his whole body would freeze and his face would become like a wax mask: this meant that he hadn't understood what I was talking about. I would have to stop walking too and explain: only then did Mel resume his usual expression and start moving and walking again.

Not that his normal face was a thing of beauty – it had a fresh scar running right across it, and a hole where his left eye should have been. This was the result of an accident he had caused himself. He had handled the explosive charge of an anti-aircraft shell clumsily, and it had blown up a few centimetres away from his face. The long series of surgical operations to reconstruct his face was not yet complete, and at this time Mel was still going around with that horrible gaping black hole on the left side of his face. It wasn't until three years later that he got a false eye, made of glass.

Mel was always like that – there was no connection between his body and his mind. When he was thinking he had to stand still, otherwise he couldn't reach a decent conclusion, and if he was performing any movement he wasn't able to think. Because of this I used to call him 'donkey' – partly in jest and partly seriously. It was mean and despicable of me, I know, but if I resorted to such behaviour it was only because I had to put up with him from morning to evening, and explain everything to him, as if he were a little child. He never took offence, but would suddenly turn serious, as if he were thinking about the mysterious reason why I called him donkey. Once he took me aback, when, quite out of the blue, in a situation that had nothing to do with the fact that I always called him 'donkey', he said to me:

'I know why you call me that! It's because you think my ears are too long!'

Then he worked himself into a frenzy defending the size of his ears.

I said nothing in reply; I just looked at him.

He was hopeless, and he made things worse by smoking and drinking like an old alcoholic.

Anyway, that February morning Mel and I were walking along the snow-covered streets. When there's not much humidity the snow is very dry and makes a funny noise: when you walk on it, it sounds as if you're walking on crackers.

It was a sunny morning and the clear sky promised a fine day, but there was a light and constant wind which might upset expectations.

We decided to go through the Centre district and stop for a snack in a little place – a mixture between a bar and a restaurant – run by Aunt Katya, the mother of a good friend of ours who had died the previous summer, drowned in the river.

We often went to visit her, and so that she didn't feel lonely we'd tell her how things were going in our lives. She was very attached to us, partly because we'd been with her son, Vitalich, on the day he'd died, and that had united us all.

Vitalich's body hadn't been found immediately. The search had been difficult because two days earlier a big dam had burst a hundred kilometres upstream.

That's another story, but it's one that deserves to be told.

It was summer, and very hot. The dam burst at night, and I remember waking up because I heard a terrible noise, like an approaching blizzard.

We came out of our houses and realized that the noise was coming from the river. We rushed to see and found gigantic waves of white water, like breakers on the ocean, coming downriver with increasing force, beating against the bank and sweeping away vessels and boats of all descriptions.

Some people had torches and shone them on the river. They picked out many objects swirling around in the water: cows, boats, tree trunks, iron drums, rags and pieces of cloth which looked like sheets. Here and there, in that chaos of water, there were pieces of furniture. Screams could be heard.

Our district, fortunately, was on the high bank, and the wall of water hadn't been too devastating: everything was flooded there too, the houses and cellars were full of water, but there was no serious damage.

Next day the river was a complete mess, and we decided to take upon ourselves the task of cleaning it up, of removing everything we could, using our own strength. There were several motorboats still available which had been spared by the waves, because when the dam had burst they had been on the bank.

My own boats had escaped as well. I had two: one large and heavy, which I used for transporting big loads (we used to spend the whole summer plundering apple orchards and food stores in Moldovan territory . . .), and one small and narrow, which I used for fishing at night. It was swift and manoeuvrable; I used it to 'guide the net' – which means to keep moving against the current, trying to close off with the fishing net the central part of the river, where most of the fish came down.

The smaller boat had escaped completely because it was at my house, where I had to do a bit of work on it. The other had escaped because it was in a boathouse on the bank: some time ago I'd asked the keeper to restore it for me with a special varnish. The boathouse keeper's name was Ignat; he was a good man, and a poor one. He'd been promising to paint that boat for me for a month, but had never found the time – he always had something more urgent to do or was getting drunk out of his mind.

We had eight boats in all, and we split up into two teams: two boats to a team, four boys to a boat.

The work was organized in such a way as to keep the river constantly 'blocked' by two boats, which fished out the rubbish. One team, equipped with long poles with big iron hooks on the ends, retrieved branches and tree trunks, bodies of animals and various large objects. All these things were then tied to the hull with ropes, and when there was no room for any more stuff the crew returned to the bank, where other boys were waiting, who jumped into the water and unloaded it all. On the bank they had created a huge bonfire. We threw the junk on the embers: within half an hour even the most sodden trunks dried out and, doused with some petrol, eventually caught fire.

By noon the fire had grown enormous; you couldn't go near it or you'd have been scorched to death. With a large number of us working all together we threw onto the flames the body of a cow, as well as various carcases of sheep, dogs, chickens and geese.

Then, at about four o'clock in the afternoon, we fished out the first human body.

It was a middle-aged man, fully clothed, with his skull cracked open. Presumably he had fallen in the river and been swept away and had hit his head against a rock or a tree trunk.

Another team was equipped with little nets, and fished out the small objects that floated on the surface: jars of preserves, bottles, fresh fruit and vegetables of various kinds, apples with peaches, water-melons with potatoes, as well as children's toys, plastic buckets and spades, photographs, lots of paper, newspapers and documents, all mixed together in one huge ratatouille.

Then there were dozens and dozens of bottles of soft drinks, both fizzy and still, because a few kilometres upstream there was a bottling factory. The water had gone through there too, sweeping away the entire contents of the warehouse.

We decided to retrieve all the bottles, put them to one side and distribute them later among the people who had helped to clean up the river. But by the end of the first hour of work we had already fished out so many that we didn't know where to put them. So two of our friends carted them away from the bank in big wheelbarrows, to free up the space for others, and dumped the bottles in the front yards of the people who lived nearby. They filled the entire first street of the district – about fifty houses – with bottles, and when they came up again with their barrows full, the people shouted:

'No, there's no more room here, boys, go on to the next house!'

We worked all day without stopping for a moment, and didn't let up till the evening, when it was so dark we couldn't see a thing.

We had thoroughly cluttered up the bank, it was almost impossible to walk along it: wherever you put your foot, you trod on something.

We stayed and slept by the fire.

Before we went to sleep we had a meal; some people had brought things from home, and there was plenty to drink – I think I drank more fizzy drinks that evening than I have in the rest of my life.

Afterwards we all lay on the ground, lit up by the firelight. We kept burping because of all the pop we'd drunk.

Ten metres away from us lay the body of the man we'd fished out in the afternoon. We put a cross and a candle in his hands so that he wouldn't be angry. Someone also brought him a glass of mineral water and a piece of bread, in accordance with the Siberian tradition of always offering something to the dead.

We decided that next day we'd better ask the people of the other districts to help us, since the river was still full of junk, as well as other corpses. With the warmth the bodies would start to decompose, and then it would be unbearable. We thought we'd be able to clear the river quickly with the help of other kids.

Next day, at around ten, the reinforcements arrived. Many boys from Centre, and some from Caucasus and Railway: they had all come to help us, and we were pleased.

To avoid any risk of them falling in the water (many of them couldn't swim – they hadn't grown up on the riverside like us), we got them to work on the bank. They carried the stuff away in wheelbarrows or bags.

We sold a lot of bottles of pop to people who came in cars to pick it up and then sell it on to shops. We asked a low price, basing it not on the number of bottles we gave them but on the number of trips they managed to make in their cars: fifty roubles per trip, and they could take as much as they could carry. If they were quick they would earn three times as much. It was a good deal for everyone – we cleared the bank quickly, and even made a bit of money out of it, they got for next to nothing goods that they could sell on.

One of the boys who worked with us was Vitalich.

Although he lived in Centre, we were good friends with him.

He often came to bathe with us in the river; he was an excellent swimmer. He competed in rowing races, so he had an athletic physique and plenty of stamina, and when we swam together he never got tired; he could keep going upstream for hours.

Since he was so strong, we got him to lead the team of boys who were untying the objects from the boat near the bank. You had to be a good swimmer to do this, because the boat couldn't get very close to the bank. Once it was untied, the object was carried to the bank by five or six swimmers. This was a tricky operation because it was impossible to see underwater – the river was clogged with earth and leaves and other stuff, so you couldn't even make out what the thing you were carrying was. One boy had been hurt the previous day – while he was moving a trunk, a branch had impaled his calf, he'd lost a lot of blood in the water, and before he'd even realized what had happened, he had passed out. Luckily the others had noticed immediately and had carried him to the bank straight away, so it had all ended well.

At noon some relatives of the people who had disappeared in the river arrived. Each of them walked round the body of the drowned man, till a woman recognized him:

'It's my husband,' she said.

She was accompanied by the man's brother and two other men, friends of the family. There was also a ten-year-old girl, a tiny little thing, with the black hair and eyes that so many Moldovans have.

The woman burst into tears, screaming and throwing herself on her husband's body. She embraced him and kissed him. Her little daughter started crying too, but silently, as if she were embarrassed to do so in front of us.

The drowned man's brother tried to calm the woman; he took her to the car, but she went on crying and screaming there.

The three men loaded the body onto the back seat of their car. They thanked us and offered us money, but we refused it. One of us filled the boot with bottles, and they looked at us with a question in their eyes.

'That way you'll save money on the drinks, at the funeral,' we said to them.

At this they thanked us profusely. The woman started kissing our hands and to evade all those kisses we went back to work.

Other people, in the meantime, were looking for their own dead. One of them offered us his help and we accepted it: poor devils, they hoped they could help us recover the bodies of their dear ones. But it's not easy to find a drowned person. Usually the bodies stay underwater for at least three days, and only later, when they begin to putrefy and fill with gas, do they rise to the surface. It had been pure chance that we had found the body of that poor Moldovan; he must have been carried up to the surface by a strong current, and if we hadn't grabbed him straight away he would certainly have gone under again.

* * *

Vitalich, with five other boys, was pulling towards the bank a tree with a lot of branches sticking out of the water – you could tell that underneath it must be enormous.

They had decided to turn it round back to front, with the foliage towards the bank, so as to create more handholds for those who had to grasp it from the land.

While they were turning it, Vitalich got his foot tangled up in the branches. He managed to shout, to let the others know that he'd got caught, but suddenly the tree worked like a propeller: it rolled over with all its weight, pulling Vitalich under.

We couldn't believe it.

Everyone jumped into the water to get him out, but he was no longer there – either close to the tree or anywhere else, for several metres around.

We immediately blocked off the surrounding area with the net, to stop the current carrying him away. Then we started to search the river bed.

We dived into the dirty water – where it was impossible to see a thing – at the risk of crashing into something. One of us did indeed get hit by a trunk, but luckily not too hard.

Of Vitalich, however, there was no trace.

I remember continually diving into the water: I went right down to the bottom, some five or six metres, and groped with my hands in the void.

Suddenly I found something, a leg! I gripped it tightly, resting it against my body, and bending down I put my feet on the river bed; I gave myself a hard shove, as if I were suddenly releasing a spring, and a second later found myself back on the surface.

Only then did I realize that it was Mel's leg I had grabbed. His head was sticking out of the water and he was looking at me in bemusement.

I lost my temper and punched him in the head, and he responded in kind.

We didn't manage to find Vitalich's body in the first hour of searching.

We were all tired and irritable, many had started quarrelling among themselves, insults flew, and everyone wanted to shake off the blame by putting it on others. At times like these, when everyone is totally disloyal, you begin to see what people are really like, and you feel disgust for what you are and where you are.

I had lost all feeling in my arms and legs and couldn't swim any more, so I returned to the bank and lay down.

I don't remember how, but I fell asleep.

When I woke up it was evening. Someone was asking me if I was okay. It was my friend Gigit; he had a bottle of wine in his hand.

The others were sitting round the fire getting drunk.

I felt full of strength again and asked Gigit if Vitalich's body had been found. He shook his head.

Then I went over to the others and asked them why they were drinking, when our friend's body was still in the river.

They looked at me indifferently; some were pissed out of their minds, most were tired and depressed.

'You know what?' I said. 'I'm going to cast the nets at the Scythe.'

The Scythe was a place about twenty kilometres downstream. They called it that because at that point the river described a wide curve resembling a scythe. On that bend the water stopped and flooded the bank, so that the current seemed almost stationary.

Everything carried away by the current fetched up there sooner or later. By blocking the passage along the river bed, we could recover Vitalich's body.

The only problem was that because of the flood the river had filled up with all that junk, so the net would have to be changed continually, otherwise it would get too full and there would be a risk of breaking it when you pulled it up.

Mel, Gigit, Besa and Speechless came with me. We went in my two boats, taking my net and Mel's.

Nets that are used for fishing out drowned people are thrown away afterwards, or kept only to be used on another sad occasion.

I had a dozen different nets for different uses; the best were the river-bed ones, which could support heavy weights and stay in the water for a long time. They had three superimposed layers, for more effective catching, and were very thick.

I took the best river-bed net that I had and we set off.

We cast the net all night, and kept clearing it of rubbish: there were all sorts of things at the bottom of the river, including many carcases of various kinds of animal. But the worst problem was the branches, because when they got stuck in the net it was hard to get them out, and they broke the mesh.

Our hands remained wet until morning; we hardly had time to dry them before they got wet again, because as soon as you finished clearing the net on one side it was already full on the other, so you would rush over there, and as soon as you emptied it you would have to go back to where you'd been before.

Eventually Gagarin arrived with the others to take over from us. We were exhausted – out on our feet. We threw ourselves down on the grass, and fell asleep instantly.

At about four o'clock in the afternoon Gagarin and the others found Vitalich's body.

It was covered in scratches and cuts; the right foot was broken, and a bit of bone was sticking out. Vitalich was blue, like all drowned people.

We called the people of our district. They took him home to his mother. We went with them, to tell her how it had happened. She was distraught; she wept continuously and embraced us all together, squeezing us so hard that it hurt. I think she understood of her own accord, or perhaps one of the boys of Centre had told her, how hard we had worked to find her son's body. She kept thanking us, and I was touched to hear her say: 'Thank you, thank you for bringing him home.'

I couldn't look her in the face, I was so ashamed at having slept when I should have been searching for her son's body.

We were all shocked, shattered. We couldn't believe that fate had taken a person like Vitalich away from us.

And so, whenever we were anywhere near Centre, we would always drop in on Aunt Katya, Vitalich's mother.

She wasn't married: her first partner, Vitalich's father, had been on the point of marrying her when he'd been called up into the army and sent off to Afghanistan, where he had been reported missing when she was still pregnant.

Aunt Katya ran that little place I mentioned earlier, a kind of restaurant, and lived with a new partner, a good man, a criminal, who dealt in various kinds of illegal trade.

Whenever we went to see her we always took her some flowers as a present because we knew she was very fond of them.

One day she had told us that what she would like more than anything else in the world was to have a lemon tree. We had decided to get her one; the only problem was that we didn't know where to get one from, in fact none of us had ever seen a lemon tree.

So someone had advised us to try in a botanic garden, because it would have plants that grew in warm countries. After a bit of time and exploration we identified the nearest botanic garden: it was in Belgorod, in Ukraine, on the Black Sea, three hours' journey from our home.

We set off in a highly organized group. There were about fifteen of us: everybody wanted to take part in the lemon expedition, because everybody liked Aunt Katya and tried to help her and please her in every way possible.

When we got to Belgorod we bought just one ticket for the botanic garden: one of us entered, went to the toilet and passed the ticket out of the window to another member of the group, and so on, till we were all inside.

We tagged on behind a visiting school party and approached our objective. It was a fairly small tree, a little higher than a bush, with green leaves and three yellow lemons dangling in the wind.

Mel immediately said the lemons were fake and had been stuck on with glue for appearance's sake, and that the tree was just an ordinary bush. We had to stop and quickly examine the tree, to see if those damned lemons were real or not. I smelled all three of them myself: they had a characteristic scent of lemon.

Mel got a cuff round the ear from Gagarin and was forbidden to speak until the end of the operation.

We grabbed the pot and went up to the second floor of a building on the edge of the garden. We opened a window and carefully tossed the little tree on to the roof of a lock-up garage. We jumped down from there ourselves and ran to the station, clutching that heavy pot with the tree inside it. In the train we realized that despite all the knocks and shakes the lemons hadn't come off: we were so pleased not to have lost them . . .

When we brought Aunt Katya our present she wept with joy, or perhaps she was weeping because she'd seen the stamp of the botanic garden on the pot which we had carelessly failed to remove. At any rate, she was so delighted that when she picked her first ripe lemon she invited us all round for a cup of lemon tea.

So on that day too – my thirteenth birthday – as Mel and I were walking across town on our way to the Railway district, we thought of taking her a plant, and called in at old Bosya's shop.

We always bought our plants and flowers for Aunt Katya in his shop; since we had no idea what they were called, we always asked him to write down their names on a piece of paper, so that we wouldn't buy the same thing twice.

Every five plants, Bosya allowed us a small discount, or gave us some packets of old seeds, which were no longer any use because they were all dry. We took the seeds anyway and made a detour via the police station. If we found the police cars parked outside the gate we'd pour the seeds into their petrol tanks: the seeds were light and didn't sink to the bottom straight away, and they were so small that they could pass through the filter of the petrol pump, so when they reached the carburettor the engine would stall. So we made good use of what in other circumstances would have been thrown away.

Grandfather Bosya was a good Jew, respected by all the criminals, although apart from having a flower shop (which didn't sell much), nobody knew exactly what he did, so secret did he keep his affairs. It was rumoured that he had links with the Jewish community of Amsterdam and smuggled diamonds. However, we never had any actual proof of this, and we always used to tease him when we went to his shop, trying to find out what he really did. It had become a tradition: we tried to get him to talk and every time he succeeded in avoiding the issue.

We would say:

'Well, Mr Bosya, what's the weather like in Amsterdam?'

And he would reply in an off-hand manner:

'How would I know that, a poor Jew like me who doesn't even possess a radio? Though even if I did have one I wouldn't listen to it: I'm so old now that I can't hear a thing – I'm going deaf . . . Oh, how I wish I could go back to the days when I was young like you, and just play around and have a good time . . . By the way, what have you boys been up to lately?'

And it always ended with us, like a bunch of idiots, telling him about our own doings instead of hearing about his, and leaving his shop with a vague sensation of having been tricked.

He had a real talent as a conman, and we fell for it every time.

The flowers in old Bosya's shop weren't all that special; I reckon some of them had been there for years. The shop was a long, narrow cubby-hole, with wooden shelves crammed with old plants that no one ever bought. When you entered you felt as if you'd landed in the middle of a jungle; a lot of the plants had grown so much their leaves intertwined with those of the ones next to them, and all the plants together formed a kind of huge bush.

Bosya was a twisted, thin old man; he wore glasses as thick as the armour of a tank and through the lenses his eyes seemed monstrously large. He always wore a black jacket, a white shirt with a black bow-tie, black trousers with impeccably ironed creases and shiny black shoes.

Despite his age (he was so old even my grandfather called him 'uncle'), his hair was quite black, and he kept it very neat, cut in the style of the 1930s, under a thin layer of brilliantine.

He always used to say that the true weapon of every gentleman is his elegance: with that you could do anything – rob, kill, burgle and lie – without ever being suspected.

When the little bell on the door of the shop rang, Bosya would get up from his chair behind the counter, creaking like an old car changing gear, and advance towards the customer with his hands wide apart, as Jesus does in those sacred paintings, to indicate acceptance and compassion. He looked funny when he walked, because he had a comical face – smiling, but with sad eyes, like those of a dog with no master. And with every step he uttered a sound, one of those groans that old men full of aches and pains utter when they move.

All in all he filled me with sadness: a mixture of melancholy, nostalgia and pity.

When we entered his shop old Bosya would emerge from his jungle and, not seeing who had come in, set off as usual with a saintly aspect, but as soon as his eyes fell on our disreputable faces, his expression would instantly change. First the smile would disappear, to be replaced by a weary grimace, as if he were having difficulty in breathing, then his whole body would become twisted, his legs a little bent, and he would start waving his hands as if to refuse something that we'd offered him. He would turn his back on us and return to the counter, saying in a quavering voice and with a slight hint of irony, in a Russian accent contaminated by the Jewish dialect of Odessa:

'*Shob ya tak zhil, opyat prishli morochit yayza . . .*'

Which meant, 'What a life I have to live!' – a Jewish expression, which they use on every possible occasion – 'You've come to pester me again . . .'

That was his way of welcoming us because, in reality, he was very fond of all of us.

He too enjoyed not letting us trick him. We always tried, but Bosya, with his wisdom and his Jewish cunning, which in his case had something humble and worldly-wise about it, would get us to fall into his trap, and sometimes we would only realize it later, after we'd left the shop. He was a genius at mind games, a real genius.

Since he always complained that he was blind and deaf, we used to provoke him by asking him what the time was, hoping he'd look at the watch he wore on his wrist. But without batting an eyelid he would reply:

'How can I know what time it is if I'm a happy person? Happy people don't measure time, because in their lives every moment passes with pleasure.'

Then we would ask him why he wore a watch, if he never looked at it, and if he didn't care about the passing of time.

He would put on an astonished expression and look at his watch as if he were seeing it for the first time, and then reply in a humble tone:

'. . . Oh, this isn't a watch . . . It's older than I am; I don't even know if it works . . .'

He would put it to his ear, hold it there for a moment and then add:

'. . . Well, I can hear something, but I don't know if it's the ticking of the hands or that of my old heart running down . . .'

Bosya's wife was a nice old Jewish lady called Elina. She was a very intelligent woman who had worked as a schoolmistress for many years and had taught my father and his brothers. They all spoke of her affectionately, and even many years later they still respected her authority. The first time my father killed a policeman – in fact two policemen – she boxed his ears, and he knelt down at her feet to ask her forgiveness.

Bosya had a daughter, the most beautiful girl I've ever seen. Her name was Faya, and she too was a schoolmistress. She taught foreign languages, English and French. But she had grown up with the idea that she was ill, because Bosya and Elina had forbidden her to do all the things that normal children did. She was unmarried and still lived with her parents; she was a calm and very cheerful person. She had a gorgeous figure: hips and curves that seemed to have been drawn with a pencil, so perfect were they, a fabulous mouth, small and with the lips slightly parted and well defined, big black eyes, and wavy hair, which hung down to her bottom. But the most spectacular thing was the way she moved. She seemed like a cat; she made every gesture with a grace all of her own.

I was obsessed with her, and whenever I saw her in the shop I tried to find some pretext for standing near her. I would go and talk to her about the plants or anything else, just to feel her close to my skin.

She would smile at me; she was happy to talk to me and she understood that I liked her. Only later, at sixteen, did I pluck up the courage to get really close to her, by talking about literature. We started seeing each other, and exchanging books, and before long we developed a relationship which polite people usually call 'intimate', but which in my district was described with a different phrase altogether: 'dirtying the sheets together'.

But that's another story, which deserves to be told separately, and not here.

The story that should be told here is that of old Bosya's life.

In his youth old Bosya was a *bander* – the term used at the beginning of the century for a member of Jewish organized crime. The word is derived from *banda*, which in Russian means 'gang'.

In the 1920s and 1930s, in Odessa, the Jewish gangs were among the strongest and the best organized: they ran all the smuggling operations and the affairs of the harbour. Their members were united by strong religious feelings and by a code of honour, a kind of internal set of regulations called the *koska*, a term which in the old

Jewish dialect of Odessa means 'word', 'law' or 'rule'. In short, contravening the *koska* was a good way of committing suicide.

In the mid-1930s the Soviet government began systematically combating crime all over the territory, and they dispatched to Odessa – which was deemed to be one of the towns worst affected by rackets and organized crime – special squads which devised a battle tactic called *podstava*, which means 'done on purpose'. Through infiltrators they provoked internal conflicts within the gangs themselves.

Donnie Brasco, the famous movie gangster played by Johnny Depp, certainly couldn't have imagined that his Soviet precursors had exploited the work of undercover agents not in order to obtain information but to create by artificial means situations where criminals went to war against each other and killed each other on an industrial scale. No, Donnie Brasco would never have dreamed of it.

In this way many of the gangs and criminal communities in Odessa were eliminated. Only the Jewish community managed to survive, because there were no Jews in the police force and no one else knew the Jewish culture, language and traditions well enough to be able to pass for one of them.

Later, when the power of the police grew in Odessa and began to threaten the Jews as well, they pooled their forces to form two big gangs, each with thousands of members.

One, the more famous, was led by the legendary criminal Benya Krik, alias 'the King', and specialized mainly in robberies and burglaries. The other was headed by an old criminal called Buba Bazich, alias 'the Squint', and dealt only in illegal financial dealing.

These two organizations worked very well together, and the police could do nothing against them. Before long they had taken over Odessa, and the Jewish community became one of the most powerful throughout the southern USSR, and especially in Ukraine.

In October 1941, when the German and Romanian occupation forces entered Odessa, most of the Jews were deported to the concentration camps and exterminated.

The criminals joined the partisan units, hiding in the underground tunnels which ran all the way across the city and right down to the sea. They hit the enemy at night, with sabotage actions: they blew up their railway lines, derailed trains carrying arms and provisions, torched and sank ships, and kidnapped and killed senior German officers, often capturing them while they were intimately engaged with the prostitutes of Odessa, who for the occasion had turned into skilful spies.

Bosya was there, in those underground tunnels.

Sometimes, when we dropped in at his shop, Bosya would tell us about the Odessa resistance; he said that for several years they had all lived in the tunnels under the city, without ever seeing the light of day. The Germans, he said, were constantly blowing up the tunnels to prevent the partisans from carrying out their sabotage attacks, but each time they shook off the dust and dug new passages.

Bosya had met his wife in those tunnels. Elina had been with her Jewish family, who had been freed by the partisans: they had fallen in love and got married there, underground. He used to say – perhaps joking, perhaps not – that when they had finally come out of the tunnels they had forgotten what the sunlight was like, and his young wife, after taking a good look at his face, had said to him:

'I'd never noticed you had such a long nose!'

They wanted a child, but for years after the war didn't succeed in having one, and were sad about this. They tried all the treatments, but in vain. So one day they decided to go and see an old gipsy woman who lived with her blind niece. People said this gipsy woman could cure diseases with magic and with folk remedies – that she was a kind of witch, but very knowledgeable. The gipsy told Bosya that neither he nor his wife had any disease, that they were only suffering from unpleasant memories. She advised them to leave Odessa and settle somewhere else, in a place where there was nothing that linked them with the past.

For a long time they didn't take this advice from the gipsy seriously, and besides, it was very difficult for them to break away from the community. Only in the late 1970s did they decide to leave Odessa and move to Bender, our town, where Bosya set up his little business and devoted himself to those mysterious activities about which nobody knew anything precise, but which soon made him rich.

And then, when Bosya and his wife were at an age when people usually become grandparents, Faya was born.

The three of them made a lovely family, and as Grandfather Kuzya often said, they were 'people who know how to live happily'.

So – to return to our story – on that cold February morning Mel and I called in at Bosya's shop to buy a plant, and he, as always, welcomed us with kind words:

'Dear me, haven't you got anything better to do in such cold weather?'

It was better for me to do the talking, because a dialogue between Mel and old Bosya would have been rather complicated.

'We've come about Aunt Katya. On business.'

Bosya peered at me over his spectacles and said:

'Thank goodness somebody still manages to do a bit of business! I've been knocking my head against these walls all my life and have never managed to do any at all!'

I gave in at once, without even attempting any repartee; trying to get the better of him was like trying to outrun a cheetah.

As always, pushing a plate towards us, with a somewhat nonchalant gesture, he offered us his revolting, ancient sweets. He knew perfectly well that they were awful; it was a ritual piece of mockery. We took them every time: we would fill our pockets and he would watch us, smiling, and repeating the words:

'Eat them, boys, eat them! But mind you don't break your teeth . . .'

When his wife caught him playing that cruel trick, she would get angry with him and insist that we empty our pockets and throw the sweets in the rubbish bin. Then Elina would take us to her house and offer us tea with biscuits filled with butter cream, the best biscuits in the world.

A few months earlier I had let Bosya in on the secret of his sweets, and he had been astonished, because he had thought that through all those years we had eaten them. 'We used them as stones,' I told him, 'to fire with our catapults.' At the windows of the police station, to be precise: they were deadly, especially the raspberry-flavoured ones. One evening I had fired one at Mel's knee as a joke: it had swollen up, and for six months he'd had to keep having the water drained from his knee with a syringe.

Mel and I took our sweets in silence and chose a small plant to give to Aunt Katya.

But I can't mention catapults like that without explaining exactly what our catapults were like.

Each of us made his own catapult, from start to finish, so they were all different and reflected in some way the individuality of their owners. The frame of the catapult had to be made exclusively of wood. A particular luxury was a thin frame, made of a pliant but strong wood. Everyone had his own little tricks which he kept to himself, but if someone liked another boy's catapult he could buy it or be given it as a token of friendship.

The catapult always had to be kept in your pocket, like your knife; not until the age of thirteen or fourteen was it replaced by a gun. But I carried my catapult around with me even later, till I was eighteen.

When my grandfather had been in Siberia he had made pipes for tobacco, using the roots of local trees, or various kinds of bush. With his help we had found a type of wood that was perfect for catapults and this was my great strategic secret; my friends tried repeatedly to make me talk but I always held out, like a brave Soviet partisan in a Fascist prison.

To make the elastic we generally used old bicycle inner tubes, but often they didn't produce enough power in the shot. Much better were the tourniquet bandages that we found in military first-aid packs: the ones that are used for compressing the arteries, to stop blood loss. If these bandages were properly attached, we could shoot a round stone or steel bolt – or one of Grandfather Bosya's sweets – over a hundred metres through a window, and it might even break something inside the room.

But the most deadly elastic of all was an invention of mine: the one made from Soviet army issue gas masks.

Fixing the elastic on, too, was something that each of us did in our own way; I preferred a secure but complicated form of attachment, and I never got hit in the eye or on the nose by the elastic, which is very painful. I used a thin thread, wound round the elastic a number of times and tied with a simple fisherman's knot. To make it extra secure I then smeared it with a little chewed-up bread, which created a kind of substance which was like glue but didn't dry the thread.

In the middle of the elastic you fixed the piece of leather where you would put the object you wanted to fire. I used leather which was not very thick but tough, because if it was too thick it would crack and eventually break.

There were a lot of little tricks for improving the ballistic capability of your catapult, once you had a good basic structure. For example, whenever possible, I always used to damp the frame of the catapult before firing it; that way it was softened and I could be confident of using it to maximum effect without breaking it. Then I would grease all the knots of the catapult: this guaranteed more precision, because it eliminated those little movements of dry materials which might influence the trajectory.

I invented the method of setting fire to the cars in the yard of the police station using a catapult. The yard was surrounded by a very high wall, and in order to fire something into it you had to venture too close and they would, inevitably, catch you as soon as they saw you arrive. Molotov cocktails were too heavy to throw, and whenever we tried they didn't even reach halfway up the wall before smashing. We would always end up exchanging disconsolate looks, thinking that all the effort we'd made to prepare those bottles was burnt up in an instant against that grey wall. We had begun to lose heart, until one day I came across some liquor belonging to my uncle in the cupboard. What I found was a lot of small bottles containing various kinds of spirit – those little bottles for alcoholic dwarves. I emptied some of them; after all my uncle was in jail, and in any case he wouldn't have scolded me, because I was making good use of them. I made a mini-molotov, then I constructed a special

catapult, slightly stronger than usual, and after carrying
out some preliminary tests, which it passed with flying
colours, I prepared a box full of mini-molotovs (which we
called 'mignons') and ten catapults for firing them.

We broke into an old abandoned printing works
near the police station and from there we had a perfect
view of our targets. We positioned ourselves carefully, and
like a battery of howitzers we fired the first shot. Ten of
us did the shooting; one boy would pull back the catapult
with the little bottle in it and another boy standing behind
him would light his bottle and that of the next shooter,
using two cigarette lighters which he held at the ready.
All our actions were perfectly synchronized. Our little
bottles flew spectacularly, whistling like bullets as they
disappeared over the wall of the police station. When I
heard the small explosions followed by the cries of the
cops and the first signs of black smoke, which rose in the
air like fantastic dragons, I felt like bursting into tears, I
was so happy.

Our position was ideal: before our victims realized
what had happened, we had already fired off our whole
arsenal and ridden calmly homeward on our bikes.

It was the talk of the town: 'There's been an attack on
the police station,' said one. 'Who was it?' asked another.
'A gang of strangers, apparently,' replied a third – and we
felt very important; every time I heard someone talking
about that episode I wanted to shout in his face, 'It was
us, us!'

I was proud, no doubt about it. I thought I was a
genius and for some time after I behaved towards my
friends like a general towards his army.

After that, we set fire to the police station car park a few more times, but then the police covered it with wire netting, so our molotovs couldn't get through. Many bounced on the netting and then hit the ground, *plof!*, on the outer side of the wall, but without exploding. It wasn't very interesting any more.

For a while we tried to think up something new, but then suddenly we grew up and someone suggested simply shooting the policemen with guns. That was interesting, too, but it wasn't like burning them with mini-molotovs. There was something medieval about those 'mignons' which made us feel like knights fighting valiantly against dragons.

And so, as we walked towards Aunt Katya's restaurant with our beautiful plant, we crossed the Bridge of the Dead. At that time this was a stretch of asphalted road with some old stones sticking out of it, but once it had been a real bridge. When the bridge was destroyed, it had first been covered with earth and then asphalted over, but for some inexplicable reason the stones kept breaking back up to the surface, making holes in the asphalt. It was weird to see those large old black, shapeless patches sticking out of the cracked asphalt. An old man of our area had told me the mystery could easily be explained as an 'engineering error'. But when I was a child I preferred another story which explained that strange movement of the stones on the Bridge of the Dead as a supernatural phenomenon.

The story ran that during the nineteenth century the workers in our town, tired of being exploited by a rich and noble lord who had a reputation comparable to that of Count Dracula, had revolted. The pretext for their revolt had been the fact that the master had raped a young peasant girl. The girl had not, like many others before her, suffered in silence, but had told everyone the truth, even at the risk of being despised and of losing her dignity. The peasants and the workers, however, had not despised her but had supported her and risen up immediately. They had killed the guards and entered the master's palace, then dragged him out of bed and taken him into the street, where they had kicked and beaten him to death. Afterwards, they had tied his body to the palace gate and prevented his family from removing it. 'It must rot up there,' they had said.

The next day, the revolt had been put down. But the people said that if the master's body were taken down from the gate and buried under a cross, a curse would fall on all his family. Naturally nobody had heeded those words, and the master had been buried with full honours, like a hero who had fallen in battle.

After a few months his wife had fallen ill and died. His eldest son, now a young man, had also died not long afterwards, having fallen off his horse. Finally, some time later, his daughter had died while giving birth to her first child, a baby boy, who did not survive either.

The palace had been abandoned and soon fell into ruins: nobody wanted to live there any more. The land of that nobleman was occupied by the peasants. Over the family tombs they built a bridge, which was accordingly known as 'The Bridge of the Dead'.

The legend says that every night the ghosts of the family gather to take the body of that cruel man out of the ground, so that they can hang it up on the gate again, because they want to lay the curse and be able to rest in peace. But they never succeed in getting him out, because the bridge was built over his grave, and all the ghosts manage to do in one night is to pull up a few stones, which the next day the people, when they pass over the bridge, put back in place.

When we were small we sometimes went hunting for those ghosts at night. To keep up our courage we carried our knives, as well as various 'magic' Siberian objects, such as the dried foot of a goose, or a tuft of grass taken from the river bank during a night of the full moon.

As we hid in a little ditch and waited for the ghosts we filled the time with horror stories to frighten ourselves so much that we stayed alert. But we soon all fell asleep, one after another.

The first would say:

'Wake me up if you see something, boys,' then we'd all fall asleep, lying at the bottom of the ditch like corpses.

In the morning the one who had held out longest would tell the others some tall tale about what he had seen.

The others, of course, would be angry.

'Why didn't you wake us up, you idiot?'

'I couldn't move, or even open my mouth,' he would claim. 'It was like being paralysed.'

Mel had once told us that the ghosts had carried him up into the air and flown him around the town. The idea of Mel flitting around in the company of aristocratic ghosts from the previous century made a deep impression on me.

Whenever we passed that way I would remind Mel of the story of his flight. He would gape at me.

'Are you taking the piss?' And I'd burst out laughing, flapping my arms to imitate the movement of the wings, whereupon Mel wouldn't be able to restrain himself any longer and he too would start laughing.

Crossing the Bridge of the Dead, both flapping our arms, we finally reached the street where Aunt Katya's restaurant was.

We found her among the tables, serving her regular customers – old criminals who lived on their own and went to eat in her restaurant every day. They had spent so long in prison that they had got used to the collective criminal life, and consequently they tried to be together all the time, though you would hardly have thought it, because they looked as if they couldn't stand each others' company. The expressions on their faces seemed to indicate great unhappiness, but in fact those were simply their normal expressions. I think they missed prison, in a way, and even missed the hardship in which they had grown accustomed to living. They continued to live the life of prisoners, despite having been free for years. Many of them couldn't get used to the rules of the civil world, to freedom. Almost all of them preferred to live in one-room flats where they'd had the walls of the bathroom and the kitchenette knocked down to create a single space that reminded them of their cell. I knew some old men who even put barbed wire and bars across their windows, because otherwise they felt uneasy and couldn't get to sleep. Others slept on wooden bunks like those of the prisons and always left the tap running, as it had in their cells. Their whole life became a perfect imitation of the one they had lived when they were incarcerated.

Aunt Katya allowed all those criminals to re-create a kind of make-believe prison in her restaurant, because they were her regular customers, but also because she loved every one of them and, as she herself used to say:

'I wouldn't presume to re-educate elderly people.'

So entering Aunt Katya's restaurant was like entering a prison cell. All the men sat with their heads bowed, as if something were preventing them from looking up. This is an unmistakable mark of the ex-convict: he'll always keep his head down, because in prison you spend most of the time lying on bunks and you have to be careful not to bang your head on the bunk above. Even people who have only spent a few years in jail don't find it easy to break this habit when they come out.

The old men usually played cards at Aunt Katya's, but not with normal playing cards: they used *kolotushki*, hand-painted cards made in prison.

They all dressed the same, in grey, and all wore the *fufayka*, the standard heavy jacket, which is thick and warm.

As in their cells, they smoked by passing a cigarette from one to another, even though they could afford to smoke one each. Out of that smoke, which filled the whole restaurant, their ravaged faces loomed, wearing an expression that was an eternal question, as if they'd been struck by some strange fact which they couldn't make head nor tail of: wide eyes that looked at you and in the space of three seconds gave you a complete X-ray, and knew who you were even better than you did yourself.

Among themselves they talked only in slang and in *fenya*, the old Siberian criminal language, but they spoke quietly and little; they communicated more in gestures, mostly secret ones.

They called Aunt Katya 'mama', to emphasize the importance of her role and of her authority.

They followed many of the prison rules of behaviour; for example, they never went to the toilet while someone was eating or drinking, even though the toilet wasn't in the same room but on the other side of the yard. Nor did they ever discuss politics, religion, or differences between nationalities.

There was strict hierarchy among them: the highest Authorities sat near the windows and enjoyed the best places; the others sat nearer to the doors. The 'garbage' – people considered to be beneath contempt – and those who had been 'lowered', or demoted to the lowest ranks of society, were not admitted: outside prison there is not the same compulsion to share the same space as there is inside. There were only two or three 'sixths'[1] – a kind of slave, people who performed tasks deemed unworthy

---

1. This term is used for the lowest-ranking members of some criminal castes: the number is that of the lowest-value playing cards in a pack.

of a criminal: they were allowed to touch money with their hands, so they paid for everyone's meals, taking the money from a common kitty. Whenever anyone ran out of cigarettes, the 'sixth' had to hurry off to get him some more: a service for which he was paid but also treated with slight contempt – not offensive, but indicative, to remind him of his place on the hierarchical scale. It was strange to see these old men being treated like little boys; they were always on the alert, constantly looking to see whether anyone in the room needed them. When they brought the cigarettes they would bow, with a humble expression on their faces, wait for the highest Authority to open the packet and offer them a few for the service, and then, thanking him, return to their place, walking backwards, like crayfish, so as not to turn their back on the person with whom they had been dealing.

So when you entered Aunt Katya's restaurant you had to follow prison rules, and behave as you would when you entered a real cell. It may seem ridiculous, but for those people, for those elderly ex-convicts, it was a sign of respect, a way of showing them that you had come with good intentions and were astute.

When you enter a cell you have to know how to greet people in an appropriate manner. You can't just say 'Hello' or 'Good morning': if you do, the criminals will immediately understand that you know nothing of their culture, and if you're lucky they'll dismiss you as 'someone who's just passing through', who is irrelevant to them; they won't communicate with you, they'll act as if you don't exist. You must greet them like this: open the door, take just one step and then stop – woe betide you if you take another step. Then say 'Peace to your (or our) house' or 'Peace and health to honest vagabonds' (this is a safe variant, worthy of a true criminal), or 'Good health to the honest company', 'It's the hour of your joys': in short, there are many forms of greeting used in the criminal world. After saying the appropriate phrase, it's essential not to move, but to wait for the reply. Usually the criminals don't reply immediately; they let a few moments pass, to assess your reaction. If you're clever you'll keep calm, gaze at a point in front of you and never look anyone in the face. The highest Authority, or one of his men, will eventually answer you, again with a set phrase: 'Welcome with honesty' or 'May the Lord guide you', or 'Enter with your soul'.

According to the rules, before doing anything else you must personally greet the highest Authority. In my case, on this occasion I knew him. He was sitting near one of the windows on the other side of Aunt Katya's restaurant. He always sat there, with his companions.

All the people present belonged to the caste of the Men, who in the criminal hierarchy are also called Grey Seed. They are hardened criminals, alcoholics, simple people, thieves and murderers, who for personal reasons had never wanted to join the caste of Black Seed, whose members formed a kind of 'aristocracy' among the criminals.

In the criminal world Black Seed was a young but powerful caste, which had succeeded in exploiting the philosophy of personal sacrifice. Its members appeared to be pure and perfect men, who devoted their lives to the welfare of people in prison. They worshipped prison: they referred to it affectionately as 'home', 'church' or 'mother', and were happy to spend time there, even their whole lives. Whereas all the other castes, including that of the Siberian Urkas, despised prison and put up with detention as you might a misfortune.

Thanks to the enormous number of scum and low-lifes that had joined its ranks, Black Seed had become the largest caste in the Russian criminal world: but for every wise and good person that you could find among them, you would meet another twenty uncouth and sadistic ones, who showed off and threw their weight around in every possible situation.

Then there was another very unusual caste: Red Seed, whose members collaborated with the police and believed in the nonsense purveyed by the prison administrations, such as 'redemption of the personality'. They were called 'cuckolds', 'reds', 'comrades', *sucha*, *padla* – all very pejorative words in the criminal community.

All the people in the middle were called Grey Seed, or neutrals. They were opposed to the police and observed the rules of criminal life, but they didn't have the responsibilities, let alone the philosophy, of Black Seed, and they certainly didn't want to spend their whole lives in prison.

The members of Black Seed were required to disown their relatives; they weren't allowed to have either a home or a family. Like all the other criminals they idolized the figure of the mother, but many of them didn't respect their own mothers; on the contrary, they treated them very badly. Many is the poor woman I've known with sons who, while they were in prison, declared to each other in a theatrical manner that the only thing they really missed was their mother and then, when they got out, turned up at home only to exploit her, and sometimes even rob her, because that is what their rule says: 'Every *Blatnoy* – member of Black Seed – must take everything away from his home; only in this way can he prove that he is honest through and through . . .'

It was madness – mothers and fathers were robbed, threatened and sometimes even killed. A short and violent life, as the Black Seed described it: 'Wine, cards, women, and then let the world come tumbling down . . .', with no moral or social commitment. Their whole life becomes one long show, in which they must always demonstrate only the negative and primitive sides of their nature.

The balance between Grey Seed and Black Seed rests on a continual series of truces: the Men are more numerous, but the *Blatnye* are better organized in prison.

The caste of the Men has no hierarchy like that of Black Seed – respect is accorded to age and profession. The highest in rank are those who take the greatest risks – robbers and murderers of policemen. After them come the thieves, conmen, cheats and all the rest.

The Men take every decision together and follow rules of life similar to those of the Siberians, but they remain more neutral in every situation. Their motto is: 'Our home is outside the village.' Their criminal units are not called gangs, but 'families', and even in prison they form families where everyone is equal and shares everything; when necessary the families get together and become a power which knows no limits. Almost all prison riots are organized by them.

The highest Authority in that restaurant – whom I had to greet personally before doing anything else – was called Uncle Kostich, nicknamed 'Shaber'. He was an old and experienced criminal, well-known all over the country; in our community and in my family he was highly thought of and treated with great affection. He was a calm, peaceful man with a very agreeable way of speaking. He expressed himself with patience and humility and was always clear and direct – if he had to tell you something he didn't beat about the bush. He lived with his mother, a woman so old she seemed like a tortoise; she moved slowly but she was otherwise in very good physical shape. They owned a house and a bit of land. Uncle Kostich kept a lot of pigeons, and I went to see him now and then to swap some of mine with his. He was honest, and would always give me a few pigeons more. He would offer me chifir and then tell me a lot of interesting stories about his life. He had a daughter somewhere in Russia, but hadn't seen her for a long time, and I think he was very sad about that.

In his youth, he told me, he hadn't been a criminal; he used to work in a big sawmill, cutting tree trunks. But then one day he'd seen a boy get cut in two, when a trunk had knocked into him and he had fallen on the

blade of a large saw. The foreman hadn't allowed anyone
to stop working even for a second; they had been forced
to go on cutting the wood, getting spattered with their
workmate's blood. From that moment he'd begun to hate
communism, collective work and everything the Soviet
system represented.

He had been given his first prison sentence under an
article of the penal code known in the USSR as the 'Idler'.
According to this article, anyone who was unemployed
could be condemned as a criminal. So Kostich had been
sent for three years to an ordinary regime prison in the
town of Tver. During that period a war between castes
was going on, and Black Seed was about to gain control
of the prisons; at first not many were happy with this
change, and the blood flowed like a river in spring.
Kostich had tried to stay aloof from everyone, not to take
sides, but gradually, as time passed, he had realized that
it was impossible to live on your own in prison. He liked
the Men better than the *Blatnye* because, he said, 'they're
straightforward and don't try to get anything by violence
and bullying; they prefer to use words and common sense'.
In prison he had joined a family which tried to live in a
neutral manner, not siding with anyone in that war, but
one day one of their elderly criminals had been killed by
a young, ruthless *Blatnoy*, who wanted to weaken Grey
Seed so that he could exploit its members, bending them
to his own interests.

So the Men first organized a kind of peaceful resistance,
and then, when they realized that this approach wasn't
producing the desired results, they decided to go to war.
And they fought the war with knives. Many of them, there

in prison, worked in the kitchens or as barbers (whereas the *Blatnye* didn't work; it was against their rules), so they easily armed themselves with knives and scissors and wrought havoc among the Black Seed.

Kostich was very good at using a knife: he'd grown up in the country, and as a boy he'd learned to kill pigs thanks the teaching of an old First World War veteran who worked as a butcher and slaughtered pigs by running them through with a bayonet. So, after his first murders, Kostich earned his nickname 'Shaber' – the name of a knife. When he got out of prison, he already knew what he was going to do: he began a long career as a robber from ships on the rivers Volga, Don and Danube.

With Uncle Kostich I could speak freely, without worrying too much about rules of behaviour. Of course I was respectful, as I was towards any Authority, but I also took some liberties: I would tell him about my adventures and ask him a lot of questions, something that is not usually done in the criminal community.

Often he asked me to recite to him the poems of Yesenin, Lermontov and Pushkin, which I knew by heart, and when I'd finished he would say to his companions:

'Did you hear that? This boy's going to be an intelligent man one day, a scholar! God bless you, my son! Come on now, let's hear the one about the eagle behind the bars again . . .'

It was his favourite piece, the poem by Pushkin which describes a prisoner's state of mind, comparing it to that of a young eagle that has been raised in captivity and forced to live in a small cage. I used to recite it to him in a powerful tone and he would look me straight in the eye expectantly, his lips moving slowly, repeating the words after me. When I ended with the lines 'Come, let's fly away! We're free birds! It's time, brother, it's time! There, where behind the clouds the mountain gleams white, there, where the blue of the sea is deepest, there, where I fly alone in the wind . . .', he would clap his hands to his head and say in a very theatrical manner:

'That's just what it's like, it's true, that's just what it's like! But even if I could have my time over again, I'd do exactly the same!'

At these moments I found it moving to see how simple he was, and how beautiful and pure his simplicity was.

One day Kostich had beaten to death a couple of young junkies who lived in Centre, and who were guilty of having starved to death their four-month old baby, leaving him to die in a corner of their apartment, among the dirty rags and the clothes that needed washing.

That couple were famous in town for their arrogance. The girl was quite good-looking; she dressed very provocatively and behaved accordingly. Her husband, the son of the manager of a car factory in a big city in central Russia, was a university drop-out, a drug addict and a pusher; he was disliked by a lot of people because he spread his poison among the young.

The neighbours, who had been aware for some time that the baby was too thin and was always crying, saw them leave home one morning without the child and go to a bar, where they stayed all day. Suspecting the worst, they had knocked down the door and found that lifeless little body. At that point all hell broke loose.

The two parents were seized by the crowd, which would certainly have killed them had it not been for the intervention of the Guardian of Centre, who took them and drove them to his home, saying that they must be judged according to the criminal laws. In reality the Guardian only wanted to exploit the occasion to blackmail the manager of the factory and force him to pay up to save his son from certain death. Everyone, though they suspected something, preferred to keep quiet. Everyone except Kostich.

Kostich made a spectacular gesture: he turned up alone at the Guardian's house, bare-chested, with a stick in his hands. The Guardian's henchmen tried to stop him, threatening him with force, but he said just one thing:

'Are you going to strike her?' pointing at the Madonna with Child tattooed on his chest. They backed off and let him go in, and he beat those two unnatural parents to death, then threw them out of the window into the street, where the people trampled them underfoot till they were reduced to a pulp.

The Guardian was furious, but only half an hour later the highest Authorities in the town, including Grandfather Kuzya, proclaimed that Kostich was right and recommended to the Guardian a simple and drastic solution: to commit suicide.

A week later the manager of the factory arrived in town, with the intention of avenging his son. It was clear that he didn't know much about our town, because he turned up with a gang of armed buffoons, comprising off-duty cops and soldiers. He had engaged them to carry out a punitive raid against the criminal who had killed his son. Well, they all disappeared in an alleyway, together with their three off-roaders. Nobody saw or heard anything; they entered the town and never left.

The authorities searched for them for a while: there were appeals in the newspapers, and on television they even showed the manager's wife begging anyone who knew anything about her husband to speak out. Nothing came of it. As they say in our community: 'drowned without leaving a ripple in the water'.

Whenever I asked Grandfather Kuzya – not straight out, of course, but in a roundabout way – whether he thought the manager had died for a just cause, he would answer me with a saying which he must have been very fond of, since he repeated it at every opportunity:

'He who comes to us with the sword shall die by the sword.'

As he said this he would smile at me in his usual way, but with the brooding look of a man who holds many stories within him which he will never be able to divulge.

To return to our story, we made our way towards Uncle Kostich's table. I walked quickly and Mel shuffled along behind me. Uncle Kostich immediately invited us to join him. It was a generous gesture and we accepted at once.

Just then Aunt Katya arrived, and showered us with kisses.

'How are you, my sons?' she asked, in her usual angelic voice.

'Thank you, Aunt, everything's fine . . . We were passing this way, so we decided to drop in to see how you were, and if you needed anything . . .'

'I'm still here with my company, thank heavens . . .' and she threw an affectionate glance at Uncle Kostich.

He took her hand and kissed its palm, as was customary in the old days as a sign of affection towards a woman – often your mother or sister. Then he said:

'May Jesus Christ be with you, mother; we breathe thanks to the labours you make. Forgive us for everything, Katyusha; we're old sinners, forgive us for everything.'

It was a real spectacle to witness these simple yet flamboyant gestures of respect and human friendship exchanged between people of such different backgrounds, united by loneliness in the midst of chaos.

Aunt Katya had sat down with us. The old man continued to hold her hand and, looking into the distance, over our heads, said:

'My daughter must be the same age as you, do you know that, Katya? I hope she's well, that she's found her road, and that it's a good and just road, different from mine . . .'

'And from mine too . . .' replied Aunt Katya, with a slight tremor in her voice.

'God forgive me, poor fool that I am. What have I said, Katyusha, may God help you . . .'

She didn't reply; she was on the point of tears.

We could only be silent and listen. The air was full of true, profound feelings.

What I liked about that circle, however violent and brutal it might be, was that there was no place for lies and pretence, cant and dissembling: it was absolutely true and involuntarily profound. The truth, I mean, had a natural, spontaneous appearance, not one that was cultivated or deliberate. The people were *truly* human.

After a short pause I said:

'Aunt Katya, we've brought you something . . .'

Mel put on the table the little bag with the plant wrapped up in old Bosya's rags to protect it from the cold.

She unwrapped the rags and on her face there appeared a smile.

'Well, what do you think? Do you like it?'

'Thank you, boys, it's lovely. I'll take it into the greenhouse straight away, otherwise with this cold . . .' and she went away with the plant in her hands.

We were delighted, as if we'd performed a heroic act.

'Well done, boys,' Uncle Kostich said to us. 'Never forget this holy woman. God only knows what it feels like to lose your children . . .'

When Aunt Katya came back she hugged us and you could see from her eyes that while she was in the greenhouse she'd been crying.

'Well, what shall I feed you on today?'

The question was almost superfluous. Everything she cooked was delicious. Without thinking twice we ordered an excellent red soup with sour cream and bread made from durum wheat. It was good bread, as black as the night.

She brought us a full saucepan and put it in the middle of the table; the soup was so hot that the steam rose solid as a pillar. We helped ourselves with a big ladle, then added to our dishes a spoonful of sour cream, which was hard and yellowish from all the fat it contained. We took a piece of black bread, spread garlic butter on it, and away we went: a spoonful of soup and a bite of bread.

On these occasions Mel was capable of emptying a whole saucepan on his own. He ate quickly, whereas I chewed slowly. I always gave myself up entirely to the pleasure of it, and often, when I twirled the ladle around in the saucepan to get a second helping, I would hear it knock sadly against the empty sides. At these moments I was strongly tempted to break the ladle over the head of my insatiable companion.

After eating that soup, I always felt as if I'd been given a new lease of life; a stream of positive emotions flowed through my body, and I felt like lying down on a warm, comfortable bed and sleeping for ten hours.

But within five minutes the second course arrived: potatoes roasted with the meat in the oven, which were floating in the melted fat and had a smell that went straight to your heart. And as usual, to accompany this course, there were three traditional dishes. Cabbages cut into long, thin strips and marinated in salt – quite delicious. My grandfather used to say they were a natural

medicine against any disease, and that it was thanks to
them that the Russians had won all the wars. I didn't
know how cabbages could cure diseases and with what
military strategies they had won the wars, but they were
tasty and, as we say, 'they went down whistling'. The
second dish was cucumbers, also marinated in salt –
delicious, and as crunchy as if they'd just been picked off
the plant, perfumed with many spices and herbs, fabulous.
The third was grated white turnips with sunflower oil and
fresh garlic. All these dishes were products of a peasant
cuisine that was very poor in raw materials, but capable
of exploiting them all in numerous different recipes. Then
there were always on the table little dishes of fresh garlic,
sliced onion, small green tomatoes, butter, sour cream,
and plenty of black bread. For me, if heaven exists, it
must include a table laden with delicacies, like that in
Aunt Katya's restaurant.

We didn't dare to drink alcohol in front of her, because
we knew it would offend her. So we drank *kompot*,
a kind of fruit salad, a cocktail of apples, peaches,
plums, apricots, cranberries and bilberries boiled for a
long time in a big saucepan. It was made in summer, and
for the rest of the year preserved in three-litre bottles with
a hermetically sealed neck ten centimetres wide. It was
kept cool in the cellars, then warmed up before it was
drunk.

But every time Aunt Katya went away, Uncle Kostich
added a bit of vodka to our glasses, with a wink:

'You're right not to let her see you . . .' We obediently
knocked back the mixture of vodka and *kompot*, and he
laughed at the faces we made afterwards.

Lunch lasted an hour, maybe a little longer. At the end there was boiling hot tea, strong and black, with lemon and sugar. And apple cake, a marvel. Mel leaped at that cake like a German invader jumping on the chickens in the henhouse of a Russian peasant. But he promptly got a friendly slap from me and his hands withdrew and vanished under the table.

The task of slicing up the cake was mine – it was my birthday. I gave the first piece, out of respect, to Uncle Kostich, the second to his friend, an old criminal called 'Beba', who was a kind of silent, invisible shadow of his. Then, taking my time, very slowly, I served Mel, who was on the point of bursting: he was staring at his slice with intense concentration, like a dog that gazes at the morsel of food in his master's hands, following its every movement. It made me laugh, so without the slightest remorse I played on his patience, performing each gesture in slow motion. Eventually Mel lost control and his legs started trembling under the table in a nervous tic, so I said to him, very calmly:

'Watch out, or you'll knock it onto the floor.'

Everyone burst out laughing, Mel even louder than the others.

After the dessert it is customary to sit still for a quarter of an hour, 'to accumulate a bit of fat', as my grandfather used to say. And people talk about all kinds of things. Mel, however, couldn't talk about anything, because to judge from the way he sat back from the table and slumped down in his chair, he had overdosed. He always did this. My uncle, ever since Mel had been small, had always called him 'pig', because like pigs Mel went into a kind of drunken state after eating.

So the only participants in the conversation were Uncle Kostich and I, with Beba occasionally putting in a word.

'Well, is everything all right at home? How's your grandfather, may God help him?'

'Thank you, he still says his prayers; it's a good thing the Lord always listens to us.'

'And what happened about that poor lad Hook?'

Kostich was referring to something that had happened a few weeks earlier: one of our friends, who had just come of age, had got into a fight with three Georgians and seriously wounded one of them with his knife. There was always a bit of trouble with Caucasus; it wasn't a real inter-district war, we were only hostile to a group of reactionary Georgians. Hook hadn't been wrong to get into the fight, but he had made a mistake afterwards: he had refused to appear at a trial that had been organized by the Authorities of the town at the instigation of a relative of the wounded Georgian. Hook was angry and out of control, and so, very thoughtlessly, he had offended the local system of criminal justice. If he had gone before the Authorities and put his case, it would certainly have been resolved in his favour, but as it was the relative had convinced everyone that the Georgian had been attacked for no reason by a cruel, merciless Siberian.

Kostich was one of the Authorities involved in the trial, and was trying to understand why Hook had behaved like that.

'What's this boy like? You know him well, don't you?'

'Yes, Uncle, he's a good friend of mine, we've been through all kinds of scrapes together. He's always behaved very well to me and the others – like a brother.' I was trying to save his face at least before one of the Authorities, hoping that Uncle Kostich would then influence the others. But I couldn't go too far and give my word; besides, my word as a minor didn't count for much.

'Do you know why he behaved dishonestly towards good people?'

Kostich had asked me a question which we call 'the one that tickles' – that is, a direct question that you can't not answer, even if the matter doesn't concern you. I decided to express my opinion, irrespective of what had happened:

'Hook's an honest person; three years ago he got stabbed three times in the fight against the people of Parkan, because he covered Mel and Gagarin with his body. Mel was still a child – he could have been killed. Sometimes it's hard to talk to him because he's a bit of a loner, but he's good-hearted and has never shown disrespect to anyone. I don't know what happened with the Georgians: Hook was on his own, there was nobody with him. Maybe that's partly why he felt betrayed. Three strangers – and from Caucasus, at that – attack you almost in front of your own house, in the heart of your own district . . . and none of your friends is there to help you stand up to them.'

I had told that story deliberately, about Hook's sacrifice in defence of Mel, because I knew that these things count far more than many others. I hoped Kostich thought so too; after all, he was still a simple man and a terrible troublemaker.

'Do you think he behaved rightly? Wouldn't it have been better to settle the matter in words?'

This question was a trap laid specially for me.

'I think it just happened like that. You know better than I do, Uncle, that every time is different. Until it happens to you, you can't know how you'll react.'

'If he was right, why didn't he want to appear before the others, to give his side of the story? He must think he's in the wrong, he can't be sure he behaved honestly . . .'

'I think he was just scared of being attacked a second time. The first time outside his house, with knives, the second through the justice of the Authorities. He lost faith in authority, he felt betrayed: they granted the Georgians' request even though they knew he'd been knifed like that, three against one, and in his own district.'

At last I'd succeeded in saying what I thought.

Kostich looked at me for a moment expressionlessly, then smiled at me:

'Thank goodness there are still some young delinquents in our old town . . . Remember this always, Kolima: it's wrong to want to become an Authority, you'll become one if you deserve it, if you were born for it.'

* * *

The question of Hook was settled three days later. The Authorities decided that the Georgians, by their request, had offended the honour of justice, and they proclaimed them 'stinking goats', an expression of extreme contempt in the criminal community. Those three quickly disappeared from Transnistria, but before leaving they threw a hand grenade into Hook's house, while he was having supper with his old mother. Luckily the grenade came from a batch that was intended for use in military exercises: it had a red circle drawn on it with ink and contained no explosive charge, so it was about as dangerous as a brick. The Georgians didn't know that; they'd bought it thinking it worked.

Although nobody had been killed, the people of our district took it as a grave insult to the community. And one evening Grandfather Kuzya said to me:

'Watch the news; you might see something interesting.'

Among the latest headlines was a report from Moscow: seven men with criminal records, and of Georgian nationality, had been found murdered in the home of one of them – brutally shot while they were having their evening meal. The pictures showed an overturned table, furniture riddled with holes, bodies gashed with wounds. On the lampshade, a hand-painted Siberian hunting belt, and hanging from the belt the fake hand grenade. The journalist commented:

' . . . a brutal massacre, no doubt a revenge attack by Siberian criminals.'

I remember that that evening, before going to bed, I took my hunting belt out of the cupboard, looked at it for a long time and thought, 'How wonderful it is to be Siberian.'

After the conversation with Uncle Kostich I woke Mel up with a couple of slaps on the cheek. We thanked Aunt Katya and went on our way. She, as always, came out onto the steps outside the restaurant and waved to us till we disappeared round the corner.

Mel started pestering me; he was desperate to know what I'd talked about with Uncle Kostich. The idea of having to summarize the whole content of our conversation was almost unbearable, but when I looked at his innocent expression I couldn't say no.

So I started to tell him the story, and when I got to the part where Uncle Kostich had asked me about Hook, he stopped and stood as stiff as a lamppost:

'And you said nothing, didn't you?'

He was angry, and this was a bad sign, because when Mel got angry we often ended up fighting, and since he was four times bigger than me I always came off worst. I only beat him once in my whole life, and we were only six years old at the time: I hit him with a stick, giving him a nasty gash on the head, taking advantage of the fact that he'd got his arms and legs trapped in a fishing net.

Now Mel was standing there, stock still on the road with a scowling face and fists clenched. I looked at him for a long time, but just couldn't guess what might be going through his mind.

'What do you mean, nothing? I said what I thought . . .'
Before I could finish the sentence he'd thrown me down
on the snow and was pummelling me, shouting that I was
a traitor.

While he was hitting me, I slipped my right hand into
the inside pocket of my jacket, where I kept a knuckleduster. I put my fingers right through the holes, then
suddenly pulled out my hand and punched him hard on
the head. I was a bit sorry to hit him right in the area
where he already had so many aches and pains, but it was
the only way of stopping him. Sure enough he released his
grip and sat down beside me, on the snow.

I lay there panting, unable to get up, watching him
closely. He was touching his head where I'd hit him and
with a disgusted grimace he kept kicking me lightly with
his foot, more out of scorn than with the intention of
hurting me.

When I got my breath back I propped myself up on
my elbows:

'What the hell got into you? Were you trying to kill
me? What did I say?'

'You talked about Hook, and now there'll be trouble.
He saved my life, he's our brother. Why did you squeal to
Uncle Kostich?'

At those words I felt a sharp pain in my stomach, I
couldn't believe it. I got up, brushed the snow off my jacket
and trousers and, before walking on, turned my back on
him. I wanted him to understand the lesson properly.

'I praised Hook, you idiot – I defended him,' I said.
'And God willing, Uncle Kostich will help us to get him
out of trouble.'

With that I set off, already knowing what would happen. For well over an hour we would walk like a theatre company: me in front, looking like Jesus just descended from the cross, with head held high and a gaze full of promises which loses itself cinematically in the horizon, and Mel behind, with shoulders drooping, all humble, with the expression of someone who's just committed a shameful crime, forced to lurch along like the hunchback of Notre-Dame and repeat the same words over and over again in a whimpering, piteous voice, like a monotonous prayer:

'Come on, Kolima, don't be angry. We had a misunderstanding. These things happen, don't they?'

'Bloody hell,' I thought, 'bloody hell!'

And so we left Centre and the last row of old three-storey houses. We now had to walk across to the other side of the park, where there stood a hideous and depressing building, a palace which had been erected two centuries earlier as a lodge for the tsarina of Russia on her journeys into the borderlands. I know nothing about architecture, but even I could see that the palace was an ill-assorted jumble of styles: a bit of Middle Ages and a bit of Italian Renaissance, clumsily imitated by Russians. It was coarse, its ornamentation was completely out of character, and it was covered with mould. This ghastly place, which I thought more suitable for Satanic feasts and human sacrifices, was in fact used as a hospital for people suffering from tuberculosis.

In Bender the hospital was known as *morilka*, which in the old Indic language means something that suffocates you. The doctors who worked there were chiefly military medics employed by the penitentiary system – prison doctors, in other words. They came from all over the USSR. They would move to Bender for a few years with their families and then go away; their place would immediately be taken by others, who in turn, before leaving would suggest new changes – trivial and pointless revolutions. Those poor patients had grown accustomed to being constantly moved from one floor or wing to another. They were forced to see their lives drawing to an end in the midst of absolute chaos.

The hospital was of the 'closed' type – that is, it was guarded, like a normal prison, because many of the patients were ex-convicts. It was surrounded by barbed wire and had bars on the windows.

Smoking was forbidden in the building, but the nurses secretly brought in cigarettes and sold them to inveterate smokers at three times the normal cost.

Among the patients there were many who were only feigning illness: Authorities of the criminal world who by exploiting their connections had managed to have false medical certificates made out which declared them to be 'terminal'. So they stayed in a comfortable hospital instead of a cold, damp, stinking prison. Whenever they wanted they had prostitutes brought in from outside; they organized parties with their friends and even meetings of Authorities at a national level. Anything was permitted and covered up, provided you paid for it.

The person who guaranteed the Authorities a happy
stay in hospital was a woman, a fat nurse of Russian
nationality and of a perennially cheerful disposition: Aunt
Marusya. She seemed healthier than Our Lord: she had
red cheeks and spoke in a loud and extremely powerful
voice. She was very popular with the criminals, because
there was nothing she wouldn't do for them.

The hospital was divided into three non-commun-
icating blocks. The first and most pleasant was exposed
to the sun: it had big windows and a warm swimming-
pool; it was the block for the terminally ill, where every
patient had his own clean, warm little room and received
constant attention from the staff. This was where the
Authorities stayed: they pretended to be moribund but
were really as healthy and strong as could be; they spent
their days playing cards, watching American films on
video, screwing the young nurses and receiving visits from
their friends, who supplied them with all they needed for
an agreeable life full of delights.

Grandfather Kuzya was critical of those people; he
called them *urody*, which means 'freaks': he used to say
they were a disgrace to the modern criminal world, and
that we had the culture that came from America and
Europe to thank for the fact that people like them existed.

The second block was intended for the chronically
ill. They slept six to a room; no television, no fridge,
only the canteen and a bed. Lights out at nine o'clock in
the evening, wake-up call at eight in the morning. They
couldn't leave their room without the permission of the
authorized staff – not even to go to the toilet. In case of
need, outside the prescribed hours they could use an old

mobile latrine which was emptied every evening. The food was reasonable and was delivered three times a day. This was the block where the genuinely sick were kept – criminals and non-criminals, and also many homeless people and vagabonds. The medical treatment was the same for everybody: pills and the occasional injection, inhalations of steam twice a week. The wards were cleaned by the nurses with a powerful disinfectant, creolin, the same one as was used for cleaning stables: it had such a strong smell that if you breathed it in for more than half an hour you got a terrible headache. In this block even the food smelled of creolin.

The third block was for patients suffering from tuberculosis in the acute phase, those who were infectious. The block was entirely in the shade, facing the trees of the park, with small windows which were always misted over; it was so damp that the water dripped from the ceiling. There were three floors, with fifty rooms to a floor and about thirty people to a room. For sleeping there were wooden bunks like those of the prisons, small mattresses, sheets that were changed once a month and rough blankets made of synthetic wool. Not everyone had a pillow. In these over-crowded rooms people were constantly dying. It was disgusting in there. Many couldn't even get to the toilet on their own, and since nobody helped them they did everything over themselves. What's more, many of them spat blood when they coughed; they spat it continually, straight on the floor. They had no television, radio or any other form of entertainment. They received no treatment, because it was deemed to be pointless. And they were given little or nothing to eat, on the grounds that since they were going to die, food would have been wasted on them.

The nurses' market, of course, didn't reach the patients of the third block, so they had invented an ingenious system for getting hold of cigarettes. They used young boys, people like us, in the street. The patients would throw out of the windows a heavy bolt with a double fishing line tied to it. When the bolt landed over the wall, the boys would hook a little bag containing the cigarettes onto the thread, and the patients would fix on another bag containing the money. By pulling the thread you propelled the two little bags, which thus began their journeys in opposite directions – the money towards the boys and the cigarettes towards the patients.

The boys sold the cigarettes more or less at market price, but they made a profit anyway because the cigarettes were stolen and hadn't cost them anything.

The patients were always hungry for cigarettes, always. The hospital administration, in an attempt to stop this kind of trade, had spread a story to scare the street boys, giving them to believe that they might fall ill and die if they touched the patients' money. But the boys, as always, had found a solution: they quickly ran the flame of a cigarette lighter around the banknotes to 'kill' the mortal bacterium. And besides, the idea of doing something forbidden and dangerous attracted them even more.

The hospital guards were under orders to intervene. Many turned a blind eye, but some bastards took pleasure in thwarting the exchange at the very last minute: they waited for the moment when the patient stretched out his hand to take the packet and – *snip!* – they cut the string. The cigarettes fell to the ground, accompanied by the despairing cries of the patient. The guards had a good laugh: they were scum that deserved to be slaughtered like pigs, in my opinion.

By now Mel and I had crossed the park. Mel continued to apologize to me, and I continued to ignore him and walk on as if I were alone.

Suddenly, as we were skirting the wall of the block, a bolt fell between my feet. I stopped and picked it up: it had the fishing line tied round it. I looked up: leaning out of a window on the third floor was a middle-aged man with a long beard and unkempt hair. He was staring at me with wide-open eyes, making the gesture of smoking, as if he held a cigarette between his fingers.

I made a sign to him that I would see to it at once. I turned towards Mel, who hadn't even realized why I'd stopped, and asked him to give me all the cigarettes he had.

Mel eyed me suspiciously, but I said to him disgustedly:

'Oh come on! These people haven't got anything to smoke. You'll be able to buy yourself another packet in a minute.'

'But I haven't got any money on me!'

I felt a terrible anger rising within me, but anger didn't get you anywhere with Mel, so I calmed myself down and told him:

'If you give me your cigarettes, I'll forgive you and I won't tell the others.'

Without a word, Mel took two packets of Temp – the Soviet Marlboro – out of his pocket.

I pointed to the area of his jacket where he kept his cigarette lighter.

'But you gave it to me, don't you remember?' he said, trying to save at least that much, but even as he spoke, he was already putting his hand into his inside pocket to get it.

'I stole it from a kiosk at Tiraspol. I'll steal you another one – a better one, with a naked woman on it . . .'

'Oh, all right, all right . . .' The ploy of the naked woman had worked, and Mel thought he had made a great bargain. 'But remember, Kolima, it's got to have a naked woman on it, you've promised!'

'I always keep my promises,' I told him, taking the lighter from his large but gullible hand.

One of the packets had already been opened and a couple of cigarettes were missing. I slipped the lighter into it and then wound the string all round the bundle, tying it up with a bow like a gift. Finally I added the only thing I had on me, my clean cotton handkerchief, slipping it in between the two packets. Then I started pulling the string. When my bundle reached the window, the man's hand stretched out through the bars and the shouts of joy carried right down to us.

I was left with the patients' little bag in my hands. I opened it: inside was a banknote, torn, dirty and wet. One rouble. Next to it, a scrap of paper with a message: 'Sorry, we can't afford any more.'

I didn't even touch the rouble; I closed the little bag again and moved the two strings, to alert the patients. The man at the window pulled the string towards him, took back his rouble and shouted to me:

'Thanks for everything!'

'God bless you, guys!' I replied, shouting as loud as I could.

At once a guard materialized to the right, waving his Kalashnikov and shouting:

'Get away from the wall! Get away or I'll fire!'

'Shut your mouth, you fucking cop!' Mel and I replied simultaneously, though each in slightly different words.

Completely unruffled, we walked on. Then we turned around. The cop was standing there silently, glaring at us with such malice he seemed on the point of exploding. From the window the patient was still watching us: he was smiling and smoking a cigarette.

'You could have taken that rouble, though,' said Mel after a while.

I couldn't kill him because I was fond of him, so I did what Grandfather Kuzya always told me to do with people who can't understand the important things: I wished him good luck. He was a real imbecile, my friend Mel, and he still is: he hasn't improved over the years, in fact he might even have got a bit worse.

By this time we weren't far from the Railway district, where Mel had to deliver the message to a criminal. Leaving the hospital behind us, we passed the food warehouse complex – a place we knew well, because we often went to steal there at night. It was an old, turn-of-the-century site comprising several brick buildings with high walls and no windows. The railway ran alongside it, so the trains stopped right there and the wagons were quickly unloaded or loaded.

In order to steal from them you didn't need the agility of a burglar, but simply a bit of diplomacy. We never forced any locks; we had one of our own men inside, an infiltrator, a kind of mole who kept us informed and told us when it was the right moment. After the goods had been loaded, the trains usually stayed where they were for a few hours; the drivers rested and then left later, at dawn. So we would open the wagons at night while they slept and carry off the stuff: it was easier to work on the trains than to break down the doors of the warehouses. We would load everything into a car and drive off.

The trains were bound for the countries of the Soviet bloc – many for Romania, Bulgaria and Yugoslavia. They carried sugar, preserves and all kinds of canned food. Sometimes they were already half-full, with clothes, warm coats, workers' overalls, gloves and military uniforms. In some wagons you might also find domestic appliances, drills, electric wiring, hardware, electric fires and fans. When we got a chance like that we would make as many as three or four trips, to carry off as much as possible. We never managed to get everything into the car: but fortunately our man let us leave the goods temporarily in certain hiding places inside the warehouse.

Our mole was in fact the elderly caretaker of the warehouses, a Japanese who, after years of living with the Russians, now went by the name of Borishka.

He was very old, and had come to our town with the Siberians in the second wave of deportation in the late 1940s, after the Russian victory in the Second World War.

He had been made a prisoner-of-war in the Russo-Japanese conflict, at the battle of Khalkhin Gol. He was knocked unconscious by a blow to the head, and only survived by pure chance, because the Russian tanks drove straight over the dead bodies lying on the ground. After the tanks, the cavalry passed by: they found him there, looking bewildered, wandering around like a ghost in the midst of the dead. Out of pity they took him with them, otherwise he would have been killed by the infantry, who were searching for any Japanese left alive to avenge their comrades who had been killed the previous night, when the Japanese forces had attacked the first Russian divisions.

The Cossacks didn't hand him over to the armed forces; for some time they kept him on as a stable hand. He had to clean and care for the horses of the Cossacks of Altay, in southern Siberia. They treated him well and a friendship formed between him and the Cossacks.

Borishka came from Iga, a land of ninjas and assassins. Since boyhood he had been trained to fight both with weapons and bare hands. The Cossacks, too, loved fighting with cold steel and wrestling, so Borishka taught them the techniques of his own country and learned theirs.

Borishka hated the Japanese, and especially the samurai and the emperor; he said they exploited the people, who were forced to submit to many injustices. He said he had enlisted only in desperation, because of an unhappy love affair. The girl he had fallen in love with had been given in marriage to another man, who was rich and powerful.

The Cossacks' ataman, or leader (a big, strong man, a typical southern Siberian), was particularly fond of him. One day, Borishka said, they had called him out of the stables. He had gone out onto the parade ground, where the Cossacks were waiting for him, standing in a circle.

'Now the Japanese are all dead,' the ataman said, 'Japan has lost its war and you can go home. But first I want you to do one thing . . .' The ataman motioned to a young Cossack, who brought two swords: one was Borishka's – he had been wearing it on his belt when the Cossacks had saved him – and the other, the *shashka*, was the typical sword of the Siberian Cossacks, much heavier than that used by the Cossacks in other parts of Russia, because the Siberians also used it for chopping wood. A sword of that kind can weigh as much as seven kilos, and the men capable of carrying it could, in battle, split a man in two from head to hip.

The ataman took the two swords and said to him, in front of everyone:

'We have treated you well and you have nothing to complain of, but now I want to find out whether trying to occupy the USSR has served as a lesson to you. Here are the two swords. If you have understood that making war on us was unjust, break your Japanese sword with our Cossack one, and we will let you stay with us and you will be a Cossack yourself. But if you think your war was a just one, break our sword with yours, and we will let you go free wherever you want, and may God assist you; we will do you no harm.'

Borishka didn't know what to do. He didn't want to become a Cossack, but nor did he think that the war against the Russians had been a good and just thing. And above all, he hated the Japanese.

So he picked up his sword, kissed it, as the Cossacks kiss their swords, and hung it on his belt, in its place.

The ataman was watching him with interest, trying to understand what he was up to. Many Cossacks were sure Borishka would break their sword.

But instead he picked up the *shashka*, kissed it too and gave it back to the ataman.

Everyone was left speechless, and the ataman burst out laughing:

'Well, Borishka . . . You're a clever man, Japanese!'

'I'm not Japanese, I'm from Iga, and my sword is from Iga too,' he replied.

'Well, you're really a good fellow, Borishka; you must never forget who you are and never betray your tradition . . . You must be proud; only in that way will you preserve your dignity!'

So Borishka stayed with the Cossacks for a long time yet, but from that day on he was allowed to carry his sword with him.

When the Cossacks returned to Siberia, and to Altay, Borishka went with them. The ataman took him into his own house, and there Borishka met his future wife, the ataman's eldest daughter, Svetlana. They got married. Out of respect for her, Borishka was baptized in the Orthodox faith with the name of Boris, so that the ceremony could be held in church. They built their house and lived there, in a little village on the River Amur.

Then one day the ataman was suddenly arrested by Stalin's secret services, and some time later shot as a traitor. Borishka was very distressed; he thought it was all his fault, whereas in fact it was nothing to do with him: during that period many Cossacks were singled out by the Soviet government because they didn't share its communist ideas and still had a certain liking for anarchy and autonomy.

After his death the ataman was declared an 'enemy of the people', and the members of his family were deported to Transnistria, along with many other Siberians.

Borishka still remembered that long journey. The trains, he said, used to stop for a long time on the rails, and you couldn't get out because they were guarded by armed soldiers. Sometimes two trains travelling in opposite directions would stop alongside each other; on the one there would be people from the European part of the USSR who were being sent to Siberia, and on the other the opposite. He would hear someone shout from one train:

'Oh God, they're taking us to Siberia! It's too cold there, we'll all die!'

And someone reply from the other:

'Oh Christ, they're sending us to Europe! There are no woods there, only empty hills, we'll die of hunger!'

During that journey Borishka met some Siberian Urkas. He joined up with them because they were the only ones who didn't seem to be in despair. In a sense they had a secure future; there was already a fairly well-developed community waiting for them in Transnistria.

Borishka told his story to one of them, an elderly man respected by all the others, and was reassured:

'Don't be afraid, stay with us: our brothers are in Transnistria. If you're a just man, you'll soon have a home and you'll be able to bring up your children with our children, may the Lord bless us all . . .'

The Urkas and the Cossacks had always been on the same wavelength and got on well: both groups respected the old traditions, loved the nation and their homeland and believed in independence of any form of power. Both were persecuted by various Russian governments in different ages, because of their desire for freedom. It was just that the Urkas were more extreme, and had a particular hierarchical structure. The Cossacks, on the other hand, regarded themselves as a free army, and so had a paramilitary structure; in peacetime their main occupation was raising livestock.

When they arrived in Transnistria, Borishka and his wife were taken in by a family of Urkas, just as the old man had promised them.

Borishka at once felt at home. To him the Urkas had a lot in common with the people of the land where he came from, Iga. They were united and extremely anarchic and had a strong criminal tradition.

He soon joined in the business activities of the Siberian criminals, who respected him because he understood everything about their law; he was a man of his word and a just one.

And little by little he became one of us. He lived in our area with his family. His wife, whom we all called Grandmother Svetlana, had borne him two sons, who followed the road of the Urkas.

In his old age Borishka exploited a connection with the manager of the food warehouses, who took him on as a caretaker. They came to an agreement: the manager wouldn't make any fuss when goods disappeared, and Borishka would share his slice of the profits with him. He organized every raid to perfection; he was very precise and serious in business matters. In particular, he was very good at controlling his emotions; I never saw him get flustered.

Once, in autumn, when in every home the people make preserves for the winter and light a big fire on which they put a large pot full of water, I saw Borishka save a child's life. As usual at our house, the women gathered to cut the greens and prepare the pulses, and the men tended the fire and prepared the glass jars. We children were nearby, playing among the adults. Old Borishka was there too, with his son and grandchildren.

Suddenly the bar under the big saucepan snapped in two, and the pot overturned and poured out a flood of boiling water in a second. A few metres away sat a little boy, the son of a neighbour of ours, Uncle Sanya. I had gone out into the garden to look for more jars. When I heard the sound of the pot overturning, I rushed into the house and saw old Borishka pick up a big steel alloy bowl, throw it on the ground and jump into it, skimming along like on a surfboard. And there in the steam, which was as thick and white as the morning fog on the river, I saw slowly emerge the figure of a man standing inside a bowl with a child in his arms, surrounded by boiling water. The child's mother fainted; his father, Uncle Sanya, started screaming; the only two people who were calm were those two, Borishka and the little boy.

He had acted instinctively, without thinking about it, and afterwards had resumed his usual serene expression, as if he did such things four times a day.

He was a very interesting person; I liked talking to him, and hearing him tell the stories of his life. He often went fishing with a rod he had made himself, and while he was fishing he would stand with his feet in the water and sing Japanese songs. When I was small he taught me a very nice one: it was about a mountain and a young man who crossed it to find his betrothed.

We had made a deal with Borishka: when we went to the stores we had to pretend not to know him. If we saw him near the gate, we mustn't even greet him. He would often be there keeping guard with an old sheepdog that had something wrong with its hind legs and couldn't move very far; both of them would usually sit on a bench, and while the dog slept, Borishka would read the paper. Borishka read only one paper: *Pravda*, which means 'The Truth' – the newspaper of communist propaganda, which was read by everyone who wanted to believe in the freest and most beautiful country in the world. In *Pravda* any

item of news whatsoever was transformed into a source of
pure propaganda: even when you read about disasters and
wars, in the end you were left with a sense of happiness
and you felt lucky to live in the USSR. I don't know why
Borishka was so fond of that paper; once I asked him, and
he replied:

'When you're forced to listen to cattle singing, you
must at least exercise your freedom to choose the cow that
sings best.'

When I passed the gate I always looked away, so as not
to see whether Borishka was there or not. But my friend
Mel could never remember this simple but important rule.
He always stared at the gate, and if he saw Borishka he
would greet him, waving his hand in the air and smiling
with that disfigured face of his. Then I would glare at him
and he would immediately remember the deal we had
made with Borishka and start hitting himself, slapping
his forehead with the palm of his hand. As Grandfather
Kuzya used to say, a person like him was enough to drive
a madman mad.

Borishka was always furious when Mel greeted him.
On his way home from work he would come looking for
me or Gagarin and say, in a voice trembling with anger,
yet quiet and lilting:

'So you're wealthy men – you've finally become rich!'

'What do you mean? We're not rich . . .'

'You must be, since you can afford to refuse to work
with me, and earn money . . .'

At those words my hair would stand on end. To refuse
to work with Borishka was to say goodbye to half our
earnings.

'We haven't done anything, Uncle Borishka.'

'Haven't done anything? Teach that imbecile of a friend of yours how to behave. And if he can't get it into his head, don't bring him past the warehouses any more, take the long way round . . .'

We would talk to Mel, explain everything to him all over again, but it was no use. The next time, as soon as we got near to the stores, he would be looking for the old man, to greet him. It was like a penance to us, having him with us.

One day, as we were walking past Borishka's house, in our district, we stopped to have a chat with him. While we were talking, we realized that Mel was some distance away, on the other side of the road, with his back turned to us. Borishka looked at us all, then pointed to him, and his face suddenly became very serious.

'For your own good, get rid of your friend,' he said. 'Don't take him around with you any more: he'll only cause trouble. In fact, I'm willing to pay him, if only he'll stay at home and not roam the streets.'

Pretending not to understand, I said:

'But Uncle Borishka . . . It's true that Mel's a bit thick, but he means well.'

Borishka looked at me as if I'd spoken to him in a language he didn't understand.

'A bit thick, you say? Look at him: he's a disaster, that one! Even he doesn't know what's going on inside his head! Listen, I like you boys, that's why I'm being frank with you. You're still young; your friend makes you laugh now, but before long he's going to cause so much trouble that you'll be crying.'

What wise words they were! A pity I understood that too late, after many years had passed.

When we left, I asked Mel why he'd kept away from us. He looked at me with the expression of a torture victim, full of suffering, and said, almost in tears:

'First you tell me not to speak to him, then I speak to him and you scold me, then I don't speak to him and you scold me anyway! I give up; for all I care this Borishka might not even exist!'

I laughed, but Borishka was right – it was no laughing matter. And that was something we should have known by then.

When we were about ten years old, we went to the cinema to see a film called *The Shield and the Sword*. The main character, a Soviet secret agent, appeared in various action scenes, shooting his capitalist enemies with his silenced gun and doing a lot of acrobatics. The guy risked his life as if he were doing something perfectly normal and routine, to combat injustice in the NATO countries. It was a kind of Russian response to the many American and British films about the cold war, where the Soviets were usually portrayed as stupid, incompetent monkeys who played about with the atomic bomb and wanted to destroy the world. We, despite the rule imposed by our elders, had gone to see it in the only cinema in town (they hadn't yet built the second cinema, which was to have a very short life, because it was destroyed in the 1992 war: the Romanian soldiers took up their positions there, and our fathers, in order to kill them, one night blew the whole complex up, including the restaurant and the ice-cream parlour). Well, at one point in the film the main character jumped off the roof of a very tall building, using a big umbrella as a parachute, and landed comfortably without getting hurt. You could say he did a Mary Poppins.

The next day, without saying anything to anyone, Mel, equipped with a big beach umbrella, jumped off the roof of the central library, a three-storey building, below which there was a pleasant green area full of chestnuts and birches. Crashing down onto a tree, a birch, he managed to break a hand and a leg, knock himself out and impale his stomach on the pole of the umbrella. The result was a sea of blood, his mother in despair, and him having to shuttle from one hospital to another for almost six months.

Making fun of him seemed a good way of getting him to understand where his naivety might lead him. Another time, when we were already fourteen or fifteen, Mel was at my house, and we were making some tea to drink in the sauna. All at once he started blathering about tropical countries, saying that it wouldn't be bad to live there; he thought it might suit us, because the weather was never cold.

'There's too much humidity,' I told him. 'It never stops raining. It's a lousy place. What would we do there?'

'If it rained we could shelter in a hut. And think about it – on an island you don't need a car, you can go around on a bike and there's always a boat available. And the Indians . . .'

They were all Indians to him. American Indians. He thought the indigenous people of every country always went around on horseback with coloured feathers on their heads and painted faces.

'. . . the Indians,' he went on, 'are clever people. It would be great to become like them.'

'That's impossible,' I provoked him. 'They wear their hair long, like homosexuals.'

'What are you talking about? They're not homosexuals. It's just that they don't have any scissors to cut their hair with. Look,' he said to me, taking out of his pocket a little plastic figure with faded colours that he always carried about with him – an Indian warrior in a fighting pose, with a knife in his hand. 'You see? If he's got a knife he can't be a homosexual, or they'd never had given him permission to insult a weapon!'

It was funny to see how he applied our Siberian rules to the Indians. He was right, in our culture a 'cockerel' – that is, a homosexual – is an outcast: if he isn't killed he is prevented from having contact with others and forbidden to touch cult objects such as the cross, the knife and the icons.

I had no wish to dismantle his fantasies about the fabulous heterosexual life of Indians. I just wanted a bit of fun. So I tried another angle of attack, teasing him about a subject that he regarded as sacred: food.

'They don't make red soup,' I said in one breath.

Mel became very attentive. He craned his neck:

'What do you mean, they don't make red soup . . . What do they eat, then?'

'Well, actually they don't have much food; it's hot there, they don't need fat to help them resist the cold, they just eat the fruit that grows on the trees, and a few fish . . .'

'Fried fish isn't bad,' he attempted to defend tropical cuisine.

'Forget fried fish: they don't cook anything there, they eat everything raw . . .'

'What kind of fruit do they have?'

'Coconuts.'

'What are they like?'

'They're good.'

'How do you know?'

'My uncle's got a friend in Odessa who's a sailor. Last week he brought me a coconut with milk inside it.'

'Milk?'

'Milk, yes – only it doesn't come from a cow but from a tree. It's inside the fruit.'

'Really? Show me!' In five seconds he had taken my bait. All I had to do was reel him in.

'I'm afraid we've already eaten the fruit, but if you want to try it I've still got a bit of the milk.'

'Yes, let me try it!' He was jumping up and down on his chair, so eager was he for this milk.

'All right, then, I'll give you some. I put it in the cellar to keep it cool. Wait a couple of seconds and I'll bring it to you!'

Laughing like a bastard, I went out of the house and over to the toolshed where my grandfather kept all things useful and useless for the house and garden. I picked up an iron cup and put a bit of white filler and some plaster into it. To give the liquid the right density I added a bit of water and some glue for sticking on wall-tiles. I stirred the mixture with the wooden stick that my grandfather used for clearing the pigeons' nests of their droppings. Then I lovingly carried the magic potion to Mel.

'Here you are, but don't drink it all, leave some for the others.'

I should have saved my breath: as soon as he took the cup in his hands, Mel drained it in four gulps. Then he grimaced, and a timid shadow of doubt appeared in his good eye.

'Maybe it's gone off a bit in the cellar, I don't know; it was delicious when we first tried it,' I said, trying to save the situation.

'Yes, it must have gone off . . .'

From that day on I started calling him 'Chunga-Changa', and he never understood why.

Chunga-Changa was a cartoon film which was much loved by children in the Soviet Union. It was rather badly drawn, in the style of a communist propaganda poster: all bright colours, figures filled in without any gradations of tone and very stylized, proportions deliberately not respected so as to create an effect like that of a puppet show.

The cartoon promoted friendship among the children of the world through the story of a little Soviet boy who went to visit a little coloured boy on an island called Chunga-Changa. The Soviet boy had a very determined look in his eye (as did all communists and their relatives), a steamship and a very small dog , and he dressed like a sailor. The coloured boy was as black as a moonless night and wore only a kind of skirt made of leaves, and his friends were a monkey and a parrot; other creatures also appeared – a crocodile, a hippopotamus, a zebra, a giraffe and a lion, who all danced together paw in paw, round and round.

The cartoon lasted a quarter of an hour in all, and more than ten minutes of that were taken up by three songs, with a few very short dialogues in between. The song that became famous, and was loved by all the children of the USSR, was the last one. In it, to a cheerful, catchy little tune, a female voice sang of the happy, carefree life on the island of Chunga-Changa:

> Chunga-Changa, a wonderful island
> Living there is easy and simple
> Living there is easy and simple
> Chunga-a-a-Changa-a-a!
>
> Chunga-Changa, the sky is always blue
> Chunga-Changa, continual merriment
> Chunga-Changa, our happiness is incomparable
> Chunga-Changa, we know no difficulties!
>
> Our happiness is never-ending
> Chew the coconut, eat the bananas
> Chew the coconut, eat the bananas
> Chunga-a-a-Changa-a-a!

After the food warehouses the first houses of the Railway district finally began. This district belonged to Black Seed, and had different rules from our own. We would have to behave ourselves, or we might not come out alive.

The boys of that area were very cruel; they tried to earn the respect of others with the most extreme violence. Power among juveniles had a symbolic value: some kids could order others about, but none of them was respected by adult criminals. So, naturally, boys couldn't wait to grow up, and to achieve this more quickly many became absolute bastards, sadistic and unjust. In their hands the criminal rules were distorted to the point of absurdity; they lost all meaning, and became little more than excuses for violence. For example, they didn't wear anything red – they called it the communists' colour: if anyone wore any red garment the Black Seed kids were quite capable of torturing them. Of course, knowing this rule, none of the people who were born there ever wore anything red, but if you had it in for someone, all you had to do was hide a red handkerchief in his pocket and shout out loud that he was a communist. The hapless individual would immediately be searched, and if the handkerchief was found, no one would listen to anything he had to say in his defence: in everyone's eyes he was already an outcast.

This sense of a constant struggle for power, or, as Grandfather Kuzya called it, 'contest of the bastards', was essential to the ethos of the district. In order to be a perfect Authority among the youngsters of Railway you had to be always ready to betray your own people, not have ties of friendship with anyone and be careful you weren't betrayed in your turn, know how to lick the arses of the adult criminals and not have any education received from any form of human contact that was deemed to be good.

Those boys had grown up thinking they had nothing but enemies around them, so the only language they knew was that of provocation.

If it came to a fight, however, they behaved in various ways. Some groups fought with dignity, and many of these we were friends with. But others always tried to 'strike from round the corner', as we say – in other words attack from behind – and didn't respect any agreement; they were perfectly capable of shooting you even if you'd previously made a pact with them not to use firearms.

They were organized in groups which, unlike us, they didn't call 'gangs', a word they considered a bit offensive, but *kontory*, which means 'bureaus'. Each *kontora* had its leader, or, as they called him, *bugor*, which means 'mound'.

I had a long-standing quarrel with a *bugor* of that district: he was a year older than me and called himself 'the Vulture'. He was a lying buffoon, who had arrived in our town four years earlier, claiming to be the son of a famous criminal who went by the nickname 'White'. My uncle knew White very well; they had been in jail together and he had told me his story.

He was a criminal of the Black Seed caste, but one of the old guard. He respected everyone, and was never arrogant, but always humble, my uncle said. In the 1980s, when a group of young Black Seed men ousted the older Authorities (with the sole aim of making money and setting up as businessmen in civil society), many old men tried with all their strength to prevent it. So the young men started killing their old folk: during that period this was happening all over the place.

White fell victim to an ambush. He was getting out of a car with his men, when some men in another passing car opened fire on him. When they fired with their Kalashnikovs, a lot of people were walking along the street, and some were wounded. White managed to take refuge behind his car, which was armoured, but he saw a woman in the line of fire and threw himself at her to cover her with his body. He was badly wounded, and died in hospital a few days later. Before he died, he asked his men to seek out that woman, ask her forgiveness for what had happened and give her some money. This gesture of his made such a great impression in the criminal society that his killers repented and apologized to the old men, but then they went on killing each other and, as my uncle said, 'at that point Christ only knew what was in that salad'.

Anyway, in our community White was very highly thought of. So when I heard that his son had arrived in town and that he'd had to leave his village because a lot of people had wanted to take revenge on him after his father's death, I was dying to meet him. I told my uncle about this at once, but he replied that White hadn't had any sons, or indeed any family at all, because he had lived according to the old rules, which prevented the members of Black Seed from marrying and bringing up children. 'He was as lonely as a post in the middle of the steppe,' he assured me.

Some time later I met the Vulture, and without wasting many words I went straight to the point and unmasked him. We had a fight, and I came off best, but from that day on the Vulture hated me, and tried to get revenge in any way possible.

One winter evening, in 1991, I was returning home dead drunk from a party. I was with Mel, who was even drunker than I was. Around midnight, on the border between our district and Centre, the Vulture appeared with three of his friends: they overtook us on their bikes and stopped in front of us, blocking our way, and the Vulture pulled a 16-bore double-barrelled shotgun out of his jacket and fired two shots at me. He hit me in the chest; the cartridges were filled with chopped-up nails. Luckily for me, however, those cartridges had been carelessly filled: in one there was too much gunpowder and only a few nails, and the stopper had been pushed too far down; so it exploded inside, and the backfire scorched that poor fool's hand and part of his face. With the other the opposite mistake had been made: it had too many nails and too little powder, and evidently the stopper hadn't been closed properly, so the nails came out at a lower velocity and only tore my jacket a little; actually, one got through to my skin, but it didn't hurt me, and I only noticed it a couple of days later when I saw a slightly red blister. Mel threw himself at them barehanded and managed to knock one of them down and break his bike, so they made off.

After that episode, with the help of the whole gang I caught the Vulture and gave him three stab wounds on the thigh, as was the custom in our community as a sign of contempt. He didn't give up, but kept saying to everyone that he wanted revenge. But back then he was still a nobody, just one of the many teenage delinquents in Railway. Later though, the Vulture had succeeded in building a successful career, and now he was the leader of a bunch of thugs with whom he did things for which we in our community would have had our balls cut off at the very least.

That February day, as we entered the Railway district, I was only thinking of getting the job done quickly and not running into this fool of an enemy of mine. So as not to bother Mel with that story and not make him anxious – because it was a very serious matter to see him looking worried – I tried talking to him about the birthday party I would be having that evening, and the dishes my mother had prepared for us. He listened attentively, and from his expression it was clear that he was already there at the table, eating it all himself.

In Railway, as in our district, the boys acted as lookouts: they observed the movements of anyone who came in or left and then informed the adults. So we were immediately spotted by a little group of boys aged six or seven. We were crossing the first yard of the district and they were sitting there in a corner, a strategic point from where they had a good view of each of the two roads that ran from the park to the district. One of the boys, the smallest, received an order from another bigger boy, whereupon he got up and started running like a bullet towards us. In our district we didn't do that: if you had to approach someone, you went in a group; you never sent just one boy, let alone the smallest. And usually you didn't go towards anyone at all; you organized things so that the outsiders came to you, so from the outset you put yourself in a position of superiority.

The little boy looked like a little junkie. He was thin and had two blue rings round his eyes, a clear sign that he sniffed glue – a lot of kids in Railway used to get high like that. We took the piss out of them, calling them 'boyfriends of the bag', because they always carried a plastic bag around with them. They would put a bit of glue into it and then stick their head in the bag. A lot of them died like that, asphyxiated, because they didn't even have the strength to take the bag off their heads; an incredible number of them were found in various little hiding places around town, in the cellars or in the central heating boiler rooms, which they turned into shelters.

Anyway, this little boy stood in front of us, wiped his snivelling nose on the sleeve of his jacket and with a voice ravaged by the residue of glue said:

'Hey, stop! Where are you going?'

To let him know who we were, I gave him a crash course in good breeding:

'Where have you put your manners? Have you left them in your pocket, along with your dear little bag? Has nobody ever taught you that there are places where if you don't say hello to people you can end up as a *baklan*?[1] Go back to your friends and tell them to come all together and to introduce themselves properly, if they want to talk. Otherwise we'll go on acting like we haven't seen them!'

Before I had even finished, his heels could already be seen kicking up the snow.

---

1. Pejorative name for a person who does not respect the rules that govern behaviour among criminals.

Soon the whole delegation arrived with its leader at its head, a small boy aged about ten who to give himself the air of a criminal was turning over in his hands a *chotki*, a piece of equipment made of bread used by pickpockets for exercising their fingers, to make them more supple and sensitive.

He looked at us for a while and then said:

'My name's "Beard". Good morning. Where are you going?'

There was a lifeless note in his voice. He too must have been ruined by glue.

'I'm Nikolay "Kolima",' I replied. 'This is Andrey "Mel". We're from Low River. We've got a letter to take to one of your elders.'

Beard seemed to wake up.

'Do you know the man you have to deliver it to?' he asked in an unexpectedly polite tone. 'Do you know the way, or do you need someone to show you?'

Strange, I thought. This is the first time I've ever heard of anyone from Railway offering to show you the way; they're famous for their rudeness. Maybe, I said to myself, they've been told not to let anyone who enters the district go around on their own. But it would be crazy trying to follow everyone – they'd be going backwards and forwards day and night.

We didn't know the addressee or the way to his house.

'The letter's for a guy called Fyodor "the Finger"; if you tell us the way we'll find him on our own, thank you.' I was trying to get out of his offer to show us the way. I don't know why, but I felt there was something wrong with that offer.

'I'll explain it to you, then,' said Beard, and he started saying that we had to go that way, turn off there, then again there, and then again there. In short, I realized after a few seconds, since I knew the district well, that he was trying to make us take a needlessly long route. But I couldn't make out why, so I heard him out to the end, feigning ignorance. Then I said deliberately, as if agreeing with him:

'Yes, it does seem very complicated. We'll never find the way on our own.'

He lit up like a coin fresh from the mint.

'I told you, without the help of a guide . . .'

'Okay then, we accept,' I concluded, with a smile. 'Let's go. Lead the way!'

I asked him to take us himself so that I could assess the gravity of the situation. No leader of a group guarding a district will ever leave his station; he will always send one of his underlings. My proposal was a kind of test – if he refused to accompany us, fine, I could relax, but if he agreed, it meant he had orders to take us somewhere, and that we were in for serious trouble.

'Great, let's go!' he replied, almost singing. 'I'll just have a word with my *kontora,* then I'll be with you.'

While Beard was talking in a corner with his group, I told Mel about my worries.

'I'll beat them up,' he said bluntly.

I told him that didn't seem to me a very good idea.

If we beat them up, we'd have to leave the district at once, without delivering the letter. And how would that make us look in front of our Guardian?

'Stupid, Mel, that's how we'd look, bloody stupid. What would we tell him? "We didn't deliver the letter because we suspected something strange was going on, so we beat up some nine-year-old kids who were so high on glue they could hardly stand upright?"'

I proposed a different, more risky plan: that we get Beard to show us the way and then, in the first convenient place, 'split' him, a verb which in our slang means 'to beat the truth out of someone'.

We had to find out what we were up against, I explained to Mel, and make him give us this Finger's right address. If we found out there was a serious risk, we could go back and tell our Guardian all about it; but if the risk was low we would deliver the letter, and when we got home we'd tell everyone about it anyway – and so become the heroes of the district.

He liked the last part of my speech very much. The idea of returning to Low River with a glorious tale to tell definitely appealed to him. He clapped his hands in support of my brilliant strategy. I smiled and reassured him that everything would be fine, but deep down I had some doubts about the matter.

Meanwhile Beard's boys were huddled in a circle around him; one or two of them burst out laughing and glanced at us. As far as they were concerned we'd already fallen into their trap, and it had all been so easy . . .

I told Mel to act normal, and when Beard came back over to us Mel flashed him a smile so wide and false that my heart sank.

We set off. Beard walked between the two of us, and we chatted about this and that. We passed a dozen or so deserted front gardens: now the weather had turned cold people were staying indoors.

We walked along the side of a closed and dilapidated old school, where in summer the Railway kids used to get together and mess around. There, two years earlier, a teenage girl had been brutally murdered – a poor down-and-out kid with no family who had been driven to prostitution to survive. It had been her friends, other teenagers like her, who had forced her to work the streets for them, and who had then taken what little money she earned. They had killed her because she had wanted to get out of the scene and go to live in another district, where she'd found a job as a dressmaker's assistant.

It was a shocking story, because they had raped and tortured her for the best part of three days, keeping her tied to an old bed frame which had lost its springs: she had been left hanging there, and her wrists and ankles hadn't been able to take the strain and had broken. She was found with cuts all over her body and cigarette burns on her face; they'd forced a large hydraulic torque wrench into her anus and pushed into her vagina the spout of an electric kettle, with which they'd burned her little by little, to heighten her sufferings.

At first the people of Railway had tried to hide this horrific murder, but soon the whole town had found out and the criminal Authorities had intervened. They had ordered the Guardian of Railway to find the people responsible within a few days, beat them to death with clubs and hang their bodies up at the scene of the crime for a week, and then bury their corpses in a grave with no cross or any identifying mark.

And so it had been. We too had gone to look at
the bodies of those murdering bastards strung up by
their legs on the veranda of the empty school; they
were swollen up like balloons and black all over from
the beating. I averted my gaze, which then fell on the
walls: they were very thick; I realized that while the
girl was being tortured nobody had heard her screams.
It must be difficult and terrifying to die in that way,
knowing that only a few steps away from the hell in which
you find yourself people are relaxing in their homes,
doing the things they always do and not imagining even
a fraction of the pain you're suffering. The tears came to
my eyes at the thought of this detail: 'all the noise that
can be made in here stays in here'; and this was nothing
compared with what that poor soul must have gone
through.

When we reached the front of the school I nudged Mel
with my elbow to indicate that it was up to him to make
the first move.

'I can't wait any longer, boys,' he said at once, 'I must
have a pee. Let's go to some place for a moment where I
can "wait for the train" in peace.'

Beard looked first at Mel and then at me with a rather
worried look on his face; perhaps he wanted to make some
objection, but he didn't, for fear of raising our suspicions,
and merely said:

'Okay, come on, I'll show you a place. Here, inside
the school.'

As soon as we got inside, Mel gave him a shove in the back and Beard fell face down on the frozen floor. He turned towards us with a terrified expression on his face:

'What are you doing? Are you crazy?' he asked in a trembling voice.

'You're the crazy one, if you think you can screw us like a couple of whores . . .' I said, while Mel opened his flick-knife; he turned it over in his hand almost sadly and longingly, so that the blade threw a thousand reflections on the grimy walls covered with vulgar graffiti.

I walked slowly towards Beard, and he backed away on the floor at the same speed as me, until he came up against the wall. I kept talking to him, pretending I knew everything, to make him feel useless and afraid:

'We came here specially to make an end of this whole business . . . You'll see, it's not nice to try and cheat the people of Low River.'

'Don't hurt me! It's nothing to do with me!' Beard started squealing sooner than expected. 'I don't know anything about your business, I'm just carrying out the Vulture's orders . . .'

'What orders?' I asked him, pressing the tip of my boot against his side.

'If anyone from Low River arrives, we have to take them straight to him!' He was almost hysterical; he spoke in a hoarse little voice.

Mel moved in close and began to tease him with his knife, pushing the blade little by little through his clothes. With each move he made, the boy cried out louder, with his eyes closed, begging us not to kill him.

I waited a while, to let him simmer properly, and when I realized he'd reached the point where he couldn't refuse me anything, I made my proposal:

'Tell me where we can find Finger, we'll deliver the letter to him and you'll live. But don't try to trick us – we know our way round this lousy dump of yours, and if you send us to the wrong place we'll realize it. And if we don't find Finger we'll kill you, but not with a knife: we'll beat you to death, breaking every bone in your body first . . .'

In a few seconds he sketched in the air the correct route to Finger's house.

We decided to lock Beard in the school so he didn't try to double-cross us. In the basement we found a door that could be barred from outside by jamming a wooden plank against the iron handle. The room was cold and dark, a real shithole. Perfect for Beard, who was humbly waiting to know his fate.

'We're going to lock you in here, and nobody will find you till summer. If you've lied and we have any problems, if they give us any bother or hurt us, you'll stay here to rot – you'll die alone. If everything goes well, we'll tell someone where you are and they'll come to let you out. Okay? You'll be able to live and remember this personal lesson we've given you free of charge.'

Mel pushed him into the darkness, then shut and barred the door. Tearful screams came from inside:

'Don't leave me here, please! Don't leave me here!'

'Shut your mouth and be a man. And pray to the Lord we don't run into trouble, or you're dead!'

* * *

Finger's house was some distance away, a quarter of an hour's walk. We had to try not to attract attention, but the further we moved into the district the less chance we had of emerging unscathed from this expedition.

In the meantime I formed a thousand ideas of the kind of surprise that fool Vulture could have planned for us, and strangely I was growing more and more curious. I was dying to know what they meant to do to us in Railway. I wasn't scared, but excited, as if I were playing a game of chance. Mel was walking along quite calmly and showing no sign of inner conflict. He wore his usual blank expression; now and then he would look at me and snigger.

'What the hell are you laughing about? We're in the shit,' I said, trying to scare him a bit. Not out of malice, just to stir things up.

But it was no use, he was imperturbable, and his smile broadened. 'We'll slaughter them all, Kolima,' he gloated. 'We'll carry out a massacre, a bloodbath!'

To be honest, a massacre was precisely what I wanted to avoid.

'As long as it's not our blood . . .' I replied; but he didn't even hear me, he was walking along like a man who had decided to exterminate half the population of the world.

Then we came to the apartment block where Finger lived, and went up to the second floor, stopping outside his door. Mel raised his hand to ring the bell, but I stopped him. First I looked through the keyhole, which was pretty big. I could see a dirty hallway, with a light which hung down very low, as if someone had pulled it down deliberately. At the end of the hall, in front of a television, a thin man with short hair was cutting his toenails with a razor blade, as people do in prison.

I took my eye away from the keyhole and said to Mel:

'Check that the letter's okay, then ring the bell. When Finger opens the door, greet him and introduce yourself, then introduce me. Don't mention the letter straight away . . .'

Before I could finish, Mel interrupted me:

'Are you going to teach me how to go to the toilet? It's not the first letter I've delivered, I know how to behave!'

He pressed the bell. The sound was strange, it kept breaking off, as if the wires didn't make perfect contact. We heard the creaking of the wooden floor at every step Finger took. The door opened without any sound of a key: it hadn't been locked. In front of us appeared a man of about forty, completely covered with tattoos, and with iron teeth which shone in his mouth like jewels. He wore a vest and some light trousers; his feet were bare on the icy cold floor.

Inside the flat it was so cold we could see his breath condense into white vapour. He looked at us calmly; he seemed a normal kind of guy. He waited.

Mel stared at him speechless, and the man raised his hand and scratched his neck, as if to indicate that our silence was making him feel ill at ease.

I gave Mel a gentle kick and he started off straight away, spraying out words as a machine gun does bullets. He did everything according to the rules, and after the introductions he said he was carrying a letter.

Finger immediately changed his expression, smiled and invited us in. He led us to a table on which stood a saucepan full of freshly made chifir.

'Go ahead, boys, help yourselves. I'm sorry, but I haven't got anything else, only this. I've only just got out – the day before yesterday . . . What a terrible thing, this freedom! So much space! I'm still feeling dizzy . . .'

I liked his sense of humour; I realized I could relax.

We sat down, saying he shouldn't worry about us. While we were passing the cup of chifir round between the three of us, Finger opened the letter from our Guardian. After a few moments he said:

'I have to go back to your district with you; it says here that they want me to speak . . .'

Mel and I looked at each other. We would have to tell him about our adventure; it would be treacherous to take a person with you without telling him you were in trouble.

I decided to do the talking; letting Mel speak would only complicate things. I filled my lungs with air and blurted it all out: my war with the Vulture, the trap set by Beard and his gang of young junkies, the school . . .

Finger listened attentively, following every little detail as prisoners do. Stories are the criminals' only entertainment in jail: they take turns at telling each other the story of their life, one piece at a time, in episodes, and when they've finished they go on to somebody else's life.

At the end I told him that if he didn't want to run a risk by coming with us, he could put off his visit to the next day.

He opposed this:

'Don't worry, if anything happens I'll be with you.'

I wasn't happy, because I knew that in Railway the young didn't respect the old. Often they would lie in ambush for them outside their houses, when the old men came home drunk, and beat them up to get something they were carrying, and afterwards show it off to the others as a trophy. Moreover, Finger wasn't an Authority; from what could be read in his tattoos he was a guy who had for some reason joined up with the Siberians in jail: he had a Siberian signature on his neck, which meant that the community protected him, perhaps because he had done something important for us.

While I was thinking about all this, Finger had got dressed, in a jacket covered with sewn-up tears, battered shoes, and a green scarf that almost touched the ground.

Along the way we got talking. Finger told us he had been in prison since the age of sixteen. He had been sent there because of a stupid incident: he had been drunk, and without realizing it had clubbed a cop a little too hard, killing him stone dead. In juvenile prison he had joined up with the Siberian family, because, he said, they were the only ones who stuck together and didn't beat people up; they did everything together and didn't take orders from anyone else. He had arrived in the adult prison as a member of the Siberian family, and the others had welcomed him. He had served twenty years in prison, and when he was about to be released an old man had suggested he go and live in the apartment we had seen.

Now he wanted to move closer to the people of our district: they, he said, were his family. So he had asked the old Siberian Authorities in prison to contact the Guardian of Low River.

He felt part of our community, and this pleased me.

While we were walking, I had an idea. Since we needed reinforcements, I had decided to drop in at the house of a friend who lived nearby. He was a boy called 'Geka', which is a diminutive of Evgeny. He and I had known each other since childhood; he was the son of an excellent paediatrician called Aunt Lora.

Geka was a well-read, intelligent, polite boy; he didn't belong to any gang and preferred a quiet life. He had many interests and I liked him for this; I had been at his house several times and had been fascinated by his collection of model warplanes, which he assembled and painted himself. His mother allowed me to borrow some books from her library; that's how I got to know Dickens and Conan Doyle, and above all the only literary upholder of justice I had ever found congenial: Sherlock Holmes.

Geka would spend the whole summer with us on the river; we taught him to swim, to wrestle and to use a knife in a fight. But he wore glasses, so my grandfather felt desperately sorry for him: to Siberians wearing glasses is like voluntarily sitting in a wheelchair – it's a sign of weakness, a personal defeat. Even if you don't have good eyesight you must never wear glasses, in order to preserve your dignity and your healthy appearance. So whenever Geka came to our house, Grandfather Boris would take him into the red corner, kneel down with him in front of the icon of the Siberian Madonna and that of the Siberian

Saviour, and then, crossing himself over and over again, say his prayer, which Geka was obliged to repeat word for word:

'O Mother of God, Holy Virgin, patron of all Siberia and protectress of all us sinners! Witness the miracle of Our Lord! O Lord, Our Saviour and Companion in life and death, You who bless our weapons and our miserable efforts to bring Your law into the world of sin, You who make us strong before the fire of hell, do not abandon us in our moments of weakness! Not from a lack of faith, but in love and respect for Your creatures, I beseech You, perform a miracle! Help Your miserable slave Evgeny to find Your road and live in peace and health, so that he can sing Your glory! In the names of the Mothers, Fathers and Sons and of those members of our families who have been resurrected in Your arms, hear our prayer and bring Your light and Your warmth into our hearts! Amen!'

When he had finished the prayer, Grandfather Boris would get up off his knees and turn towards Geka. Then, making solemn, spectacular gestures, like those of an actor on the stage, he would touch Geka's glasses with his fingers and, saying the following sentence, slowly remove them:

'Just as many times You have put Your strength into my hands to grip my knife against the cops, and have directed my pistol to hit them with bullets blessed by You, give me Your power to defeat the sickness of Your humble slave Evgeny!'

As soon as he had taken off the glasses, he would ask Geka:

'Tell me, my angel, can you see well now?'

Out of respect for him, Geka couldn't bring himself to say no.

Grandfather Boris would turn towards the icons and thank the Lord with the traditional formulas:

'May Your will be done, Our Lord! As long as we are alive and protected by You, the blood of the cops, the contemptible devils and the servants of evil will flow in abundance! We are grateful to You for Your love.'

Then he would call the whole family and announce that a miracle had just occurred. Finally he would return Geka's glasses to him in front of everyone, saying:

'And now, my angel, now that you can see, break these useless glasses!'

Geka would put them in his pocket, mumbling:

'Don't be angry, Grandfather Boris: I'll break them later.'

My grandfather would stroke his head and tell him in a gentle, joyful voice:

'Break them whenever you like, my son; the important thing is that you never wear them again.'

The next time, so that he wouldn't be angry, Geka would turn up at our house without his glasses; he would take them off outside the door before coming in. Grandfather Boris, when he saw him, would be overcome with joy.

Well, to return to our story: Geka lived with his mother and an uncle who had had an incredible life; he was the embodiment of divine anger, of the living doom to which this likeable, kindly family was predestined. His name was Ivan, and he had been nicknamed 'the Terrible'. The allusion to the great tyrant was ironical, because Ivan was as good-natured as they come. He was about thirty-five years of age, short and thin, with black hair and eyes, and abnormally long fingers. He had been a professional musician before he had fallen into disgrace; at the age of eighteen he was playing the violin in an important orchestra, in St Petersburg, and his musical career seemed to be rocketing upwards like a Soviet intercontinental missile. But one day Ivan had ended up in bed with a friendly tart who played in the orchestra, a cellist, the wife of an important member of the communist party. He had become infatuated with her, made their relationship public and even asked her to leave her husband. Poor naive musician, he didn't know that party members couldn't get divorced, because they and their families had to be an example of a perfect 'cell' of Soviet society. And what kind of cell are you, if you get divorced whenever you feel like it? Russian cells must be as hard as steel, made of the same stuff as their tanks and their famous Kalashnikov assault rifles. Have you ever seen a faulty Soviet tank? Or a Kalashnikov that jammed? Families must be as perfect as firearms.

So our friend Ivan, as soon as he tried to follow the motions of his heart, was crushed by his lover's husband, who hired some agents of the Soviet secret services, who pumped him so full of serums they reduced him to a zombie.

Officially he had disappeared, nobody knew where; everyone was convinced that he'd escaped from the

USSR via Finland. A few months later he was found in a psychiatric hospital, where he had been interned after being picked up on the street in a serious state of mental confusion. He couldn't even remember his own name. The only thing he had with him was his violin; thanks to that the doctors traced him to the orchestra, and later were able to hand him back to his sister.

By this time Ivan's health was permanently impaired, and his face was that of a person tormented by one long, enormous doubt. He could communicate perfectly well, but he needed time to reflect on questions and think about his answers.

He still played the violin; it was his only link with the real world, a kind of anchor which had kept him attached to life. He would perform twice a week in a restaurant in Centre and then get drunk out of his mind. When he was drunk, he used to say, he managed to have moments of mental lucidity, which unfortunately soon passed.

The faithful companion of his life, who had always shared in all his drinking bouts, was another poor wretch called Fima, who had caught meningitis at the age of nine and since then been out of his wits. Fima was extremely violent, and saw enemies everywhere: when he entered a new place he would put his right hand inside his coat as if to take out an imaginary gun. He was bad-tempered and quarrelsome, but nobody reproached him for it, because he was ill. He went around dressed in a sailor's overcoat and shouted out naval phrases, such as 'There may be few of us, but we wear the hooped shirt!' or 'Full ahead! A hundred anchors in the arse! Sink that damned fascist tub!'

Fima divided the world into two categories: 'our boys' –
the people he trusted and regarded as his friends – and
the 'fascists' – all those he considered to be enemies and
therefore deserving to be beaten up and insulted. It wasn't
clear how he determined who was one of 'our boys' and
who a 'fascist'; he seemed to sense it, on the basis of some
hidden, deep-seated feeling.

Together Ivan and Fima got into a lot of trouble. If
Fima was wild, Ivan would attack with a natural violence:
he would pounce on people like a beast on its prey.

In short, because of these virtues I really hoped we
would find them at home.

When we arrived, Geka, Ivan and Fima were playing
battleships in the living room.

Geka was relaxed and was laughing, mocking his
competitors in the game:

'Glub-glub-glub,' he repeated derisively, imitating the
sound of a sinking ship.

Fima, with trembling hands, disconsolately clutched
his piece of paper: his fleet was evidently in a desperate
plight.

Ivan was sitting in a corner looking crestfallen, and
his piece of paper thrown on the floor indicated that he
had just lost the game. He was holding his violin and
playing something slow and sad which resembled a distant
scream.

I briefly explained our situation to Geka and asked
him if he could help us to get across the district.

He immediately agreed to help us, and Fima and Ivan followed him like two lambs ready to turn into lions.

We went out into the street; I looked at our gang and could hardly believe it – two Siberian boys and an adult fresh out of jail, accompanied by a doctor's son and two raving lunatics, trying to escape unharmed from a district where they were being hunted. And all of this on my birthday.

Geka and I walked in front and the others followed. While I was chatting to Geka, I heard Mel telling Finger one of his miraculous stories, the one about the big fish that had swum all the way up the river, against the current, to get to our district, because it had been attracted by the smell of Aunt Marta's apple jam. Every time Mel told that story, the funniest part was when he demonstrated how big the fish had been. He would open his arms like Jesus crucified, and with an effort in his voice would shriek 'A brute as big as *that*!' As I waited for that phrase with one ear and listened to Geka with the other, I felt really great. I felt like I was out for a stroll with my friends, without any dangers.

When Mel came to the end of his story, Fima commented: 'Holy fuck, the number of fish like that I've seen from my ship! The whales are a real pain in the arse! The sea's full of the buggers!'

I turned round to see what expression he had as he was saying those words, and saw something fly past close to my face, so close it almost touched my cheek. It was a piece of brick. At the same moment Geka shouted:

'Shit, an ambush!' and a dozen boys armed with sticks and knives emerged from each of two opposite front yards, and ran towards us, shouting:

'Let's kill them, kill them all!'

I put my hand in my pocket and took out my pike. I pressed the button and with a *clac* the blade, pushed by the spring, shot out. I felt Mel's back lean against mine and heard his voice say:

'Now I'm going to do someone!'

'Go for their thighs, you fool; their jackets are stuffed with newspapers, don't you see they're prepared? They've been waiting for us . . .' Before I could finish the sentence I saw a big guy armed with a wooden stick in front of me. I heard his stick whistle past my ears once, then a second time; he was quick, the bastard. I tried to get closer so I could stab him with my blade, but I was never fast enough; his blows were growing ever quicker and more accurate, and I was in danger of being hit. Suddenly another guy attacked me from behind; he pushed me hard and I bumped into the giant with the stick. Instinctively I gave him three quick stabs in the thigh, so quick that I felt shooting pain in my arm, a kind of electric shock, from the released tension. The snow beneath us was spattered with blood, the giant elbowed me in the face but I kept stabbing him till he fell on the ground, clutching his leg in the blood-red snow, grimacing in agony.

From behind, the boy who had pushed me tried to stab me in the side, but I was thin and my jacket was big, and he didn't manage to reach the flesh. The jacket ripped, however, and his hand went through the hole along with the knife. I turned and wounded him with my pike, first on the nose and then above the eye: his face was instantly covered with blood. He was trying to get his hand out of the hole in my jacket, but his knife had got stuck in the material, so he abandoned it there. He put his hands to his face and, screaming, fell on the snow, away from me.

I put two fingers into the hole in my jacket and carefully pulled out the blade: it was a hunting knife, wide and very sharp. 'Bloody hell,' I thought, 'if he'd got through I'd have been killed. When I get home I'm going to light a candle in front of the icon of the Madonna.'

Stepping over my enemy's body and holding his knife in my left hand, I went towards Geka, who was down on the ground, trying to avoid the blows from a stick wielded by a sturdy boy. He was leaning on his right arm and trying to fend off the blows with his left. I surprised his attacker from behind and plunged the blade of my pike into his thigh.

The blade of my knife was very long and slipped easily into the flesh; it was the ideal thing for putting people out of action, because it had no problem in penetrating muscle right through to the bone.

Simultaneously, using the hunting knife, I cut the ligaments behind the knee of his other leg. With a cry of pain the stocky boy fell to the ground.

Geka got to his feet and picked up the stick, and together we rushed towards Mel, who had caught one of them and, yelling like a madman, was stabbing him with his knife in the area of the stomach, while three guys tried to stop him by raining down blow after blow from their sticks on his head and back. If I had taken so many hits I'd have been killed for sure; it was only thanks to his physique that Mel managed to stay on his feet.

I rushed with my knife at a guy who was about to unleash a powerful blow at Mel's head. I came up from behind, and cut one of his ligaments.

Geka hit another boy on the head, who immediately passed out, blood oozing from his ear. The third ran off towards one of the yards from which they had all emerged a few moments before.

Meanwhile Fima and Ivan, armed with sticks, were standing close to the pavement, clubbing two guys who had fallen on the ground. One was in a very bad way. Fima had definitely broken his nose and his face was covered with blood – he was instinctively holding up his quivering hands to shield his face from the blows, but Fima was hitting him anyway, with such violence that the stick bounced off those hands as if they were made of wood, like a puppet's: it was clear that Fima had broken them. Angrily, furiously, Fima hit him, shouting:

'Who is this guy who wants to kill a Soviet sailor? Eh? Well? Who is this damned fascist?'

In the meantime Ivan was trying to club the face of the other attacker, who was doing well to avoid the blows by twisting to one side and the other. At one point he almost hit him, but at the last moment the stick missed his face and slammed into the frozen asphalt covered with red snow – red with the blood which as soon as it fell on the ground became as hard as ice. The stick broke in two; Ivan lost his temper and threw away the piece that was left in his hand. Then he jumped two-footed on the boy's head and started stamping on his face, letting out a strange war-whoop, like the Indians when they attack the cowboys in American westerns.

They were really crazy, those two.

In an instant the battle was over.

On the other side of the street was Finger, with a knife and a stick in his hands, and at his feet a boy with a cut which started from his mouth and ended in the middle of his forehead: it was too deep: a nasty wound. The boy lay there, conscious but not moving – terrified, I think, by the blood and the pain.

Mel was holding fast by the lapel the guy he had previously been stabbing in the stomach with his knife. He was gazing in astonishment at his blade, which had snapped in two. I went over to him and with a sharp tug ripped open the boy's jacket, which was full of holes. Out onto the snow fell a couple of dozen thick newspapers, glued together: the missing part of Mel's blade was sticking out from that pack of paper.

Surprised and incredulous, Mel looked at the scene as if it were a magic show.

I picked up the pack of paper from the ground and held it in my hand for a moment, feeling its weight. Then, putting all the strength I had into it, I slapped Mel across the face with that bundle of newspapers, making a loud noise, like when an axe splits a stump of wood.

His cheek immediately went red, he let go of the boy's neck and put his hand to his face. In a plaintive voice he asked me:

'What's the matter with you? Why the hell are you angry with me?'

I hit him again and he took two paces backwards, putting one hand in front of him, to stop me.

I replied:

'What did I tell you, you fool? Go for the thighs, not the chest! While you were messing around with that junkie and getting whacked by his three friends, I got the real blade. Shit, it was a damn close thing, I nearly got killed! And where were you? Why didn't you cover my back?'

He immediately put on a mournful expression – lowered eyes, bowed head, mouth slightly open – and in the voice of a beggar asking for alms he started mumbling incomprehensible words, as he always did when he was in the wrong:

'Uh-m-m-m . . . Kolima . . . o-o-only wa-a-anted . . . mm-hm-hm . . . so-o-orry . . .

'Fuck your excuses,' I interrupted him. 'I want to go home and celebrate my birthday, not my funeral. Now listen to me. This is no time for pissing about, we're risking our necks in this fucking business. And don't forget we're not alone; there are other people with us, they're giving us a hand; we can't expose them too much. And thank God they are here, because with more friends like you I'd already be dead.'

Mel shrank even smaller and, as he always did on such occasions, began to cover my back, though it was a bit late now.

The street was like the scene of a massacre: all the snow was red with blood; our assailants were dragging themselves over to the sides of the pavement, looking decidedly the worse for wear.

I went over to the one Mel had been trying to stab: he was frightened, even though he didn't have a scratch on him. I had to play tough. I grabbed him by the neck and tried to pull him up, but I couldn't lift him – he was heavier than me – so I bent down and stuck my knife into his thigh, till a little blood started to ooze out. He screamed and started crying, begging me not to kill him. I gave him a hard slap, to shut him up:

'Shut your mouth, you little pansy! Do you know who you've taken on, you dickhead? Don't you know us guys from Low River are baptized with knives? Did you really think you could kill us? I've been fighting since I was seven; I've ripped open so many guys like you, it would take me a lifetime to count them.'

I was exaggerating the number of victims, of course, but I had to scare him, sow fear, because a terrified enemy is already half defeated.

'I won't kill you this time, seeing as today's my birthday and it's the first time we've come up against each other; but if you cross my path again I'll have no mercy. When you see the Vulture, tell him Kolima sends his regards, and if I meet him before this evening I'll slit him open like a pig . . .'

That poor idiot, with the blood welling out of his thigh and his face distorted with terror, looked at me as if I were taking possession of his soul.

We set off again: Fima with a big stick, Ivan with a broken truncheon that he'd picked up off the ground, Geka with an iron bar, Finger with a knife and a stick, I with two knives in my pocket, and lastly my second shadow, Mel, with a sheepish look on his face, holding a stick and a knife with only half a blade.

As we went away, the 'survivors' started to come out of the yard. We were twenty metres away when one of them shouted after us:

'Siberian bastards! Go back to your fucking woods! We'll kill you all!'

Mel turned round and quick as a flash hurled his broken knife at him. It flew in a strange trajectory and landed smack in the face of a boy standing next to the one who had shouted. More blood, and they all scattered again, leaving another wounded comrade on the snow.

'Holy Christ, what a massacre . . .' said Geka.

We walked fast. When we came out into wide open spaces we almost ran. We tried to avoid yards and narrow passageways.

We passed the last row of houses before the food warehouses and hid among the illegally built garages and lockups. I suggested we should explore the area carefully before crossing the road in a group: I sensed that there were surprises in store for us.

'Listen,' I said. 'I'm going to take off my jacket so I can run faster. I'll cross the road further down, where it bends round and goes into the trees, then I'll go on to the warehouses and see what the situation's like. If there are a lot of them waiting for us, we'll go another way. If there are only a few of them we'll attack them from behind, and rub them in the shit . . . It'll take me a quarter of an hour, no more; in the meantime, have a look in the garages, maybe there's something handy we could use as a weapon, but be careful not to attract attention . . .'

Everyone agreed. Only Mel didn't want to let me go on his own: he was worried.

'Kolima, I'll come with you: anything might happen . . .'

I couldn't tell him he was a burden; I had to find a kinder way.

'I need you here. If they discover where you guys are, it'll be your job to defend the group. I can get away from any shit on my own, but do you think they can?'

At these words Mel became serious, and his face took on the same expression the Japanese kamikazes might have worn before boarding their aircraft.

I took off my jacket and was about to leave, but Mel stopped me, putting the iron bar in my hand, and in a trembling voice he said:

'You might need it . . .'

I looked at him in wonder: what a fool that human being was, and how he loved me!

The fewer things I carried in my hands the better it was. But to avoid pointless explanations I took the bar and ran off. I threw it away as soon as I disappeared behind the garages. I was moving fast; the air was cold and breathing was easy.

I got to the bend, crossed the road and headed toward the stores. From a distance I saw a dozen boys sitting around an iron bin, where they had lit a fire to warm themselves. I counted the sticks and bars leaning against the wall. I waited a moment, to make sure there wasn't anyone else there, then I turned back.

When I reached them, my friends had already opened five garages. Mel had turned out a cupboard full of gardening equipment and armed himself with a small hoe which had on one side an iron blade for hoeing and on the other a little fork, which I think was for picking things up: I don't know the first thing about gardening – in our district gardens were only used for hiding weapons.

Mel had also filled his pockets with some spare cutters for a circular saw; they were round and had large sharp teeth.

'What are you going to do with those things? Do you think you can slice people up?'

'No, I'll use them as missiles,' he replied proudly, and I saw his eye gleam as it always did when he was about to do something really stupid.

'Mel, this isn't a game. Be careful you don't hit any of us, or I'll be forced to shove all those missiles up your arse.'

He looked offended, and sloped out of the garage hanging his head.

Fima was walking around with an enormous axe, which worried me a lot, so I persuaded him to abandon it in favour of a nice length of stainless steel piping.

'Look how shiny it is,' I said to him. 'It looks like a sword, doesn't it?'

He seized the pipe without comment, his eyes suddenly full of the desire to fight.

Ivan had got himself a long hatchet, the kind that's used for lopping off branches. I took it out of his hands, replacing it with an iron bar. They were too violent, those two. They would have carried out a full-blown massacre; their armaments needed scaling down.

Finger had found a long, stout axe-handle, Geka a big skiving knife and a heavy wooden stick.

Perfect.

I searched one of the garages and found a crate of empty bottles. I'd had an idea: I wanted to do something horrible, but very useful in our situation. I looked in the other garages; in one I found some sand for preserving apples in winter. So I called Geka and we got a little tube and siphoned the petrol out of the cars' tanks. We filled all the bottles with a mixture of petrol and sand, and made the stoppers out of some old rags we found lying around.

The molotovs were ready.

We had a quick meeting, at which I outlined my elementary plan:

'We'll cross the road directly from here and get to the wall of the warehouse, then we'll creep towards them, getting as close as possible. They're expecting us to appear from the other direction; we'll take them by surprise, attacking them with the molotovs, and then close in and beat them up. That's our only chance of getting out of the district on our own legs.'

They all agreed.

We ran across the road all together, very fast. When we reached the wall we slowed down. Geka and I were carrying the crate full of molotovs.

Suddenly we started to hear their voices: they were just around the corner. We stopped. I stuck my head out a little and took a peek at them: their position was a perfect target. They were all close to the wall, sitting round the fire in the bin.

One of them I knew, he was a thug about four years older than me, a born imbecile, called Crumb. He'd killed three cats that belonged to an old woman, a neighbour of his, and then gone on boasting to everyone about this heroic deed for a long time. He was a real sadist.

One day we'd all got together for a swim on a beach by the river, and one of the boys of our district, Stas, nicknamed 'Beast' – a really nasty type, a guy who was angry with the whole world – heard him boasting about his exploit with the cats. Beast didn't waste any words: he went over to him, grabbed hold of his hands and crushed them so hard you could heard the sound of the breaking bones. Crumb went white in the face and passed out; his hands became swollen and purple, like two balloons. His family carried him away. Later I heard they'd fixed his hands in hospital, and that he'd resumed his life as a hooligan, telling everyone that he was going to take his revenge one day. But he never had time to, because Beast died soon afterwards, killed in a shoot-out with the cops. So Crumb swore vengeance on our whole district, and made a pact with the Vulture, vowing to destroy us. There was a rumour that they had held a black mass in the town cemetery, during which all of us Low River boys had been cursed.

I took two molotovs and gave another two to Geka and Finger. I didn't give any to Mel, because when he was small he'd thrown one too high and it had come apart and spilt part of its contents over us. Since then he had always been given the job of holding the match or cigarette lighter at the ready.

I shook the bottles well, raising the sand from the bottom, set fire to the two rags, jumped out from behind the wall and threw two molotovs simultaneously at the group. A moment later I already had two more in my hands, lit them and threw them, in rapid succession.

The enemy were in a panic – boys with burnt faces threw themselves in the snow; there was fire everywhere; someone ran off so fast he vanished from our sight in a flash.

The three of us emptied the crate in less than a minute. Before Mel had even had time to put out his match, we had finished.

I pulled out my knives and rushed towards a guy who had just got up off the ground and was about to pick up a stick. He had no burns: the fire had only reached his jacket and he'd had time to roll in the snow. He was very angry, and kept whooping like a warrior. He tried to hit me a couple of times, always keeping me at a distance. Suddenly I dived towards his feet, avoiding a swipe from the stick, and plunged my knife into his leg. He kicked me in the face with the other leg and split my lip; I tasted blood in my mouth. But in the meantime I had managed to give him several stabs in the thigh and to cut the ligament behind his knee.

Behind me Mel had already felled three, one with half his face burnt, another with three holes in his head from which serious blood was oozing: the black stuff, the kind that comes out when they get you in the liver, only thicker. The third one had a broken arm. Mel was furious, and was walking around with a knife stuck in his leg.

Finger was standing by the wall. At his feet were three others, all wounded in the head; one had a broken bone sticking out of his leg, below the knee.

Geka, too, was leaning against the wall; he had taken a blow to the forehead, nothing serious, but he was clearly scared.

Meanwhile, those two maniacs Fima and Ivan were both laying into a giant, a colossus stretched out on the ground who, for some reason, wouldn't let go of the wooden club he held in his fist. His face looked like a lump of minced meat, and he must have passed out some time ago, but he still didn't release the club. I bent down over him and noticed that the club was fixed to his wrist by an elastic bandage. To leave him a souvenir from Siberia I cut the ligaments under his knee. He didn't even utter a moan, he was completely unconscious.

I pulled the knife out of Mel's leg, then retrieved the elastic bandage and divided it into two: one part I put over the wound as a plug and with the other I made a tight bandage. Mel had taken off his trousers to simplify the operation and now said that he didn't want to put them back on. He said he wanted to get a bit of air, the nutcase.

Finger was looking at Fima and Ivan with a smile that didn't fade. They waved their iron bars proudly, like heroes.

I helped Geka to his feet. He was fine, except that after the blow he felt a bit groggy and at the same time agitated. I took a sweet out of my pocket.

'Take this, brother; chew it slowly. It'll calm you down.'

This was bullshit, of course, but if you believe it a sweet works like a tranquillizer. 'The psychological factor', my uncle called it; he had induced one of his cellmates to give up smoking by telling him the cock-and-bull story that if he massaged his ears for half an hour a day he would lose the habit in a month.

Geka took the sweet and felt better. He had a long purple bruise which ran across his forehead and down to his left ear. I told him we had to get away fast, leave Railway as soon as possible.

Geka was scared to go home in case they knew where he lived.

'Don't worry, little brother,' I reassured him. 'When we get to our district I'll tell the Guardian the whole story. Uncle Plank will sort things out.'

I tried to explain to him that with us he was safe, protected.

'How can you be sure we're in the right and not in the wrong?' he asked me.

At the time his question seemed stupid to me. Only later, with time, did I come to see how profound it was. Because the real question was not whether we boys were right or wrong in that situation, or in other similar situations, but whether our values were right or wrong with respect to the world around us.

He was a philosopher, my friend Geka, but I wasn't clever enough with words, so I answered him with the first ones that came into my head:

'Because we're genuine, we don't hide anything.'

When he heard my reply he smiled in a strange way, as if he wanted to say something but preferred to keep it for another time.

Meanwhile Mel had searched our enemies' pockets and come up with three knives, six packets of cigarettes, four cigarette lighters – one of which was made of gold, and which he immediately slipped into his pocket – more than fifty roubles and a plastic bag full of gold rings and chains, which those thugs had no doubt just stolen from someone.

We found more booty inside a cloth bag near the bin. A thermos full of badly made but still quite hot tea, about ten cheese sandwiches and the biggest surprise – a short double-barrelled shotgun, with no butt, and a lot of cartridges scattered here and there, even inside the sandwiches. I checked the cartridges: the original ones I kept, the home-made ones I threw away, because I didn't trust cartridges made by strangers, especially guys from Railway.

Mel was surprised and kept asking over and over, like a cracked record:

'Why didn't they fire at us? Why didn't they fire at us? Why didn't they fire at us?'

'Because they haven't got the balls . . .' I replied, but only to stop him asking that question, because in fact I couldn't understand it myself. Maybe the guy who had brought that shotgun with him had been taken by surprise and hadn't had time to get it out . . . Maybe, maybe not. The only certain thing was that if he had used it our whole story would have taken a different course and I might not be here now to tell it.

Mel wanted to take the shotgun, but by right of seniority it was due to Finger: I gave it to him, and he hid it well under his jacket. Luckily Mel wasn't offended, on the contrary he agreed with the decision; he just started teaching Finger how to shoot with the thing.

We set off at a brisk pace towards the park. As I walked along, chewing a frozen sandwich, I thought to myself what a bad omen it was that I'd got into all this trouble on my birthday.

'Okay, I'm in for a hard life,' I said to myself. 'I only hope it's not too short.'

By the time we entered the park it was already dusk. In the winter the darkness falls quickly; the daylight retreats without much of a battle, and before half an hour has passed you can't see a thing. There were no lamp-posts in the park; all we could see was the weak lights of the town twinkling between the trees.

We walked along the main path. As we drew level with the sanatorium I expounded to Geka my theory that the crisis wasn't over yet. I felt in my heart that there was another ambush waiting for us, and since the park was the best place for laying one, isolated and dark as it was, I feared for all of us.

Geka was of the same opinion:

'It can't be a coincidence, can it, that Vulture hasn't shown himself yet?'

He suggested we all walk close together, so we'd be

ready to cover each other's backs if they jumped out on us suddenly.

We bunched together in an instant, and all walked in step, like soldiers, expecting the enemy attack at any moment.

We went right across the park, but nothing happened. When we saw the lights of Centre we were so pleased we were almost jumping for joy. Mel even started hurling bizarre insults in the direction of Railway.

We entered Centre; walking along the lighted streets we were already quite relaxed and even able to crack jokes. Everything seemed so natural and simple . . . I felt such a lightness in my body that I said to myself: 'If I wanted to, I could fly.'

Mel started making snowballs and throwing them at us; we all laughed as we walked homeward.

We took a short cut near the library, along a quiet little street that went past the old houses of the original town centre. I was dying to get back to celebrate my birthday with the others who were waiting for us.

'They'll be pissed out of their minds,' joked Mel. 'They'll already have eaten everything, and when we get there we'll have to do the washing up.'

'If we do, boys, the next time I have a birthday I'm going to spend it on my own; you can all go . . .' I didn't finish the sentence: something or someone struck me a violent blow on the right side. I fell down on the frozen ground, banging my head. I was in pain, but I reacted at once, and when I leaped to my feet, I already had the knives in my hands.

The street was narrow and dark, but somewhere, a little way off, there was a lighted window, and thanks to that light it was possible to see something. There were shadows coming towards us.

'Shit, what was that? Are you all right?' Mel asked me.

'I think so; somebody pushed me. It's them, I'm sure of it . . .'

'Holy Christ, I've already thrown away my stick,' he looked at me despairingly.

'Take one of my knives. What happened to those blades for the circular saw?'

Mel put his hand in his pocket and gave them to me.

'Throw them at their faces, boy.'

I didn't need telling twice. I hurled a blade at the nearest shadow, and a few seconds later there was a terrible scream.

I saw Fima jump forward with the iron bar, shouting:

'You damned fascists, I'm going to tear you to pieces!'

He threw himself at a boy who by now was so close to us you could see his face; the boy tried to dodge the blow but the bar hit him full on the back of the head and he fell down without a moan.

Out of the darkness three of them charged at Fima; Ivan tried to hit them with his iron bar as best he could.

Geka was on the ground; he had a broken hand, he was getting beaten by a giant – another one – armed with a stick. In a second Finger threw himself at the giant with his shotgun lowered: he shot him at point-blank range, right in the chest. The giant collapsed in an unnatural way, as if pushed by an invisible force.

I set about helping Fima: I kept throwing blades, hitting two attackers full in the face. Another one I stabbed in the side; I felt the knife go deep into the flesh through a layer of cloth, then I realized they'd been so sure of taking us by surprise that they hadn't even stuffed their jackets with newspapers. I stabbed him twice more in the same place, in the region of the liver. I hoped to kill him. Immediately afterwards I felt a sensation of weakness in the hand that was holding the knife. It was as if I was losing control of the arm, a kind of paralysis.

'That was all I needed . . .' I thought.

I tried to pull myself together, to grip the knife more tightly, but my right hand wasn't obeying me, wasn't responding any more. So I grasped the knife with my left hand and at the same moment, from behind, Mel seized me by the neck and dragged me away. Meanwhile I heard a lot of footfalls in the dark: the sound of people running away.

I was winded, struggling to breathe. The place where I'd been struck on my left side hurt, but I didn't think it was anything serious. I thought that at worst they'd broken a couple of my ribs, and indeed the pain increased when I breathed in.

The giant was on the ground, motionless, and groaning. There wasn't a drop of blood. The bullets Finger had used to shoot him must have been those rubber ones with an iron ball inside them: specially made not to kill, but when fired from close range they can do serious damage.

* * *

We started walking again – or rather, without realizing it, we started running. We all ran; in front was Finger with Geka, who held his broken hand against his chest, supporting it with the other. Then Fima, shouting curses as he ran, and behind him Ivan, who was silent and focused. Although I was in pain I ran like mad too, I didn't know why: maybe that sudden attack, just when we had been feeling as if we were out of harm's way, had put a new fever into us.

Mel ran slowly behind me, he could have run faster, but he was worried because I couldn't run as well as I usually did: the side where I'd been hit was hurting like hell.

At last we reached the border of our district. We slowed down to a halt in the middle of the road that led to the river. Three friends arrived, who were on guard at the time. We gave them a brief account of what had happened, and one of them went straight off to tell the Guardian.

We arrived at my home. My mother was in the kitchen with Aunt Irina, Mel's mother, and when they saw us come in they froze on their chairs.

'What happened to you?' my mother stammered.

'Nothing; we had bit of trouble, nothing much . . .' I hurried into the bathroom to hide my torn jacket, and to wash my blood-stained hands. 'Mama, call Uncle Vitaly,' I said, going back into the kitchen. 'We've got to get Geka to hospital, he's broken his arm . . .'

'Are you all crazy? What? He's broken his arm? Have you been fighting with someone?' My mother was trembling.

'No, ma'am, I fell down, it was an accident . . . I should have been more careful.' Poor Geka, in a voice that seemed to come from the other world, tried to save the situation.

'If you fell down, why has Mel got a bruise on his face?' My mother had her own special way of saying that we were a bunch of liars.

'Aunt Lilya,' said that genius Mel to my mother, 'the fact is, we all fell down together.'

At that Aunt Irina slapped him hard across the face.

I went back into the bathroom and locked myself in. I turned on the light, and when I looked in the mirror my heart sank: the whole of my right leg was soaked in blood. I got undressed and turned towards the mirror. Yes, there it was: a very thin cut, only three centimetres wide, from which a piece of broken blade was sticking out.

I picked up the tweezers my mother used for her eyebrows, and at that moment she knocked.

'Let me in, Nikolay.'

'Just a second and I'll be out, mama. I just want to wash my face!'

I gripped the broken piece of blade and gently pulled. As I watched the blade emerge and grow ever longer, I felt my head throb. I stopped halfway, turned on the tap and damped my brow. Then I pinched the blade again and pulled it right out. It was about ten centimetres long; I couldn't believe my eyes. It was part of the blade of a saw for cutting metal, filed by hand till it was razor sharp on both edges, and with a thin, fragile tip. They'd chosen that weapon specially, so they could jab it in and then snap it off, so that it would stay in the wound and be more painful.

The wound was bleeding. I opened the wall cupboard and treated myself as best I could: I put a bit of cicatrizing ointment on the cut, and all around it a tight bandage, to stop the blood. I threw all my clothes and my shoes out of the bathroom window and put on some dirty clothes from the basket next to the washing machine. I washed and dried the knife and went back into the other room.

Mel and Aunt Irina had already left. Uncle Vitaly had arrived; he had his car keys in his hand, ready to take Geka to hospital.

Fima and Ivan were sitting at the kitchen table, and my mother was serving them soup with sour cream and meat stew with potatoes.

'Well, bungler, what have you all been up to this time?' asked Uncle Vitaly, who was in a cheerful mood, as always.

I was drained of strength; I didn't feel much like joking.

'I'll tell you later, Uncle, it's a nasty story.'

'Did you have to go and get into trouble on your birthday, of all days? All your friends are already drunk, they're waiting for you . . .'

'No party for me, Uncle. I can hardly stand up, I just want to sleep.'

I spent two days in bed, only getting up to eat and go to the bathroom. On the second day Mel came to see me with the Guardian, Uncle Plank, who wanted to hear what had happened.

I told him the whole story, and he promised me he would sort it out in a matter of hours and prevent any reprisals being taken against Geka, Fima and Ivan in Railway. Finger, meanwhile, would be staying on in our district.

About a week later Plank called me round to his home to speak to a man from Railway. He was an adult criminal, an Authority of the Black Seed caste; his nickname was 'Rope', and he was one of the few criminals in Railway who was respected by our people.

I found them sitting round the table; Rope got up and came to meet me, looking me in the eye:

'So you're the famous "writer"?'

A writer, in criminal slang, is someone who's skilled at using a knife. Writing is a knife wound.

I didn't know what to say in reply or whether I was allowed to reply, so I looked at Plank. He nodded.

'I write when I feel the urge to, when the Muse inspires me,' I replied.

Rope smiled broadly:

'You're a smart young rascal.'

He had called me young rascal – that was a good sign. Maybe the matter was going to be resolved in my favour.

Rope sat down and invited me to join them.

'I'll ask you only once what you think about this business, then we won't discuss it again.' Rope talked with a great calm and confidence in his voice; you could tell he was an Authority, a man who was able to handle things. 'If, as far as you're concerned, the matter ends here and you don't want to take revenge on anyone, I give you my word that all those who have bothered you and your friends will be severely punished by us, the people of Railway. If you want to take revenge on someone in particular, you can do so, but in that case you'll have to do it all on your own.'

I didn't think about it for a moment; the reply came to my lips at once:

'I've got nothing personal against anyone in Railway. What's done is done, and it's right that it should be forgotten. I hope I didn't kill any of your people, but in a fight, you know how it is – everyone's intent on his own survival.'

I wanted him to understand that revenge wasn't important for me, that well-being and peace in the community came first.

Rope looked at me earnestly, but with a kindly, amiable expression:

'Good, then I promise you the person who organized this shameful action against you, while you were guests in our district, will be punished and expelled. Your friends can live their worthy lives and walk with their heads held high in Railway . . .' He paused, glancing at a door on the other side of the room. 'I want to introduce you to my nephews; you've already met them, unfortunately, but now I want you to accept their apology . . .' At these words, two boys with gloomy faces and bowed heads came in. One I recognized immediately – it was Beard, the little bastard whom we had beaten up and locked in the school –

while the other's face seemed familiar, but I couldn't place it. Then I noticed he was limping, and that under his trousers, on his left leg, there was the swelling of a bandage: it was the guy I'd stabbed when I was giving him my message for Vulture, after the first fight.

The two boys approached and stopped in front of me, with all the enthusiasm of two condemned prisoners in front of a firing squad. They greeted me in unison. It was very sad and humiliating; I felt sorry for them.

Rope said to them sternly:

'Well, then? Begin!'

Immediately, Beard, the little junkie, jabbered out what was clearly a prepared speech:

'I ask you as a brother to forgive me, because I've made a mistake. If you want to punish me I'll let you, but first forgive me!'

It wasn't as moving as it might sound; it was clear that he was just going through the motions.

I too had to act my part:

'Accept the humble greetings of a fond and compassionate brother. May the Lord forgive us all.'

It was pure Grandfather Kuzya, that speech. If he'd heard me he would have been proud of me. Poetic tone, Orthodox content, and spoken like a true Siberian.

After my words Plank sat with a contented smile on his face, and Rope looked astonished.

Now it was the other wretch's turn:

'Please, forgive me like a brother, for I have committed an injustice and . . .'

His voice was less resolute than Beard's; it was clear that he couldn't remember all his lines, and had shortened them. He threw a helpless glance at Rope, but Rope remained impassive, though his hands involuntarily clenched into fists.

Then I decided to kill them all with my kindness, and after taking a deep breath I reeled off the following sentence:

'As our glorious Lord Jesus Christ embraces all us sinners in His gentle love, and affectionately impels us towards the way of eternal salvation, so with equal humility and joy I enfold you in brotherly grace.'

Saintly words: my feet were almost lifting off the ground and it seemed as if a hole were going to open up in the ceiling for me.

Plank didn't stop smiling. Rope said:

'Forgive us for everything, Kolima. Go home and don't worry; I'll sort everything out myself.'

A month later I heard that Vulture had been given a savage beating: they had 'marked' his face, giving him a cut that started from his mouth, ran right across his cheek and ended at his ear. Then they had forced him to leave Railway.

One day someone told me he'd moved to Odessa, where he'd joined a gang of boys who stole wallets on trams. People who had no respect for any law, neither that of men nor that of the criminals.

Some time later I heard he'd died, killed by his own cronies, who had thrown him out of a moving tram.

* * *

Geka soon recovered; no sign of the fracture remained on him – later he went to university to study medicine.

Fima, to his misfortune, was taken by his family to Israel. I heard that when they tried to get him to board the plane he started to protest, shouting that it was shameful for a sailor to travel by air. He punched a co-pilot and two customs officials. In the end they had to knock him out with a sedative.

Ivan continued to play the violin in the restaurant, and after a while found a way of consoling himself for the absence of his friend: he met a girl and went to live with her. In fact it was rumoured among the girls of the town that Ivan had been endowed by nature with another talent besides his musical one.

Finger lived in our district for a while, then robbed banks with a Siberian gang, and finally settled in Belgium, marrying a woman of that country.

After the trouble in Railway, for a couple of years I would occasionally bump into boys I didn't know around town, who would greet me and say:

'I was there that day.'

Some of them showed me the cuts behind their knees and the scars on their thighs, almost with a sense of vanity and pride, saying:

'Recognize that? It's your work!'

I remained on friendly terms with many of them. Luckily no one had been killed that day, though I had wounded one boy quite seriously, by stabbing him near the liver.

Grandfather Kuzya, after hearing from Plank how I'd behaved towards Rope's nephews, congratulated me in his own way. A lopsided smile and a single sentence:

'Well done, Kolima: a kind tongue cuts and strikes better than any knife.'

I didn't get any birthday presents that year – my father was angry with me and kept repeating: 'You can't keep out of trouble, even on your birthday.' My mother was offended because I'd kept from her what had happened to me that day, and in the midst of all this mess nobody gave me anything, except Uncle Vitaly, who brought me a genuine leather football, a beautiful one, but my dog tore it to shreds that very same night.

No presents, and above all a nasty wound which encouraged me to reflect on, and to understand better and put into perspective, the life I was leading.

After much pondering and debating with myself I came to the conclusion that knives and fisticuffs didn't get you anywhere. So I moved on to guns.

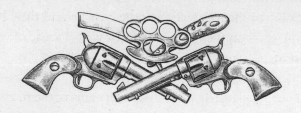

JUVENILE PRISON

One evening I was returning home with Mel; the weather was hot: it was late August. We were coming from the Centre district, and we had almost reached Low River when from a little garden about twenty metres away from us three boys aged about sixteen came out, rolling drunk, with empty bottles in their hands.

From the many curses that they uttered we immediately realized that there was going to be a fight.

Mel said in a sad and very calm voice:

'Holy Christ, these bastards were all we needed . . . Kolima, if they make a single move towards us I'm going to kill them, I swear to you . . .' He put his hand in his pocket and slowly pulled out his knife. He propped it against his hip, pressed the button to open the blade and

hid the knife behind his back. I did the same, but hid the
hand holding the knife in front of me, under my T-shirt,
pretending to tighten my belt.

'I hope for their own sakes they're intelligent. Who
needs trouble at this time of night . . .' I said as we walked
on.

Suddenly, when we had gone past them, one of the
three threw an empty bottle at Mel's back. I heard an
unnatural noise, like that of a snowball against a wall.
Then immediately afterwards another more natural noise:
that of a bottle smashing as it hits the ground.

In a second, before I could even react, Mel was already
punching one of them, and the other two were surrounding
him, trying to hit him with their bottles. I jumped on
the first one I could reach and stabbed him in the side.
Another smashed a bottle on the ground and cut my face
with the piece that was left in his hand. I flew into a rage
and gave him a series of stabs in the leg. At that moment,
behind my back I heard the sound of the cocking lever
of a Kalashnikov, and immediately afterwards a burst of
gunfire. I dropped to the ground, instinctively. A voice
shouted:

'Throw your weapons well away from you! Hands
up, legs apart, face down! You're under arrest!'

I felt as if I'd fallen into a bottomless pit.

'No, it can't be. Anything in the world, but not this.'

Pending further inquiries, which in the event took exactly
two weeks, they locked me up in a cell in Tiraspol police

station. The three guys who had attacked us withdrew their accusations, after my father sent the right people round to their houses.

Mel was released after a week, because he hadn't used his knife.

I had used mine, though – it was found on the spot – and although the victims weren't pressing charges, all the legal system needed was the reports of the policemen who'd arrested us, and my fingerprints on the weapon.

The trial was as quick as lightning: the prosecutor asked for three years' confinement in a high security juvenile prison. The defending counsel – who was a lawyer paid by the state, but nonetheless did his job well, partly because, as I later learned, he had received a certain amount of money from my family – insisted on the peculiarities of the case: the lack of any complaint from the victims, my good behaviour during my first sentence, which I had served at home, and above all the impossibility of proving that the weapon belonged to me. I might have found it on the spot, or even taken it from one of the victims, who indeed in their second statement had declared themselves to be the 'aggressors'. In the end the judge, a plump old woman, announced in a funereal voice:

'One year's detention in the strict-regime colony for juveniles, with the possibility of a request for early release after five months' detention in the event of good behaviour.'

I wasn't in the least frightened or surprised. I remember feeling as if I were going on a camping trip somewhere, to rest up for a while and then return home. Indeed I felt like

I was about to do something I had been waiting for all my life, something great and important.

And so I was taken to prison, to a place called Kamenka – 'The Place of Stone', a big jail with various blocks and sections. It was an old construction dating from the time of the tsar, built on three floors. Each floor had fifty rooms, all the same size, each seventy metres square. In each room there were two windows, or rather apertures, which had neither frames nor glass, but only a sheet of iron soldered on from the outside, with little holes in it to let the air through.

They escorted me to a room on the third floor. The iron doors opened in front of me and the warder said:

'Move! Go in without fear, come out without crying . . .'

I took one step and the doors slammed shut behind me. I looked in there and couldn't believe my eyes.

The room was crammed with wooden bunks on three levels, set alongside each other, with very little space in between – just enough to get through. The boys were sitting on the bunks, walking around naked and sweaty, in an air full of the stink of latrines and cigarette smoke and some other disgusting odour, the smell of a dirty, damp cloth which after a while begins to rot.

Only half of the room was visible: a metre and a half from the floor the air became increasingly dense, and from there right up to the ceiling there was a thick cloud of steam.

I stood there trying to work out what I should do. I knew the prison rules very well: I knew I mustn't move a single step inside that room until the Authorities of the cell said I could, but I looked around and couldn't see anyone who was interested in my arrival. What's more, my clothes seemed to me increasingly heavy, because of the humidity in the room. Then I felt something fall on my head; I brushed at it with my hand, but immediately other objects fell on my shoulders. So I moved quickly, to shake them off.

'Don't worry, it's only cockroaches . . . There are lots of them by the door, but they don't go into the room, because we put poison under the bunks . . .'

I looked towards the voice that was speaking to me and saw a very thin boy in dirty, wet underpants, with a shaven head, a gap in his front teeth, and glasses. I couldn't bring myself to say anything to him; I felt as if I was completely cut off from the rest of the world.

'I'm Dwarf – I'm the *shnyr* here. Who are you looking for? Tell me and I'll find him.' He came a bit closer and started looking at the tattoo on my right arm. *Shnyr* in criminal slang means 'the one who darts about': this figure exists in all Russian prisons, he's someone who is not regarded as an honest criminal, but is the slave of the whole cell and takes messages from one criminal to another.

'Are there any Siberians here?' I asked him coldly, to make it clear to him from the outset that he must keep his distance from me.

'Yes, there certainly are: Filat "White" from Magadan, Kerya "Yakut" from Urengoy . . .

'All right,' I interrupted him brusquely. 'Go to them quickly and tell them a brother has arrived. Nikolay "Kolima" from Bender . . .'

He immediately vanished behind the maze of beds. I heard him saying, as he went from one bunk to the other:

'A new arrival, he's Siberian . . . Another Siberian's arrived, another one . . . A Siberian from Bender has just arrived . . .'

In no time at all the whole cell had been informed.

A few minutes later Dwarf popped out from behind the beds. He leaned against the wall, looking back at the area from which he had just emerged. Eight boys came out from there and stood in front of me. The one in the middle did the talking; he had two tattoos on his hands. I read them and quickly learned that he came from a gang of robbers and belonged to an old family of Siberian Urkas.

'Well, are you Siberian?' he asked me in a relaxed tone.

'Nikolay "Kolima", from Bender,' I replied.

'Really? You're actually from Transnistria . . .' His tone had changed, becoming a little more animated.

'From Bender, Low River.'

'I'm Filat White, from Magadan. Come this way, I'll introduce you to the rest of the family . . .'

Contrary to my expectations, the juvenile prison where I had been sent bore no resemblance to the serious prisons I had always heard about and which I had been prepared for since childhood. Here there was no criminal law;

everything was chaotic and completely unlike any existing model of prison community.

The harsh living conditions and the lack of freedom, at such a delicate stage in the growth of any human being, complicated everything. The boys were very angry, like animals: they were evil, sadistic and deceitful, with a strong desire to sow destruction and raze to the ground anything that reminded them of the free world. Nothing was safe in that place; violence and madness burned like flames in the minds and souls of the inmates.

Each cell held a hundred and fifty boys. The conditions were awful. There weren't enough beds for everyone, so you had to take turns at sleeping. There was only one bathroom, at the end of the cell, and it stank so much that even if you just went near it you felt like vomiting. The ventilation was non-existent; the only source of air was the holes in the sheets of iron covering the two windows.

It was hard to breathe in there, so a lot of weak boys, who had cardiac or respiratory diseases, couldn't take it for long: they fell ill; often they fainted and sometimes never came to. A few weeks after my arrival, a boy who had a serious lung condition started spitting blood. Poor kid, he asked for something to drink, but the others dumped him in a corner and wouldn't go near him for fear of catching tuberculosis. After he had spent a night on the ground, lying in the pool of blood that had formed from his continual spitting, we asked the administration to move him to the hospital.

The light was always on, night and day. Three feeble lamps lit the space inside a kind of sarcophagus made of iron and thick glass, screwed to the wall.

The tap was always running; the water came out as white as milk, and hot – almost boiling – in winter and in summer.

The beds were three-level bunks, and very narrow. All that was left of the mattresses was the covering; the filling had been worn down, so you slept on the hard surface, on the wood. Since it was always infernally hot, nobody used the blankets: we put them under our heads, because the pillows were as thin as the mattresses, with nothing inside them. I preferred to sleep without a pillow and instead put the blanket under the mattress, so as not to break my bones on the wood.

There was no timetable to follow; we were left to ourselves for twenty-four hours a day. Three times a day they brought us some food – in the morning a mug of tea which looked like dirty water, with a faint trace of something which might have been tea in a previous existence. On top of the mug they put a piece of bread with a knob of white butter which had been thinned in the kitchen by the cooks, who stole the provisions, as though they were the criminals, not us.

Since the third floor, where I was, was that of the 'special purpose' block reserved for the most dangerous juveniles, we didn't deserve the honour of having spoons or other metal objects at breakfast. We spread the butter on our bread with our fingers. We dipped the buttered bread in the mug of tea and ate it like a dunked biscuit. Afterwards we drank the tea with the grease floating in it; it was very tasty and nourishing.

Three boys would stand by the little window in the door: they would take the food from the guards' hands and pass it to the others. Taking anything from the cops was considered 'dishonest'; those who did it were sacrificing themselves for everyone, and in exchange for the favour nobody touched them – they were allowed to live in peace.

For lunch we had a very light soup, with half-cooked vegetables floating in the dishes like starships in space. The luckiest boys found a piece of potato or a fishbone, or the bone of some animal. That was the first course. For the main course they gave us a dish of *kasha*: that's the Russian name for cracked wheat boiled and mixed with a little butter. Usually they put in it pieces of something which looked like meat but tasted like the soles of shoes. We also got a piece of bread and the usual knob of butter, and to eat this exquisite fare they even gave us a spoon. To drink we again had tea, identical to that of the morning, but not nearly as warm. The spoons were counted, however, and if at the end – after the quarter of an hour allotted for lunch – there was a single one missing, the squad from the 'educational' unit would come into the cell and beat us all up, without bothering to make many inquiries. At that point the spoon would be given back, or rather thrown towards the door by someone who preferred to remain anonymous, because otherwise his cellmates would have tortured him and, as we say in such cases, 'made even his shadow bleed'.

For supper there was *kasha* again, a mug of tea with bread and butter, and once again spoons, but this time we were only given ten minutes for eating.

A lot of trouble arose from food. Little groups of bastards, united by their common love of violence and torture, terrorized all the boys who were on their own and didn't belong to any family. They would systematically beat them up and torture them, and make them pay a kind of 'tax', forcing them to give up most of their portions.

If you wanted to survive and have a quiet life in juvenile prison, you had to join the families. A family was made up of a group of people who had some common characteristic, often their nationality. Each family had its internal rules, and boys happily obeyed them in an effort to simplify their lives. In a typical family you would share everything. Anyone who received a parcel from home would give some of his stuff to the others. In this way everyone was constantly getting something from outside, which was very important psychologically: it helped to stop you becoming demoralized.

The members of one family protected each other, and ate and organized all their daily affairs together.

Each family also imposed some particular rules, some obligations that had to be met. For example, in our Siberian family it was forbidden to participate in gambling or any similar activity together with people from other families. And if anyone did anything to a Siberian, the whole family would jump on him, even if he were on his own, beat him up and force him to 'soap his skis' – that is, to ask the guards for an immediate transfer to another cell. He also had to justify his request by saying that he feared being killed. It was a gesture which everybody else looked upon as dishonest, and so when he was transferred that poor wretch would be very badly treated and despised by everyone.

* * *

Once a member of our family, a twelve-year-old boy called Aleksy and nicknamed 'Canine Tooth', had some problems with one of the sympathizers of Black Seed, who are known as *Vorishki*, or 'Little Thieves', because in Black Seed *Vor*, or 'Thief', is the name of the highest Authority. In prison the Little Thieves imitated the members of Black Seed in everything they did: they played cards and cheated while doing it, they bet on all kinds of things, and they had homosexual relations, often raping the weaker boys and then terrorizing them, using them as slaves.

Anyway, Canine Tooth went to the toilet with another Siberian (in prison people always move about together, so that if anything happens to a brother of yours he is not on his own), and, as the regulations stipulate, he informed everyone in the cell that he was about to go and relieve himself. It is customary to let people know, because many believe that if someone goes to the toilet you mustn't eat or drink at the same time, otherwise the food and water will become dirty, and any person who touches that food will become *zakontacheny*, which in criminal slang means contaminated or tainted: a class of despised and maltreated people, who stand on the lowest level of the criminal hierarchy, from where they will never be able to rise again for the rest of their lives.

When Canine Tooth made his announcement, one of the Little Thieves, a sadistic fool by the name of Pyotr, piped up that Canine Tooth had better repeat what he'd said, because he hadn't heard it clearly.

This was a clear provocation, to which Canine Tooth retorted equally rudely, suggesting that Pyotr should wash his ears more carefully, if he had trouble in hearing things.

After which Canine Tooth went to the toilet, relieved himself and returned to the area of the Siberian family.

After dinner fifteen Little Thieves came to see us, demanding that we give Canine Tooth up to them, because he was due a punishment for offending an honest criminal. Since our idea of honesty was very different from theirs, none of us would have dreamed of leaving a brother of ours in their hands. Without saying a word in reply, we jumped on them and gave them a sound thrashing. The biggest of us, Kerya, nicknamed 'Yakut', who was a pure native Siberian and had Indian features, tore off a piece of one of their ears with his teeth, and chewed and swallowed it in full view of everyone.

We forced eighteen people to ask for a transfer all at once, and from cell to cell, all over the prison, people began to tell this story, saying we were cannibals. After a month, a boy who had been transferred from the first floor to our cell told us in terror that it was rumoured downstairs that the Siberians on the third floor had eaten a boy alive, and that nothing had been left of him.

We Siberians had made friends with the Armenian family. We had known the Armenians from way back; there was a good relationship between our communities and we resembled each other in many ways. We had made a pact with them: if there was ever any serious trouble we would support each other. In this way the power of our communities had increased.

We celebrated our birthdays and other special days together; sometimes we even shared our parcels from home. If anyone needed something urgently, such as medicine, or ink for tattoos, we would help each other without hesitation.

We were good friends with the Armenians, and also with the Belarusians, who were good people, and with the boys who came from the Don, from the Cossack community: they were rather militaristic but good-hearted, and all very brave.

We had problems with the Ukrainians, though: some of them were nationalistic and hated Russians, and for some strange reason even those who didn't share those sentiments ended up supporting them. And our relationship with the Ukrainians deteriorated markedly after a Siberian from another cell killed one of them. A real hatred grew up between our communities.

We kept well away from the people from Georgia; they were all supporters of Black Seed. Each of them was desperate to become an Authority, invented countless ways of making others respect him, and conducted a kind of criminal electoral campaign to win votes. The Georgians I met in that jail knew nothing about true friendship or brotherhood; they lived together while hating each other and trying to cheat everyone else and make them their slaves, by exploiting the criminal laws and changing them to suit their own purposes. Only by doing this did they have any hope of becoming chiefs, and of gaining the respect of the adult criminals of the Black Seed caste.

The supporters of Black Seed exercised a reign of terror over the mass of inmates whom they called 'heels'. Heels were ordinary prisoners, boys who had no connection with any criminal community, and who had ended up in jail purely through bad luck; many were the sons of alcoholics and had been convicted of vagrancy, a little respected article of the law. These poor souls were so exhausted and ignorant that everyone pitied them. The supporters of Black Seed, the Little Thieves, exploited them as slaves and mistreated them; they tortured them for sadistic pleasure and sexually abused them.

According to the Siberian tradition, homosexuality is a very serious infectious disease, because it destroys the human soul; so we grew up with a total hatred of homosexuals. This disease, which among our people has no precise name and is simply called 'the sickness of the flesh', is transmitted through the gaze, so a Siberian criminal will never look a homosexual in the eye. In the adult prisons, in places where the majority of inmates are of the Orthodox Siberian faith, homosexuals are forced to commit suicide, because they can't share the same spaces with the others. As the Siberian proverb says: 'The sick of the flesh do not sleep beneath the icons.'

I never fully understood the question of hatred for homosexuals, but since I was brought up in this way, I followed the herd. Over the years I have had many homosexual friends, people with whom I have worked and done business, and I have had a good relationship with many of them; I found them congenial, I liked them as people. And yet I have never been able to break the habit of calling someone a queer or a pansy if I want to insult them, even though immediately afterwards I regret it and feel ashamed. It's Siberian education speaking for me.

The Little Thieves despised passive homosexuals, even though most of them were active homosexuals. In the cells where there were no strong families and most of the boys were left completely to themselves, the Little Thieves gang-raped them, forcing them to participate in real orgies. They maltreated, insulted and provoked them continually, calling them all sorts of offensive names and forcing them to live in inhuman conditions.

Some of the guards often raped the boys, too; this usually happened in the showers. You were allowed to take a shower once a week if you were in the ordinary regime, whereas in the special regime, where I was, you could only do so once a month. We used to improvise with plastic bottles, rigging up a shower over the toilet, since we always had plenty of hot water. When we went to the shower block it was like a military operation: we all walked close together; if there were any weak or sick boys among us we put them in the middle and always kept an eye on them; we moved like a platoon of soldiers.

The reason for this was that there were often violent brawls in the showers, sometimes for no special reason, and just because someone was feeling irritable. It only took someone stealing your place under the water for all hell to break loose. The guards never intervened; they let the youngsters work off their anger and stood there watching; sometimes they bet on the boys, as if they were fighting dogs.

One day, after a fight in the showers between us and the Georgians, I was running after a guy who had just snatched from me a towel embroidered by my mother. Suddenly my enemy stopped, and motioned to me not to make a noise. His attitude made me curious; I suspected a trap. I stopped running and approached him slowly, fists clenched, ready to hit him, but he pointed towards a cubicle from which a strange noise was coming, as if someone was slowly rubbing some iron object against the tiled wall. We guessed something nasty was happening. I felt uneasy; I wasn't sure I wanted to see what was going on behind that partition.

Together with that boy, whom only a moment earlier I had wanted to beat to a pulp, I moved from one cubicle to another, hiding, drawing ever closer to the place the noise was coming from. I felt sick at the scene that appeared before our eyes: a large middle-aged warder with his trousers down, his head up and his eyes closed, was buggering a small thin boy, who was crying softly and not even attempting to escape the grip of his rapist, who was holding him still, with one hand on his neck and the other on his side.

The noise we had heard was that of the bunch of keys that hung from the belt of the paedophile's lowered trousers: the keys scraped against the floor with every movement he made.

We were there for no more than a second, because as soon as we realized what was going on we fled in silence. As we approached the running showers where our friends were already washing, I signed to the Georgian to keep quiet and he replied with a nod.

* * *

The guards weren't all alike. Some had a bit of humanity in them and didn't treat us badly – that is, by not beating us up, not humiliating us and not abusing us, they were already helping us a lot. Others, however, forced some boys to prostitute themselves.

There was one disgusting old screw: he had been a guard in an adult prison all his life, and after studying child psychology had asked for a transfer to a juvenile institution. He wielded a lot of power in our prison. Although he was only a warder, he rivalled the director, because he had links with people who organized a new activity which had arrived from abroad along with democracy, as a form of free life. These people made paedophile films and forced the boys to prostitute themselves, having sex with foreigners, people who arrived from Europe and the USA, people who had pots of money and hence, in the new democratic system, immense power.

Many boys were picked up at a particular time of day from the cells and came back the next day with bags full of food and all kinds of stuff, such as glossy magazines, colouring pencils and other things which nobody in jail could dream of possessing. Their cellmates were forbidden to touch them or mistreat them; they were untouchable, nobody dared to raise a finger against them, because everyone knew those boys were the old warder's whores. They called him 'Crocodile Zhena', after a character in a Soviet cartoon. The whores they called by women's names. Their bunk was usually down at the end, near the door, and they stayed there all the time.

Nobody talked to them, they were completely isolated, we all pretended they didn't exist. We Siberians, in particular, thought they were infectious, so we avoided even more than the others any form of contact even with their possessions, or with anyone who had come into contact with them or their possessions.

Once a sixteen-year-old boy called 'Fish', one of the Little Thieves, decided he wanted to rape a whore, a fourteen-year-old boy whom everyone called 'Marina'. Marina was regularly picked up from his cell, but one morning he had come back with whip-marks on his arms, and with his neck red as if someone had been throttling him. But he didn't seem upset; he was happy: he ate fruit and read comic books. To cut a long story short, Fish went over to him and asked him for a piece of fruit. Marina gave him a piece, Fish sat down with him on the bunk, they got talking and eventually he persuaded him to give him a blow-job in front of the whole cell.

We Siberians were in a precarious situation at the time: we had just been in a fight and we had to keep quiet for a while, otherwise – from what the disciplinary unit guys had said – they would split us up and send us to different cells, where we had a serious chance of ending up in the shit. So, while Fish was plunging his genitals into Marina's mouth in front of his whole escort and other idiots who had gone to enjoy the show, we sat on our bunks fuming with rage because we couldn't even afford to give him a thrashing.

We could hear the Little Thieves' shouts of encouragement:

'Go on, pansy, eat it all!'

'That's the way, Fish, make him swallow the fish!'

'Open that mouth wider and I'll stick mine in too!'

We soon realized that a lot of people wanted the same treatment from Marina. Marina's weak voice could be heard whispering in an obviously feminine tone which was disgusting to hear:

'No, boys, I did it to him because I like him, but that's enough . . .'

But there was no stopping the crowd now.

'What are you talking about? Open your little mouth, darling! There's a good girl, go on like that, or I'll break that pansy nose of yours!'

'Yeah, that's the way, suck it hard! Then it's our turn!'

You could hear the moans, and now and then the cries, of people having orgasms. Marina coughed and spat. Others shouted at him cruelly:

'No spitting, you queer! You've got to swallow, or I'll smash your face in!'

That poor devil, Marina. He sounded pitiful; he was crying, and in a thin voice, like that of a seriously ill man who hasn't got the strength to breathe, he begged:

'Please, I can't do any more, let me be! I'll suck you all off later, but let me rest, please . . .'

'Later's no good, you queer! If you're tired, lie down on the bunk, but face down!' Fish wouldn't let up.

One of our group was about to go and give him a beating, but we stopped him; we couldn't afford to get into trouble again. We were forced to witness that disgusting scene. None of us looked, but we could hear it all perfectly well; we were only a few metres away from the scene of the rape. We heard them throw Marina onto the bunk, while someone said in an obviously proud voice:

'Let me through! I'm going to be the first to fuck him in the arse!'

A moment later Marina gave a kind of cry, but then started sighing, just like a girl making love. The bunks moved; the movement passed from one bunk to another and reached ours like a gentle knocking; it made us wild with rage, that swaying; if only we'd been free to do so, we'd have torn them to pieces, every one of them.

A voice said:

'Come on, boys, let's take turns at sticking it in his mouth, too, or he'll relax too much, the queer!' And everyone laughed and joked, and Marina again started begging, and promising to suck them all off later, and do anything else, if only they'd leave him in peace for a while. But no one was listening to him. Again there were moans, again the cries of boys coming in his mouth, again Marina coughing and spitting, coughing and spitting.

Then someone gave him the first slaps in the face, and he started screaming. They squeezed their hands round his neck and continued to rape him. Now and then they slackened their grip and he started coughing and spitting again, and also trying to say something, but he couldn't, because he had a fit of coughing. Everyone was whooping with joy; they were pleased. Fish said to the others:

'Well? How do you like my girl? She's mine! Tonight she's free to you, but from tomorrow you'll have to pay me! Otherwise you'll have to just wank yourselves off!'

This madness had begun at about nine in the evening, and it went on all night. The guards didn't come even once to see what was going on. The rapists took turns: they would go away for a rest and then start all over again.

They joked among themselves:

'Hey, boys, are you sure he's still alive?'

'Well, the important thing is he's still warm . . .'

'He's alive – just look at him sucking away!'

By about six in the morning the party was over.

Everyone was laughing and joking; Marina was lying on his bed, motionless; now and then you would hear him sob and whisper something in his girlish voice.

Three days later he was picked up again by the guards.

But first Fish had a good talk with him, to make sure he wouldn't report him to the disciplinary unit.

'Marina, if you talk I'll kill you with my own hands . . . Keep quiet and behave yourself and no one will touch you again; no one will come and see you except me. Me or anyone who pays me. Understand? Without me, they'd fuck you in every hole, like the other night!'

Fish thought he'd been convincing, and as soon as Marina had left the cell he started arranging with his friends who would be the first to screw him when he got back.

A few hours later six men from the disciplinary unit arrived, with Crocodile Zhena himself. They called out by their surnames all the boys who had taken part in the rape. Panic spread among the Little Thieves. Someone said:

'I didn't do anything! I was there, but I didn't do anything.'

We watched the scene with interest.

When the warder had finished reading out the names on the list, the disgusting voice of Crocodile Zhena rang out:

'Well, are we all here? March, in single file!'

So we saw them leave the cell. For two days we heard nothing. Expectation hung in the air; nobody mentioned it, but many were worried about what might have happened.

During the night of the third day, when we were all asleep, the doors opened and the Little Thieves came in. The guards forbade us to get up and, sticking our heads out from the bunks, we tried to see what state they were in. When the doors closed, the groans started. Some of them cried, others talked out loud, saying senseless things.

I noticed that the first thing many of them did was to take a towel and go to wet it under the tap. Then I saw two of them pass between the bunks: they were holding the wet towel under their pants, against their backsides. Some of them started to quarrel about the toilet:

'Let me through, let me through! I can't wait any longer, I'm bleeding . . .'

Our boys laughed:

'Look at the fucking queers run!'

'They wanted to fuck him in the arse, didn't they? Well, if you give it you've got to take it . . .'

'Yeah! What kind of queer would you be otherwise? A semi-queer?'

'Hey, look at that one! They certainly gave him a good buggering!'

'He deserved it, the bastard, the fucking pansy . . .'

Our Filat White got up from his bed and shouted out:

'You're all contaminated! Go and sleep in the corner by the door! It disgusts us to have you anywhere near us!'

None of the Little Thieves dared to talk back, they were scared; they must have really been through it. They picked up their things and obediently moved into the corner by the door.

'Hey, look at that, a migration of queers!' said another of our group. And we all laughed.

The next day, putting together the rumours that were going round and the scraps of conversation between the Little Thieves, we reconstructed the whole story. Crocodile Zhena had taken them down to the first floor, to the room that was used for meetings with relatives: a large bedroom, with a number of beds, where visiting parents could stay for a day and a night with their children. There they'd been raped for two and a half days by Crocodile Zhena's friends, who had also filmed the whole thing with a videocamera. It was said that they had rammed a bottle into Fish, and consequently lacerated his anus, and those of a few others, till it bled.

From that moment Fish became a kind of shadow; he moved around the room silently and always looked at the floor. He went to the toilet at night, and by day tried never to leave his bunk.

The Little Thieves mainly took advantage of boys who were defenceless and frightened. Usually they took them, by threats or force, into their 'black corner', a block of bunks on which they lived, and there performed the most sophisticated and terrible tortures in front of the others.

They raped someone almost every day; afterwards they would beat the boy up and make him dance on the floor stark naked, with a paper tube stuck up his anus. First they would set fire to the tube, then they would tell the poor bastard to dance. That ritual even had a name: 'calling a little devil out of hell'. Every torture had a name, almost always a humorous one.

'The battle with the rabbit', for example, went like this: the poor bastard in question was stood in front of a wall on which there was a drawing of a rabbit wearing boxing gloves, and he had to hit it as hard as he could. They would all shout 'Go on! Harder!' at the tops of their voices. The victim would hit the wall and in a few minutes his hands would be a bloody mess. Then the others would force him to hit the wall with his head and his legs, threatening him:

'Go on, you pansy, what are you scared of? It's only a stupid rabbit! Hit it harder – with your leg, with your head! Hit it, or we'll rip your arse open like a rag!'

And the poor devil would be exhausted, then they'd force him to throw his whole body at the rabbit, but usually he would collapse before then, and pass out from the pain. Then they would leave him there on the floor, saying:

'You're a wuss, a sissy! You're useless! You let a rabbit beat you up, do you realize that? When you come to, we'll make you into a pretty little girl!'

In this way the Little Thieves sowed fear and chaos among the inmates.

Another torture was 'the flight of Gagarin': the victim was forced to throw himself off the highest bunk holding his feet with his hands, forming a kind of ball with his body. Sometimes they would wrap a towel round his head to 'protect' him at the moment of impact, but nevertheless this torture would end with broken bones, and the hapless victim would go straight to hospital.

Then there was 'the Ghost': they would force someone to go round with a blanket over his head for a couple of days. Anyone could go up to him and hit him at any moment, and he had to reply every time:

'I can't feel a thing, because I'm a ghost.'

Usually they hit him with something hard, preferably the tea kettle, with a bag of sugar inside it to make it even heavier. Once in a cell near ours they killed a boy by hitting him too hard on the head. The next day, during the recreation hour, they boasted about it in the courtyard; I heard them with my own ears say, laughing:

'The ghost was too weak.'

The staff let all acts of violence between juveniles pass as accidents. There were an incredible number of boys who 'fell out of their bunks in their sleep'; many of them died, some were left permanently disabled.

Nobody dared to tell the truth.

We Siberians were opposed to any manifestation of sexual perversion, bullying and unmotivated violence, so whenever one of us saw that the Little Thieves were about to torture someone, we would start a serious fight, which sometimes ended very badly.

In our cell the Little Thief who dominated all the weaker ones was a really sadistic bastard nicknamed 'Bulgarian'. He was the son of a Black Seed criminal and the younger brother of a *Blatnoy*. Bulgarian was quite a

thin little boy, more or less like me, except that I did gym
and was quite active, whereas he smoked and was always
loafing around, so he looked like a little mummy. His skin
was a very strange colour, like that of patients suffering
from hepatitis, so we Siberians called him 'Yellow', not
'Bulgarian'.

When Bulgarian arrived in our cell the Little Thieves
started telling stories about him, to build up the legend.
For a week his name was always at the centre of every
conversation – Bulgarian here and Bulgarian there – and
everything in the world was either him or in some way
connected with his legendary figure. We Siberians said to
each other:

'Another bastard, for sure. Let's just hope he's not a
troublemaker . . .'

Two weeks after his arrival, Bulgarian managed to
pick a quarrel with the Armenians, calling them 'Black
Arses' (that's what the Russian nationalists often called
anyone who came from the Caucasus and had a darker
skin); he shouted that he would use his connections in the
criminal world to have them all killed. He was a clown,
a spoilt child, who had clearly never seen anything apart
from the view from his father's knees, which he had never
got down from until he went to prison.

The Armenians told us about the incident, and we
assured them of all our support in the event of a fight,
guaranteeing the support of the Siberian community
outside the prison as well. We knew that sooner or later
the situation between us and the Little Thieves would
lead to a war; we were just waiting for the right moment
and, above all, an opportunity. They would have to make

a mistake, because if we wanted to go through with it and have the backing of our elders, we would have to give them a serious reason which was approved by the Siberian criminal law. This too made us different from them. The Little Thieves could pick on anyone who didn't belong to their community, infringe the rules of behaviour or do other far more serious things, and they were always supported by the people of Black Seed: confident of their protection, they stopped at nothing. We, by contrast, had a very strict law: any mistake that was made, any insult to a person considered honest by our community, had to be punished. No one, neither a relative nor a friend, would dream of protecting someone who had broken the law.

So we were just waiting for Bulgarian and his gang of bumboys (as we called them, because of their propensity for homosexual rape) to show their ugly faces and stir up some trouble, which we would then use as a pretext for mincing them up like raw meat. But those bastards exceeded all our expectations.

One day our family was gathered around the 'oak' (that's what they call the table bricked into the floor which is found in every cell). According to an agreement, the families, or 'brigades' (as the groups of those who modelled themselves on Black Seed were known) were allowed to gather around the oak for a certain length of time. In every cell it was different, but usually you stood at the oak to eat, at mealtimes. The stronger ones stood around the table first; they would eat, chat and then leave the table free for others who were weaker than them but stronger than those who came after them. Most of the inmates didn't even stand at the table, but would eat on their bunks, otherwise they wouldn't have had time to eat their meal. Eating at the oak was a kind of privilege; it emphasized the power of the group you belonged to. In our cell we were the first to eat at the oak, together with the Armenians and the Belarusians. In all there wasn't room for more than forty people at the table, but we managed to squeeze sixty of us in. We did this to show the others that our alliance in the cell was superior to everyone else. The Little Thieves who were in the same cell as us couldn't stomach this, because they felt they were in second place but couldn't do anything about it; what's more, the Little Thieves in the other cells were always ribbing them about it. But to attack us would have been like committing suicide, so one day they found an excuse for not eating at the oak any more: they started to say that the table was tainted, that someone had washed it with the floor cloth and that therefore, according to their rules, they couldn't even touch it with a finger now. It was a lie, a story they'd thought up so as not to lose their dignity entirely.

So that day we were having our lunch; the Armenians had brought to the oak a piece of cheese which one of them had just received in his parcel from home. After cutting it up into little cubes we were all eating it with relish: it was a taste that came from freedom, a delicious flavour, which reminded us of home, of the life we were all waiting to live again.

Suddenly we heard a shout; I was facing the door, so I didn't really grasp what was going on, but a group of my Siberian brothers near the bunks got up, announcing angrily:

'Honest people! While we're eating what the Lord has sent us to keep us alive, those bastards are uncorking someone!'

To 'uncork' meant to rape. What was happening was a very serious matter. Serious in itself, certainly, but there was more to it than that: although we were often forced to turn a blind eye to the homosexual acts of the Little Thieves, this time it was quite impossible. Having sexual relations while, in the same space, in the cell – which in the criminal language is called 'home' – people are eating, or reading the Bible, or praying, is a flagrant violation of the criminal law.

We got up and ran towards the Little Thieves' black corner. They were holding down one of the usual poor wretches on a bunk, and, wrapping a towel round his neck – so tightly his face had gone all red, and he was croaking for air – they were screaming at him that if he didn't keep still and take it up the arse while he was alive, he would do it when he was dead.

Filat White grabbed one of them by the neck – Filat was a very strong boy but one without heart, as they say in Italian, or with an evil heart, as they say in Siberia (and it's not exactly the same thing): in short, he had no pity for his enemies – and started pounding him with his fists, and his fists were like cannon balls. After a few seconds the guy lost consciousness and his face turned into a raw steak. Both of Filat's hands were covered in blood.

From the Little Thieves' bunks there came a torrent of abuse and threats of revenge, with which they are usually very liberal.

Filat went up to the one who had been about to rape the boy and still had his underpants down. Everyone was half-naked and dripping with sweat in that hellish heat; we Siberians were in our underpants too, but ready to tear those bastards to pieces.

Filat grabbed the rapist by the arm and started hammering him against the corner of the bunk. The guy starting yelling:

'I'm Bulgarian! You've laid hands on me! All of you here are my witnesses! This guy's a dead man, he's a dead man! Tell my brother! He'll kill his whole family!'

He squealed like a drunken country cop's rusty whistle. Nobody took his words seriously.

Filat stopped banging him against the bunk and released his grip, and the boy staggered and fell on the floor. Then he pulled himself together, got to his feet and said:

'Your name, you bastard, tell me your name, and this very evening my brother will rip your mother's guts out . . .' At the word 'mother' Filat unleashed an incredibly hard punch. I heard a strange noise, as if someone, somewhere, a long way off, had split a plank of wood. But it wasn't wood: it was Bulgarian's nose, and now he lay flat on the ground, senseless.

Filat looked at him for a moment, then gave him a kick in the face, then another, and another, and yet another. Each time, Bulgarian's head jumped so far off his shoulders that it seemed not to be attached to his spine; it was as if his skull and the rest of his skeleton were separate: his neck seemed no more than a thin thread, made of rubber.

Filat said to them all:

'Isn't wanking enough for you any more? Don't you want to wait to get out so you can make love to girls? Do you prefer arses? Have you all turned into bumboys?'

At his last word a ripple of surprise ran along the bunks: to insult a whole group of people is very wrong; according to the criminal law it's an error. But Filat had been clever: he had expressed his insult in the form of a question, and according to our law, in such situations, especially if the name of your mother has been insulted, a slight hint of an insult to a whole group is quite acceptable.

Without another word, Filat put one foot on Bulgarian's genitals, which were sadly shrunken on his inert body, and started crushing them with all his strength. Then he leaped on Bulgarian like a madman, and hurling a fearful yell into the air jumped up and down on his stomach until we all heard a terrible *crack*. I didn't know much about anatomy, but this much was clear to me – he'd broken his pelvis.

The Little Thieves sat there speechless, terrified. Filat said to all of them:

'Now I'll give you one minute to soap your skis. After that, if any of you remains in this house he'll get the same medicine as . . .'

Before he had even finished the sentence, the Little Thieves had jumped down from their bunks and rushed to the doors, shouting and pummelling on the iron:

'Guards! Help! They're killing us! Transfer! Immediately! We request a transfer!'

A few moments later the doors opened and the guards of the disciplinary squad came in, armed with truncheons. They carried away the two injured boys, dragging them along like sacks of rubbish, leaving a long trail of blood behind them. Then they started ejecting the Little Thieves.

The following week a letter arrived from outside. It said Bulgarian had died in hospital, and his brother had tried asking the Siberians for justice but they had turned him down flat, so he had started threatening vengeance, at which point they had killed him by knocking him down with a car. He had tried to run away from his murderers, but hadn't succeeded. To remove any doubt a Siberian belt had been left next to the corpse.

And so the war had ended. Nobody sought revenge any more, and everyone kept quiet and behaved themselves. Some other Little Thieves arrived in our cell a few months later, but they didn't make any more mistakes.

For nine months I was in that place, in that cell, in the Siberian family. After nine months they released me for good conduct, three months early. Before leaving I said goodbye to the boys; we wished each other good luck, as tradition requires.

After I left, for a long time I kept dreaming about the prison, the boys, that life. Often I would wake up with a strange sense that I was still there. When I realized I was at home I was happy, certainly, but I also felt a mysterious nostalgia, sometimes a regret that remained in my heart for a long time. The thought of no longer having any of my Siberian friends around me was an unpleasant one. Gradually, though, I resumed my life, and the faces of those boys became ever more distant.

Many of them I never heard of again. Years later, in Moscow, one day I met Kerya Yakut, who told me a few things about some of them, but he too no longer moved in those circles; he was working as a private bodyguard to a rich businessman now, and had no intention of returning to the criminal life.

He seemed to be in good form. We talked a little, reminiscing about the times of our Siberian family, and then we parted. Neither of us asked for the other's address; we were part of that past which is not remembered with pleasure.

Ksyusha

Ksyusha was a very beautiful girl with typical Russian features. She was tall, blonde and shapely, with freckles on her face and eyes of a dark, deep blue.

She was the same age as me, and she lived with her aunt, a good woman whom we called Aunt Anfisa.

Ksyusha was a special friend of mine.

I remember the day I first saw her. I was sitting with my grandfather, on the bench. She was walking towards our house with her slightly timid yet at the same time strong and decisive step: she seemed like a wild animal padding through the woods. When she approached, my grandfather looked at her for a moment and then said, as if speaking to someone I couldn't see:

'Thank you for sending another angel into the midst of us sinners.'

I realized that she was a 'God-willed' child, as our people say, one who in other places would simply have been called mad.

She suffered from a form of autism, and had always been like that.

'She has suffered for us all, like Our Lord Jesus Christ,' my grandfather told me. I agreed with him, not so much because I understood the reason for Our Lord's suffering, but simply because I had learned that in my family, if you wanted to survive and have some chance of prospering, it was essential always to agree with Grandfather, even in cases which exceeded the limits of the intellectual faculties, otherwise no one would get anywhere.

Since my childhood I had been surrounded by handicapped adults and children, such as my close friend Boris, the engine driver, who met the tragic end that I have already described. Many mentally ill people lived in our area, and they kept coming to Transnistria until the 1990s, when the law against keeping the mentally ill at home was abolished.

Now I realize that Siberian culture developed in me a profound sense of acceptance towards people who outside my native society are described as abnormal. For me their condition was simply never an anomaly.

I grew up with mentally ill people and learned many things from them, so I have come to the conclusion that they have a natural purity, something you cannot feel unless you are completely freed of earthly weight.

Like many God-willed children and adults, Ksyusha was a frequent visitor to our house: she entered and left whenever she wanted; sometimes she stayed until late at night, when Aunt Anfisa would come to fetch her.

Ksyusha was expansive, and could be positively garrulous. She liked to tell everyone the latest news she'd managed to gather.

She had been brought up by the criminals, so she was aware that the cops were the baddies and the people who lived in our district the goodies, and that we were all one family.

This fact had created an atmosphere of protection around her, and she felt free to live her life as she wished.

Even when she was older, Ksyusha continued to come into our house as freely as before: without asking anyone's permission she would start cooking whatever she liked, or she would go out into the vegetable garden to help my aunt, or stay indoors to watch my mother knitting.

Often she and I would go up onto the roof, where my grandfather kept his pigeons. She liked the pigeons very much; when she saw how they walked about and ate, she would laugh and stretch out her hands, as if she wanted to touch them all.

Together with my grandfather we used to fly them. First Grandfather would take a female pigeon, small and poor of colour and feather, and throw her; she would start to rise into the air, and would fly higher and higher, and when she became as small as a dot in the sky Grandfather would pass one of us a big strong male with a rich, glossy plumage, an absolutely beautiful pigeon. At Grandfather's signal we would throw this second, larger pigeon upwards, and he would rise towards the female, turning somersaults in the air to attract her attention. He would beat his wings hard, making a sound like the clapping of hands. You should have seen how Ksyusha laughed at that moment; she was the real beauty.

She liked to imitate Grandfather's gestures and phrases. When she saw a handsome new pigeon she would put her hands on her chest just as Grandfather Boris did, exactly like him, and in a tone of voice identical to his she would say, as if she were singing:

'What a miracle of a pigeon this is! It has descended straight from God!'

We would all burst out laughing at the way she succeeded in catching Grandfather's manner and the peculiarities of his Siberian pronunciation; and she would laugh with us, realizing that she had done something clever.

Ksyusha didn't have any parents, or any other relatives; her aunt wasn't a real aunt – she let herself be called that for simplicity's sake. Aunt Anfisa had a past as a *klava* or *zentryashka* or *sacharnaya*: these terms in criminal slang denote a female ex-convict who after her release settles down with the help of the criminals, finds a normal job and pretends to live an honest life, so as to deflect the attention of the police from herself. To criminals in difficulty – guys on the run from the police, say, or escaped convicts – such women are a means of support in the civil world; it is thanks to them that they communicate with their friends and obtain help. These women, who are clean and above all suspicion, are highly respected in the criminal world and often run secondary criminal affairs, such as black marketeering or selling stolen goods. According to the criminal law they cannot marry, because they are and must remain the brides of the criminal world. The former USSR is full of these women: people say of them that they haven't got married because they had some bad experience with men in the past, but the truth is different. They live in isolated spots, outside town, in quiet areas; inside their apartments there is no trace of that world to which they are closely and inextricably linked. The only visible sign of their identity might be a faded tattoo on some part of the body.

The addresses of these women don't appear in any directory, and in any case it's no use simply knowing who they are – you must be sent by someone, by an Authority. They will never open the door to you if they haven't been forewarned of your arrival, or if they don't recognize the signature on your arm.

* * *

Before moving to Transnistria, Aunt Anfisa had lived in a small town in central Russia, and occasionally put criminals up in her flat. They would go to her house as soon as they got out of prison, partly just to spend some time with a woman who was capable of loving as a criminal was used to being loved, and partly to inquire about the whereabouts of their friends, find out what was going on in the criminal world and ask for help in their new life.

One evening Aunt Anfisa was visited by a fugitive whom the police had been hunting for some time. He and the rest of his gang had carried out several bank robberies, but one day something had gone wrong and the police had succeeded in catching them at it. A violent chase had ensued, and the criminals, as they fled and endeavoured to throw the cops off the scent, had shared out the loot and split up. Each had gone his own way, but, as far as Anfisa knew, only two of them had managed to get away; the other six had been killed in clashes with the police. The group had killed more than twenty officers and security guards, so as far as the police were concerned it had been a matter of pride not to let any of the robbers escape and to give them all an exemplary punishment, so as to deter other people from doing the same.

This fugitive turned up at Anfisa's house with a baby girl, who was only a few months old. He explained to her that his original plan, to escape via the Caucasus, Turkey and Greece, had never even got off the ground: the police had burst into his flat, and one officer had killed his wife, the child's mother; but he had made his escape, and now had come to Anfisa's house, sent by a friend.

He left Anfisa his little girl – along with a bag full of money, a few diamonds, and three ingots of gold – and asked her to take care of the child. She agreed, and not only because of the money: Anfisa couldn't have children herself, and like any woman who longs for children, had found the prospect irresistible.

The man told her that if she wanted a quiet life she would have to disappear. He advised her to go to Transnistria – to the town of Bender, a land of criminals, where he had the right connections and where no one could find her and harm her.

That same night Anfisa, with a bag full of money and food and with the little girl in her arms, had left for Transnistria. Later she heard the child's father had been killed in a shoot-out with the police while trying to reach the Caucasus.

Anfisa didn't know what the little girl was called: in all the confusion the man had forgotten to tell her his daughter's name. So she had decided to give her the name of the patron saint of parents, Saint Ksenya: or 'Ksyusha', as we called her affectionately.

Right from the start Anfisa had understood that Ksyusha was different from other children, but that never stopped her being proud of her: they had a wonderful relationship, those two – they were a true family.

Ksyusha was always going off on her own, all over the place, and wherever she went she found open doors and people who loved her.

Sometimes her autism was more obvious than usual: all of a sudden she would freeze and stand motionless for a long while, gazing into the distance, as if concentrating on something a long way off. Nothing, it seemed, could wake her or bring her back to her senses. Then she would suddenly come out of that state and resume whatever she had been doing before.

There was an old doctor who lived in our area, who had a theory of his own about Ksyusha and her moments of absence.

He was an excellent doctor, and a man who loved literature and life. He lent me a lot of books, especially ones by American authors who were banned in the Soviet Union, and also some uncensored translations of European classics, such as Dante.

Under Stalin's regime he had been put in a gulag for hiding in his apartment a family of Jews who, like many Jews in those years, had been declared enemies of the people. Since he had collaborated with 'enemies of the people' he had been given a harsh sentence, and like many political prisoners during that period, had been sent to a gulag together with ordinary convicts, who hated political prisoners. Already on the train journey to the camp he had made himself useful to the outlaw community by setting the broken bones of an important criminal who had been savagely beaten by the soldiers on guard. In the camp he had been officially declared a *lepíla*, or doctor of the criminals.

After several years in the gulag he had developed such a close relationship with the criminal community, despite not being a criminal himself, that when he was released he no longer felt he belonged to the civilized world. So he decided to go on living in the criminal community, and therefore had come to Transnistria, to our district, where he had a friend.

This doctor was a very interesting individual because he was a complex character of many layers: a physician, an intellectual who had preserved the taste and refinement of a person with a university education, but also a man with a past as a convict, a friend of criminals, whose language he spoke fluently and whom he resembled in almost every respect.

On the question of Ksyusha he used to say it was very important not to disturb her when she was motionless, but that one thing in particular was essential: when she returned to her senses, everything around her must be just as it had been at the moment of separation.

So we boys knew we mustn't touch her when she went into that state. We knew this, and we tried as hard as we could to protect our Ksyusha from any possible shock, but as often happens among youngsters, sometimes we overdid things in our attempt to follow the doctor's advice.

Once, for example, we were out in a boat. There were three of us plus Ksyusha and we were going upstream along the river when suddenly the motor conked out. We put the oars into the water, but after a few minutes I noticed that Ksyusha had changed: she was sitting with her back erect and her head quite still, like a statue, and staring at the unknown . . . So we, poor fools, started frantically rowing against the current, because we were scared that if on Ksyusha's reawakening the scenery around her was different, her health would be seriously affected.

We rowed like mad for almost an hour; we took turns but were still exhausted. People watched us from the bank, trying to make out what these idiots were doing on a boat in the middle of the river, where the current was strongest, and why they kept rowing against the current in order to stay in the same position.

When Ksyusha woke up we all gave a sigh of relief and we went straight home, though she kept asking us to go on a little further . . .

We thought the world of our Ksyusha; she was our little sister.

When I was released from prison after my second juvenile conviction, I went wild for a week. Then I spent a whole day in the sauna: I fell asleep under the hot steam, perfumed with pine essence, which pinned me to the boiling hot wooden bed. Afterwards I went fishing with my friends.

We took four boats and some large nets, and travelled a long way: we went upriver as far as the hills, where the mountains began. There the river was much wider – sometimes you couldn't see the opposite bank – and the current was less strong. A whole plain scattered with small pools among wild woods and fields, and a scent of flowers and grass carried on the wind; when you breathed it you felt you were in heaven.

We fished at night and relaxed by day; we would build a fire and make fish soup or fish baked in the earth, our favourite dishes. We talked a lot: I told the others what I had seen in jail, the everyday stories of prison, the people I had met and the interesting things I had heard from others. My friends filled me in on what had happened in our area while I'd been in prison: who had left, who had been put inside, who had died, who had fallen ill or disappeared, the troubles in our part of town and the conflicts with people from another area, the quarrels that had broken out during my absence. Someone talked about his previous conviction, someone else about what he'd heard from his relatives who had returned from jail. And so the days went by.

About ten days later we returned home.

I tied my boat to the jetty. It was a beautiful day – warm, even though a bit windy. I left everything in the boat – the bag containing my soap, toothbrush and toothpaste. I even left my sandals there: I wanted to walk with nothing to encumber me. I felt good, as you feel when you're aware of being really free.

I set my eight-triangled hat askew on the right side of my head and put my hands in my pockets, my right hand touching my flick-knife. I picked a sprig from an aromatic herb on the river bank and clenched it between my teeth.

And so, barefoot in the company of my friends, I strolled homeward.

Already in the first street of our district we realized that something was wrong: people were coming out of the houses, the women with little children in their arms were walking behind the men, and an immense line of people had formed. Following the crowd and increasing our pace we caught up with the end of the queue and immediately asked what had happened. Aunt Marfa, a middle-aged woman, the wife of a friend of my father's, replied with a very scared, almost terrified expression on her face:

'My sons, what a dreadful thing has befallen us, what a dreadful thing . . . The Lord is punishing us all . . .'

'What's happened, Aunt Marfa? Has somebody died?' asked Mel.

She looked at him with a grief-stricken expression on her face and said something I'll never forget:

'I swear to you by Jesus Christ that even when my son died in prison I didn't feel so bad . . .'

Then she started crying and muttering something, but it was incomprehensible; we only caught a few words, 'residue of an abortion' – a very bad insult for us, because as well as offending the person who is called that it offends the name of the mother, who according to Siberian tradition is sacred.

When one woman, a mother, insults the name of another mother, it means that the person at whom that insult is aimed has done something really horrible.

What was going on? We were bewildered.

Then a few seconds later all the women in the procession started screaming, crying and uttering curses together with Aunt Marfa. The men, as Siberian law prescribes, let them scream but kept calm themselves: only the angry expressions on their faces, and the narrow slits of their eyes, near-closed with rage, indicated their state of mind.

Uncle Anatoly came over to Aunt Marfa. He was an old criminal who as a young man had lost his left eye in a fight and was consequently nicknamed 'Cyclops'. He was tall and sturdy and never wore a bandage over the hole where his eye had once been: he preferred to show everyone that terrible black void.

Cyclops had the job of looking after Aunt Marfa and taking care of her family, while her husband, who was his best friend, was in jail. That's the custom among Siberian criminals: when a man has to serve a long prison sentence, he asks a friend, a person he trusts, to help his family to make ends meet, check that his wife doesn't cheat on him with another man (something almost impossible in our community) and watch over his children's upbringing.

Embracing Aunt Marfa, Cyclops tried to calm her down, but she kept on screaming louder and louder, and the other women did the same. So the little children started crying too, and then the slightly older ones joined in.

It was hellish: I felt like crying myself, though I still didn't know the reason for all this despair.

Cyclops looked at us, and realized from our faces that nobody had told us yet. He murmured in a sad and angry voice:

'Ksyusha's been raped . . . Boys, this is a world of bastards!'

'Be quiet, Anatoly, don't make Our Lord even angrier!' said Grandfather Filat, a very old criminal whom everyone called 'Winter', though I never understood why.

It was said that when he was a boy Filat had robbed Lenin himself. He and his gang had stopped a car carrying Lenin and some senior members of the party on the outskirts of St Petersburg. Lenin, the story went, had refused to hand over his car and money to the robbers, so Winter had hit him on the head, and the shock had given Lenin his famous tic of involuntarily turning his head to the left. I was always very sceptical about this story – goodness knows how much truth there was in it – but it was amusing to see grown people telling these tales in the belief that they were true.

Anyway, Winter was an old Authority, and whenever he expressed his opinion everyone took notice. It was his job to rebuke Cyclops, because he had spoken too angrily, blurting out blasphemies which a well-bred Siberian criminal should never utter.

'Who are you, my boy, to call this world "a world of bastards"? It was created by Our Lord, and there are plenty of just men in it too. Surely you wouldn't want to insult all of them? Mind your words, because once they have flown they never come back.'

Cyclops hung his head.

'It is true,' went on Grandfather Filat, 'that a great misfortune and injustice has befallen us; we have failed to protect the angel of Our Lord, and now He will make us pay for it. Perhaps you yourself will be given a long prison sentence tomorrow, someone will be killed by the cops, someone else will lose his faith in the Mother Church . . . Retribution awaits us all, for we all share in the sin. I too, old as I am, will be punished in some way. But now is not the time to lose our heads; we must show the Lord that we are attentive to His signals, we must help Him to accomplish his justice . . .' The rest of Winter's speech I missed, because I had dashed off towards Ksyusha's house.

* * *

All the doors and windows were wide open.

Aunt Anfisa was wandering around the house like a ghost: her face was white, her eyes swollen from weeping, her hands shaking so much they transmitted their tremor to the rest of her body. She didn't scream or say anything; she just kept emitting a long-drawn-out whine, like that of a dog in pain.

To see her standing in front of me in that state scared me. I was paralysed for a moment, then she came towards me and clutched my face with her trembling hands. She looked at me, weeping, and whispering something I couldn't understand. At the same time, I couldn't hear anything; in my ears there was a growing noise like a whistle, like when you swim underwater, going further and further down. I had a violent headache; I closed my eyes, squeezing my temples as hard as I could, and at that moment I understood the question Aunt Anfisa kept whispering to me:

'Why?'

Simply a short, sharp 'Why?'

I felt sick; I had lost all sensation in my feet. I lost all my strength; it must have been obvious I wasn't well, because as I tried to walk to Ksyusha's room I noticed two of my friends holding me up with their arms round my waist, gripping my elbows. As I walked, I realized I was swaying, as if drunk; a new pain had appeared in my chest, I felt a weight in my heart and lungs, and couldn't breathe. Everything was whirling around me; I tried to focus my gaze, but the carousel in my head was going faster, ever faster . . . suddenly, though, I managed to catch the image of Ksyusha. It was blurred, but shocking in its very imprecision: she was lying on the bed like a newborn baby, with her knees tucked right up to her face and her arms wrapped around them. Closed, completely closed. I wanted to see her face, I wanted to stop my head spinning, but I couldn't control myself; I saw a bright light and lost consciousness, falling into the arms of my friends.

I woke up outside in the yard, with my friends standing around me. One gave me some water to drink; I got to my feet and at once felt well, strong, as if I'd slept for a long time.

Meanwhile the people had filled the yard; there was a long queue leading back to the gate and out into the street. Everyone kept asking Aunt Anfisa's forgiveness; the women kept weeping and screaming curses at the rapist.

I was obsessed by a single thought: that of finding out who could have done such a thing.

Our friend, 'Squinty' – who owed his nickname to the fact that he'd been cross-eyed as a child, though his sight had later corrected itself – came over to us boys and told us Grandfather Kuzya was expecting us all at his house for a *chyodnyak*, which is a kind of big meeting between criminals of all levels, attendance at which is compulsory, even for children.

We asked him if he knew who had raped Ksyusha, and how it had happened.

'All I know,' he said, 'is that two women from our area found her in the Centre district. Near the market. Lying among the rubbish bins, unconscious.'

* * *

As a sign of respect, these meetings are always held in the houses of old criminals who have tied the knot: thanks to their experience they are able to give valuable advice, but since they have retired and no longer have any responsibilities they are in a sense not involved. Holding meetings in houses that are not their own enables all criminals who hold a certain responsibility to say what they think without being bound by the law of hospitality, whereby the master of the house must avoid contradicting his guests. In this way they can debate freely without having to be absurdly evasive and indirect.

When we reached Grandfather Kuzya's house, the door was wide open, as usual. We went in without asking for permission. This too is a rule of good behaviour: you must never ask an old Authority for permission to enter his house, because according to his philosophy he has nothing of his own – nothing belongs to him in this life, only the power of the word. Not even the house he lives in is his: he will always tell you he is a guest. Grandfather Kuzya, as a matter of fact, really was a guest, because he lived in the house of his younger sister, a nice old lady, Grandmother Lyusya.

There were many criminals of Low River in the house, including my Uncle Sergey, my father's younger brother. We greeted those present, shaking hands with them and kissing them three times on the cheeks, as is the custom in Siberia. Grandmother Lyusya invited us to sit down and brought us a large jar of kvas. We waited until everyone had arrived, then our Guardian, Plank, gave the sign that we could begin.

* * *

The aim of these meetings is to solve difficult problems in the area in such a way that everyone agrees with the solution and everyone contributes in whatever way they can.

As I have already mentioned, each area has a Guardian. He is responsible to the highest Authorities, who never participate in meetings like this, for the application of the criminal laws. The Guardian's job is a very difficult one, because you always have to keep abreast of the situation in your area, and if anything serious happens the Authorities 'ask' you, as the phrase runs in criminal slang – that is, they punish you. Nobody ever says 'punish'; they say 'ask' for something. Asking can be of three kinds: mild, which is called 'asking as if one were asking a brother'; more severe, which is called 'putting a frame round someone'; and definitive and very severe, which changes the criminal's life decidedly for the worse, if it does not actually put an end to it, and is called 'asking as if one were asking the Gad'.[1]

The old Authorities don't usually solve individual problems themselves; that is the purpose of the Guardian, who is chosen by them and in a sense represents them, at least as long as he behaves properly. But if the situation is difficult and beyond his abilities, the Guardian may appeal to an Authority and, in the presence of witnesses chosen from among the ordinary criminals, present the case without mentioning the names of the people involved.

---

1. An old Jewish name, Gad was used to mean someone utterly evil; it was supposedly the name of the serpent in the Garden of Eden. Here it means a person who does not deserve the slightest consideration or forgiveness.

This is done to guarantee impartiality of judgement; if the Guardian dares to name someone, or in some way makes it clear who the person is, the elder can punish him, withdraw from the case himself and pass it on to another, usually a person distant from him, with whom he has few connections. The purpose of this is to ensure that the process of criminal justice is as impartial as possible: it focuses solely on the facts of the case.

Clearly, when a job happens the Guardian has a strong incentive to clear it up quickly and effectively, so as not to allow the case to become too complicated and not to involve the Authorities.

Plank was an old robber who had been brought up in the old way. To open the meeting he gave a Siberian greeting, as is customary among our people, which consisted in thanking God for making it possible for everyone to attend.

He spoke slowly in a very deep voice, and we listened to him. Every now and then someone would heave a sad sigh, to emphasize the gravity of the situation we were faced with.

The gist of Plank's speech was simple – something very serious had happened. Any act of violence against a woman is inadmissible for the Siberian criminal community, but an act of violence against a God-willed woman is an act of violence against the entire Siberian tradition.

'You have one week,' he concluded, looking at us boys. 'You must find the culprit – or culprits, if there were many – and kill them.'

The task was our responsibility. Since Ksyusha was below the age of majority, the rules of our district decreed that other juveniles must make the inquiries and carry out the final execution.

They wouldn't just leave us to ourselves – on the contrary, they would give us a lot of help – but we alone must appear before the other communities, to show how our law worked.

It's the Siberian rule: adults never do something which concerns juveniles – they can help, advise and support them, but it is up to the youngsters to act. Even in our fights no adults get involved, whereas the boys of the other districts can call adults in as reinforcements. In Siberia an adult will never dare to raise his hand against a juvenile, otherwise he loses his criminal dignity, and at the same time the juvenile must keep to his place and not bother the adults.

In short, to demonstrate to others that our law is strong, we Siberian boys must show that we can look after ourselves.

'First of all, you will go from district to district in search of information,' Plank told us. 'And this will be useful to you,' he concluded, handing us a parcel of money. It was ten thousand dollars, a very large sum.

The meeting was over, and with the blessing of our pack we could now leave for the town.

But before I left the house, Grandfather Kuzya beckoned me over, as he always did when he had something to tell me 'eye into eye', as we say in our language.

'Hey, Kolima, come here a minute.'

I followed him up onto the roof, to the shed where he kept the pigeons. I entered after him. He turned round abruptly and eyed me, as if sizing me up:

'Go into town and check that everything is all right. Let the others do the talking; you just listen. And watch out, especially with the Jews and the Ukrainians . . .' He removed a layer of hay which covered the floor and pointed to a small gap between the wooden boards. 'Lift up the loose plank and take what you find. Never part with it, and if someone gets among you, use it. I've loaded it.' Then he went out, leaving me alone facing the little trap door. I lifted the plank and found a Nagant, the legendary revolver loved and used by our old criminals.

What Grandfather Kuzya had said to me had a precise meaning in the criminal language: receiving a loaded pistol from an Authority is like having permission to use it in any situation. You're protected; you don't need to worry about the consequences. In many cases, if the situation becomes critical, you only have to say 'I have a pistol loaded by . . .' and everything will be resolved in your favour, because at that point to act against you would be equivalent to acting against the person who loaded your gun.

Outside Grandfather Kuzya's house two adult drivers were waiting for us – two young criminals from our area who had been given orders to take us wherever we wanted but not to intervene unless it was a matter of life or death.

Before getting into the cars we talked for a while, to make a rough strategic plan. We decided that Gagarin, the oldest of us, would look after the money, and that he

would also have the responsibility of talking to people.
The rest of us would split up into two groups: the first
would cover Gagarin's back, and the second, while he was
talking, would go round sticking their noses into other
people's business, looking for clues.

'This is the first time we've had to work as cops,' said
Gagarin.

We had a bit of a laugh about this, then set off for
our tour of Bender. In reality there was nothing to laugh
about: it was like descending into hell.

In the car Mel told me he was a bit worried and handed
me a gun, saying:

'Here – I know you'll only have come with a knife,
as usual. But this is a serious business; take it, even if you
don't like the idea. Do it for me.'

I told him I already had one, and he relaxed, giving
me a wink:

'Been round to your uncle's, then, have you?'

I felt too important to give away the secret of the gun
I was carrying, so I just smiled and sang softly:

'Mother Siberia, save my life . . .'

We arrived in Centre, at a bar run by an old criminal,
Pavel, the Guardian of the district. Pavel was not Siberian
and didn't live according to our rules, so with him we had
to be diplomatic, though not excessively so: after all, we

came from the oldest and most important district in the criminal world, Low River, and we deserved respect for the mere fact of being Siberian.

Pavel was in the bar with a group of friends, people from southern Russia who followed no precise rules except those of the god Money – people who flaunted their wealth, wore fashionable clothes and plenty of gold chains, bracelets and rings. We didn't like this custom: according to the Siberian tradition a worthy criminal has nothing on him but his tattoos; the rest is humble, as the Lord teaches.

We greeted those present and entered. A man got up from the table where the owner was playing cards with his friends. He was a thin man of about thirty, adorned with gold and wearing a red jacket which was as sweetly scented as a rose in springtime or, as my Uncle Sergey would say, 'as a whore between the legs'. He addressed us very aggressively: his opening remarks alone, according to our laws, would have been enough to earn him a knifing.

He was a troublemaker; men of his kind are like dogs that bark to frighten passers-by. That's the only function they have. A well-bred, experienced criminal knows that, and ignores them; he doesn't even glance at them, so that it's immediately clear he's not a *fraer*, a clown.

We walked on and headed for the table, leaving the idiot shouting and cursing.

Old Pavel looked at us closely and asked us in a very coarse manner what we wanted.

Gagarin had done three spells in juvenile prison and a year earlier had killed two cops. In his seventeen years of life he had already garnered enough experience to know how to speak to people like that, so he gave him a brief outline of the situation.

He told him about the money, and about the need to find the culprits.

Instantly everything changed. Pavel got up and ripped open his shirt aggressively, displaying his chest, which was covered with tattoos and gold chains. At the same time he shouted:

'There can be no forgiveness for someone who's committed such a crime! I swear to God if I find him I'll kill him with my own hands!'

Gagarin, as cool and calm as a dead man on the day of his funeral, said there was no need to kill him – we would do that; but if he could spread the word around and help us find him it would be very useful. Then he repeated that we would give a big reward to anyone who could help us.

Pavel assured us that he would do all he could to find out who the bastard was. Then he offered us a drink, but we asked permission to leave, since we still had a lot of calls to make.

As we left we noticed that cars and scooters were already beginning to arrive outside the bar: clearly old Pavel had called the people of his district together to explain the matter to them.

Our second port of call was the district of Railway. The criminals of Railway specialized mainly in burglaries from apartments. Theirs was a multiethnic community, with criminal rules which also applied in most of the prisons in the Soviet Union. It was all based on collectivism; the highest Authorities, the Thieves in Law, handled everyone's money.

Railway, as I have already mentioned, was an area dominated by Black Seed, the caste that officially governed the Russian criminal world because of the large number of its members, and above all of its supporters.

Between Black Seed and us there had always been a kind of tension; they described themselves as the leaders of the criminal world, and their presence was very evident both inside prison and outside, but the foundations of their criminal tradition, most of their rules, and even their tattoos, were copied from us Urkas.

Their caste emerged at the beginning of the century, exploiting a moment of great social weakness in the country, which was full of desperate people – vagabonds and small-time criminals who were happy to go to prison for the sake of the free meals and the certainty of having a roof over their heads at night. Gradually they became a powerful community, but one with a lot of flaws, as many Authorities of Black Seed themselves acknowledged.

In Railway everything was organized more or less as it was among us. There was a Guardian responsible for what happened in his area, who was answerable to the Thieves in Law; and there were checks on those who entered and left the district.

And sure enough, at the border of Railway our car was stopped by a roadblock of young criminals.

To show that we were relaxed, we waited in the car until one of them came over and started talking to

Gagarin. The others leaned against their cars, smoking, and now and then threw an abstracted glance at us, but casually, as if by chance.

I knew one of them; I had stabbed him in the fight in Centre. Afterwards, however, everything had been sorted out, and according to the rules, once settled, the matter must never be mentioned again. He looked at me; I waved to him from inside the car and he grimaced as if he were still in pain from where I had wounded him. Then he laughed and made a sign to me with his index finger which meant 'watch out' – a playful gesture, as if to say that he wasn't angry with me.

I answered him with a grin, then I showed him my hands: I showed them empty, with the palms upwards, a positive gesture, which is made to emphasize your humility and straightforwardness and indifference to what is happening.

While I was exchanging gestures of goodwill with this guy, Gagarin was explaining to one of them the reason for our visit. They called someone on a mobile phone, and a few minutes later a boy arrived on a scooter. He was our guide; he had to take us to the Guardian of the area, 'Barbos', who was so nicknamed because he was a dwarf, and *barbos* is a joking name for small, weak dogs.

Barbos was a remarkable person – very well-educated, intelligent, shrewd, and with a rare sense of humour which enabled him to laugh about everything, even his stature. But there was also a less positive side to his character:

he was very quick-tempered, and in forty-six years of life had accumulated no fewer than four convictions for murder.

A lot of crazy stories were told about him. For example, that his mother was a witch and had made him immortal by feeding him on the ashes of diamonds. Or that he had devoured his twin brother in his mother's womb, and because of this she had cursed him, stunting his growth.

My uncle, who had known him all his life, said that when he was a boy Barbos used to go to the butcher's to practise hitting people on the head with an iron bar: he used to bash the skinned beasts hanging on the hooks, and thus perfected his technique with the iron bar until he became a skilled assassin.

It was very strange that in the community of Black Seed, where murder was almost despised as a crime, at least by the highest Authorities, a man like him had succeeded in reaching such an important position in the hierarchy: I suspect he had been given the role of Guardian to keep everyone quiet during a delicate period for Black Seed, which in recent times had been getting a bit out of control and seemed to be in need of a firm hand.

Following the guy on his scooter we entered the side streets behind the railway tracks. Suddenly the boy stopped and pointed at an open door. We got out of the cars and at the same moment Barbos emerged, with three young criminals.

He came over to us and we exchanged greetings. Following the Siberian rules, as our host he first inquired after the health of some elders of Low River. Each time, after our replies, he crossed himself and thanked the Lord for showing His goodness to our elders. After the formalities he asked us the reason for our visit.

Gagarin briefly explained the whole story to him, and when he mentioned the money offered as a reward for accurate information about the rapist the dwarf's face changed, becoming like a sharpened blade, taut with anger.

He called one of his assistants, whispered something in his ear, and then hurriedly apologized to us, assuring us that he would soon explain everything. After a few minutes his man returned with a small holdall, which he handed to Barbos. Barbos gave it to Gagarin, who opened it and showed it to all of us: it was packed with wads of dollar bills and two guns.

'There are ten thousand here; I take the liberty of adding them to your reward for the head of that bastard . . . As for the guns,' the dwarf gave an evil smile, 'they're for you too: when you find him, pump lead into him on behalf of all the honest thieves of our area, since we wouldn't presume to do it ourselves. This justice is yours.'

We couldn't refuse – it would have been rude – so we thanked him.

We left the district feeling pleased at the welcome Barbos had given us and at his generosity, but I was miserable. I felt even worse than before: the thought of Ksyusha continued to haunt me. Something told me the wound had been too deep; I realized I was thinking of her almost as if she were dead.

The next call we had to make was at a district called 'Bam', an acronym of *Baykal-Amur Magistral*, the railway line connecting the famous Lake Baikal with the great Siberian river.

A motorway had been built alongside the railway, and in the 1960s many new industrial towns had been erected where large numbers of people had come to live, their purpose being to work in order to guarantee the progress of the socialist country. All these towns were identical: they consisted of five or six areas known as 'microdistricts', and altogether they presented a very dreary landscape. The houses were all built to the same model: nine-storey apartment blocks in rows of three with small front gardens where the grass never grew and the trees never lasted more than one season for lack of sunlight. On those little plots of land there was also a playground for children, with monstrous toys made of remnants of iron and cement, full of sharp edges and painted in the communist style – in a single colour, regardless of what they were supposed to represent, just like the ideal of communist society, where everyone is obliged to be the same as everyone else. Although Mother Nature had made the crocodile green and the lion tawny, both animals were painted red, so that they seemed like the creations of some maniac painter. All these toy animals, which were supposed to be for the children's entertainment, were cemented into the asphalt, and after the first few showers of rain became covered with rust. The risk of getting tetanus by cutting yourself was extremely high.

This brilliant playground initiative in the new towns was immediately dubbed 'goodbye kids', because of the many injuries to children that occurred every day. So after a few years, the first thing anyone who came to live there did was to dismantle those playgrounds, to guarantee their offspring a healthy and happy childhood.

In our town, Bam was the area of nine-storey houses inhabited by poor people, down-and-outs: most of them were hooligans, or the kind of people who in Siberia are described as 'off limits' – delinquents who because of their ignorance are not able to follow the laws of an honest, worthy criminal life.

Addiction had almost become a social convention in Bam. Drugs were always circulating, day and night. Kids started using them at twelve years old and were lucky if they reached adulthood; the few who did already seemed old by the age of eighteen – they were toothless and had skin that looked like marble. They committed minor crimes such as burglary and pickpocketing, but also a lot of murders.

Some of the stories that were told about Bam were chilling – terrible illustrations of the depths of ignorance and despair to which man can be driven: newborn babies thrown out of windows by their mothers, sons who brutally murdered their parents, brothers who killed their brothers, teenage girls forced into prostitution by their brothers or fathers or uncles.

It was a fairly multiethnic area – there were a lot of Moldovans, gipsies, Ukrainians, people from southern Russia, and a few families from the Caucasus. They had only one thing in common: their total inability to live in a civilized manner.

There was no law in Bam, and no person who could take responsibility before honest criminals for all the terrible things that went on there.

Consequently, the people who lived there were described as *zakontachenye*, 'contaminated'. According to the criminal laws you cannot associate with them as with normal people. It is forbidden to have any physical contact with them; you are not allowed to greet them, either vocally or with a handshake. You cannot use any object that has previously been used by them. You cannot eat with them, drink with them or share their table or their house. In jail – as I've already mentioned – tainted prisoners live in a corner of their own; often they are made to sleep under the bunks and to eat with plates and spoons that have been marked with a hole in the middle. They are forced to wear dirty, torn clothes, and are not allowed to have pockets, which are removed or unstitched. Every time they use the latrine they have to burn some paper inside it, because according to the criminal beliefs only fire can cleanse a thing that has come into contact with a tainted person.

People who have once been classified as tainted can never rid themselves of that stigma; they carry it with them for the rest of their lives; so outside prison they are forced to live with others like them, because nobody else wants them anywhere near them.

Homosexual relations are common among them, especially among the young drug addicts, who often prostitute themselves in the big cities of Russia and are much appreciated in homosexual circles for their youth and their modest demands. In St Petersburg many respectable citizens abuse them, then pay them with dinner in a beer hall or by letting them spend the night in a hotel room, where they can sleep in a warm bed and wash under the shower. The age of these boys ranges from twelve to sixteen: by seventeen, after four years spent in the 'system' – as drug addiction is called in criminal slang – they're completely burnt out.

According to the criminal rules, a tainted person can never be struck with the hands: if it is necessary to strike him it must be done with the feet, or better still with a stick or an iron bar. But he mustn't be stabbed, because death by knife is considered to be almost a sign of respect for your enemy, something the victim has to deserve. If an honest criminal stabs a tainted person, he too is permanently tainted and his life is ruined.

So when dealing with the people of Bam you had to be careful and know how to behave, otherwise you risked losing your position in the community.

There was a place in Bam called 'the Pole'. On this site there stood a real pole, made of concrete, which had been put there at some time in the past for an electric cable which had never in fact been completed. The criminals who represented power in the area at the time used to assemble around this pole; it was like a king's throne, you might say. Power changed hands so often that the honest criminals of Low River jokingly called the continual internal wars in Bam 'the dance around the pole'.

In Bam, since there was no criminal code or morality, the wars between criminals were very violent; they seemed like the chaotic scenes of a horror film. The clans gathered around an old criminal, who with the help of his warriors, all junkies and juveniles, tried to take control of the drugs trade in the area by physically eliminating their adversaries – the members of the clan which was handling the drugs at the time and was therefore the most powerful. They used knives, because they didn't have many firearms, and in any case they weren't very expert at using them, not having been brought up to have a familiarity with pistols and rifles. During their wars they even killed the women and children of the clans they were fighting against – their ferocity knew no bounds.

Entering the district, we headed straight for the Pole. We drove along a series of streets the mere sight of which induced sadness and anguish, but also a certain relief, if you thought how lucky you were not to have been born in this place.

The Pole was in the middle of a small square, round the sides of which there were benches, as well as a school desk with a plastic chair. Sitting round the desk were some kids, about fifteen in all, and on the chair sat an old man whose age was impossible to tell, he was so decrepit.

We got out of the cars. According to the rules we had to act tough, so we took out the sticks we'd brought in the boots of the cars and advanced towards them. The air was filled with a tension which, when we stopped a few metres away from them, became pure terror. It was important not to go too close, to keep our distance, so as to emphasize our position in the criminal community. They said nothing and kept their eyes down; they knew how to behave towards honest people. According to the rules, they could not initiate the conversation; they were only allowed to answer questions. Without giving any greeting, Gagarin addressed the old man, telling him we were looking for the guy who had raped a girl near the market, and that we would give twenty thousand dollars to anyone who helped us find him.

The old man immediately jumped down from his chair, went over to a bench and grabbed by the lapel a little boy whose face was disfigured by a large burn. The boy started screaming desperately, saying it was nothing to do with him, but the old man hit him repeatedly on the head till he drew blood, shouting:

'You son of a bitch, you bastard! I knew you'd rape her in the end, you scum!'

The other boys, too, jumped down from their benches and all started hitting their classmate.

Leaving him in their hands, the old man turned towards us, as if he wanted to say something. Gagarin ordered him to speak, and he immediately started pouring out a flood of words (mingled with various curses and insults which in our district would have got him killed), the gist of which was what we had already gathered: the person who had raped the girl was the little boy with the disfigured face.

'We were together at the market,' said the old man. 'I saw him follow the girl; I shouted to him not to, but he disappeared. I didn't see him again; I don't know what happened afterwards.'

His story was so stupid and naive that none of us believed it for a second.

Gagarin asked him to describe the girl, and the old man became flustered; he started whispering something incomprehensible, gesticulating with his hands, as if to sketch a female figure in the air.

A moment later I saw the stick that Gagarin was holding come down with tremendous force and speed on the head of the old man, who fell down unconscious, bleeding from the nose.

The others immediately stopped hitting the accused rapist – who looked so weak and demoralized he wouldn't even have been able to wank himself off, let alone rape a girl – and fled in all directions.

The only people left under the Pole were the old man with the broken head, sprawling in his own blood, and the boy they had intended to use as a scapegoat in exchange for the money. That scene, and the thought of that treachery, made my already sad and despairing heart sink even further.

So without having achieved anything we left the area, hoping the boys who had fled would start searching for the real rapist in order to sell him to us.

We decided to go to a place called 'Grandmother Masha's Whistle'. This was a private house where an old woman cooked and ran a kind of restaurant for criminals. The food was excellent, and the atmosphere friendly and welcoming.

In her youth Grandmother Masha had worked on the railways, and she still wore round her neck the whistle she had used to announce the departure of the trains: hence the name of the joint.

She had three sons, who were serving long sentences in three different prisons in Russia.

People went to the Whistle to eat or spend a quiet evening discussing business and playing cards, but also to hide things in the cellar, which was like a kind of bank vault, full of stuff deposited by the criminals: sometimes grandmother gave them a receipt, a piece of paper carefully torn out of her notebook on which she wrote in her almost perfect handwriting something like:

'*The honest hand* (i.e. a criminal) *has turned over* (in slang the phrase means 'to deposit something carefully') *into the dear little tooth* (a safe place) *a whip with mushrooms preserved in oil, plus three heads of green cabbage* (these are an automatic rifle with silencer and ammunition, plus three thousand dollars). *May God bless us and avert evil and dangers from our poor souls* (a way of expressing a wish for criminal luck, the hope that some business done together will have a successful outcome). *Poor Mother* (a way of referring to a woman whose sons or husband are in prison; in the criminal community it is a kind of social definition, like 'widow' or 'bachelor') *Masha.*'

Grandmother Masha made excellent *pelmeni*, which are large ravioli filled with plenty of meat, a Siberian dish that was common all over Soviet territory. When she decided to cook them she spread the word a couple of days beforehand: she would send out the homeless boys whom she took into her house in exchange for help in the kitchen and the occasional errand. The boys would get on their bikes and ride round all the places where the right people gathered, to tell them what Grandmother Masha was cooking.

Besides doing this, the boys also passed round the latest news: if you wanted to spread some information around, you only had to offer the boys a little money or a couple of packets of cigarettes and within two or three hours the whole town would know about it. They were also very useful in the struggle against the police: if there were trouble in any district of Bender and the police came to arrest someone, the boys would spread the word and the people concerned would turn out to set the arrested man free or to have a little gunfight with the police, just for the hell of it.

We needed the help of Grandmother Masha's boys now, to spread the news around town about our inquiries and our honest offer, but we were a little tired, and we were hungry.

When we reached the Whistle, darkness was falling. She welcomed us as she always did, with a smile and kind words, calling us 'little ones' and kissing us on both cheeks. To her we were all children, even the older ones. We sat down at a table and she joined us; she always did this with everyone: she would chat a bit before bringing you something to eat. We told her about our disaster; she listened to us, then said she'd already heard the story from her boys. We sat for a while in silence while she, with the cloth she always had in her hands, dried the tears from her wrinkled face. To look at that face you felt as if you were in the presence of the incarnation of Mother Earth.

Grandmother Masha started bringing us cutlery and something to drink. In the meantime we called over one of her boys, a thin little lad with one eye missing and snow-white hair, who was the brightest of them all; his name was 'Begunok', which means 'the one who runs fast'. He was a very serious boy; if he said he would do something you could be sure he would do it. We asked him to spread the word among the people he knew in town, and in particular to go round all the bars where people gathered to drink and hang out together. Mel slipped a packet of cigarettes and a five-dollar bill into his hand, and a second later we heard his bike setting off at top speed.

We ate our supper in silence, with none of our usual lively chatter. I was ravenous but found it very hard to eat. As I chewed the food I felt a pain in my chest. I couldn't swallow anything without washing it down with alcohol, so before long I was drunk and beginning to get maudlin. The others were in a similar state. Supper went slowly, without enthusiasm. Everyone's eyes became increasingly glazed, and the atmosphere was really gloomy.

Suddenly, amidst the heavy sighs and whispered moans, one of us started crying, but very softly, ashamed at this manifestation of weakness. It was the youngest of the gang. He was thirteen and his name was Lyocha, nicknamed 'Grave' because of his cadaverous appearance:

he was thin and always ill, as well as being constantly in a bad mood. He had already tried to hang himself ten times, but had always been saved by one of us. Once he had even tried to shoot himself in the heart with his uncle's gun, but the bullet had only punctured his lung, further impairing his already poor health. Another time, when blind drunk, he had jumped in the river, trying to drown himself, but hadn't succeeded because he was a very good swimmer, and the survival instinct had prevailed. The only reason he had never tried to slit his veins was that he couldn't stand the sight of blood: even in fights he never used a knife, but only hit people with a knuckleduster or an iron bar.

Grave was a boy with a lot of problems, but in spite of everything he fitted in well with our group, and he was like a brother to all of us. His suicidal tendency was like a ghost that lay hidden inside him; none of us could be sure when it would pop out, so he was constantly watched over by an older boy, Vitya, who was nicknamed 'Cat', because his mother said that just after he was born their cat Lisa had given birth to four kittens and at night she used to go into his cradle and suckle him, so that, according to his mother, he had become half cat. The two of them, Grave and Cat, always went around together, and their main occupation was fishing and stealing motorboats; they were the experts on the river, they knew all the particular points – where the water was still or swift, where the current swirled back, where the bed was deepest – and always knew with absolute precision where to find the fish, all year round. They never returned from a fishing expedition with empty boats, never.

At parties, and whenever we drank together, a sudden flood of tears from Grave was a sure sign that he would soon try to kill himself: so, in accordance with a rule laid down by us and approved by Grave himself (who when sober, despite all his psychological problems, had a great zest for life), we would take away his drink, and in extreme cases even tie him to his chair with a rope.

So on this occasion too, at the Whistle, while Grave was trying to stop crying, wiping his face with a handkerchief, Gagarin made a sign to Cat, who instantly replaced the bottle of vodka in front of Grave with a fizzy drink called Puppet, a kind of Soviet Coca-Cola. Grave stopped crying and drained the bottle of Puppet, ending with a long, sad burp.

Gagarin was talking to our drivers, Makar, known as 'Lynx', and Ivan, known as 'the Wheel'. They were in their early twenties, and both had just finished a five-year prison sentence. They were bosom pals. Together they had carried out a lot of robberies, and in the last one, after a gunfight with the police, the Wheel had been wounded and Lynx had refused to desert him and so he had been arrested too, because of his loyalty.

During our mission, according to the rules, they couldn't help us to communicate with the criminals of the various areas of the town, which was a pity: it would have been very useful, since we were all under age, and the criminals who didn't embrace our Siberian faith took the idea of dealing with juveniles as a personal insult. What Lynx and the Wheel could do was advise us how to behave, how to negotiate with people who obeyed rules different from our own, and how to exploit the peculiarities of each person and each community. It was important, part of our upbringing, this continual relationship between youngsters and adults who explained each individual situation according to the law observed by our elders.

While Gagarin listened to what Lynx and the Wheel had to say to him, the others started talking amongst themselves; perhaps Grave's crying had woken us all up and somehow helped to make us united and focused again.

Suddenly Mel started telling me a story he always repeated whenever he got drunk, and had done since the age of ten – a childhood fantasy of his. He had met a girl, he claimed, on the river bank, and had promised to take her to the cinema. Then they had made love; and when he reached this point in the story he always commented:

'It was like screwing a princess.' Then he would launch into a detailed description of the sex they'd had, depicting himself as a vigorous and expert lover. The story ended with her weeping on his shoulder and asking him to stay a little longer, and him reluctantly having to leave her because he was late for fishing.

It was the most incredible, ridiculous nonsense, but since Mel was a friend I listened to him with feigned interest and genuine patience.

He would talk to me with such rapture that his only eye became as thin as a slit. He would accompany the story with ample gestures of his gigantic hands, and whenever

one of his hands passed over the bottle of vodka I would
have to grab it, to stop it falling over.

The supper, as always, turned into a drunken binge.
We went on and on drinking, and to stop us getting too
drunk, Grandmother Masha kept bringing us plates of the
food we ate as an accompaniment to vodka.

Shortly before midnight Begunok returned, with
some news: a group of boys from the district of Caucasus,
during the very hours when Ksyusha had been raped, had
seen some strangers wandering about in Centre.

'They were hanging around near the phone boxes,'
said Begunok, with a serious expression on his face,
'pestering a girl.'

Without waiting to hear more, we dashed out to the
cars.

Caucasus was a district almost as old as our own. It
was so called because many of its inhabitants came from
the Caucasus, but also because of its position: it stood
on a cluster of hills. The criminals of Caucasus belonged
to various communities, but the leading one was the
so-called 'Georgian Family'. Then came the Armenians,
who formed the *Kamashchatoy* – Armenian organized
crime – and lastly people from many other regions:
Azerbaijan, Chechnya, Dagestan, Kazakhstan and
Uzbekistan.

The Georgians and Armenians got on well together,
being united by the fact that they were both Caucasian
peoples of Orthodox Christian religion, whereas the

other inhabitants of the area were either Muslims or atheists of Islamic tradition. The criminal communities of the Georgians and Armenians had a family structure: in order to become an Authority you didn't need to earn the respect of others, as among us Siberians; you merely had to be in the right family. The clans were made up of the family members, and they dealt in various kinds of criminal business, black marketeering, protection rackets, minor thefts and murder.

Because of their way of operating the Georgians were viewed with distaste by our community: often our criminals refused to communicate with them simply because they introduced themselves as the sons or relatives of some Authority. Among the Siberians such behaviour is unacceptable, because in our culture everyone is judged for what he represents as a person, and his roots come second; in Siberia you appeal to the protection of the family when you really can't avoid it, solely in matters of life or death.

For these and other reasons there was a lot of friction between us and the people of Caucasus: if we met up somewhere in town, it always ended in a fight, and occasionally someone got killed.

Two years earlier a friend of ours, Mitya, known as 'Julich', which in slang means 'little criminal', had stabbed a Georgian because he had insulted him by speaking the Georgian language in his presence. Julich had warned him, saying he was behaving in an offensive manner, but the other had made it clear that he intended to go on speaking Georgian because he despised the Russians, whom he called 'occupiers'. That was a political provocation: Julich reacted by stabbing him, and he later died in hospital. After his death the Georgians appealed to the old criminals of Black Seed for justice, but the verdict went against them, because according to the criminal law the Georgian had committed two serious errors: first, he had been discourteous to another criminal for no reason; secondly, he had dared to make a political allusion, which is condemned by the criminal regulations as a grave form of insult to the entire criminal community, because politics is cops' stuff, and criminals must have nothing to do with it.

After the verdict, however, the Georgians didn't calm down at all. They tried to get revenge a couple of times: first they shot a friend of ours called Vasya, who fortunately survived, then they tried to kill Julich in one of the discotheques in the town. They started a fight to tempt him outside the disco, where a number of them then attacked him. Luckily we were with him on that occasion, and we plunged into the fray to cover his back.

While we were fighting we noticed that they kept launching 'torpedoes' at Julich: that's what we call a method of killing a particular person during a fight, while pretending that it's an accident. Some guys, two or three of them, bump into the person – the victim, or 'client' – as if by mistake, and in the confusion they give another guy – the torpedo – the chance to make a precision strike to kill him, after which they merge back into the crowd; and in the end, if the torpedo has been skilful, nobody will have noticed anything and the whole action will have been carried out in a swift, professional manner. The client's death is treated as a normal consequence of the fight, and therefore forgotten immediately afterwards, because a fight is considered to be an extreme method of obtaining satisfaction, and every participant knows from the outset the risks he is running. But if during the brawl someone is caught launching a torpedo, he must be killed for violating the rules of the fight: his action is interpreted as outright murder. The premeditated murder of a colleague, a criminal, is considered an act of cowardice. The murderer's criminal dignity dies at that moment, and as the criminal law says, 'when his criminal dignity dies, the criminal himself dies too'.

On this occasion there were far fewer of us than there were of them. They intended to beat us up and launch the torpedo at Julich, but unfortunately for them, after a couple of minutes we were interrupted by the boys of Centre, the district where we were at the time. Exercising their right as the 'owners' of the area, they ordered us to stop fighting.

Just at that moment the Georgians' torpedo charged at Julich in full view of everyone, trying to stab him, but Julich managed to ward off the blow. The torpedo fell on the ground and started screaming something in his own language, ignoring the requests of the owners of the area that he calm down and put away the knife. In the end he actually cut the hand of one of the Centre boys, who had only asked him to give him his knife.

About three seconds later the Georgians were attacked en masse by the Centre guys, about thirty of them, and savagely beaten.

We apologized and explained the situation. Then we made an orderly retreat, taking a lot of bruises and plenty of cuts home with us.

When we got back to Low River we told the Guardian what had happened. To obtain justice against the Georgians we needed an external witness, someone who was not part of our group. Luckily three people of Centre testified to the old Authorities that they had seen the torpedo with their own eyes.

So a week later the Siberians made a punitive raid into the Caucasus district, which ended with the death of eight Georgians who had participated in the plot against Julich.

Naturally this unpleasant episode considerably worsened our already difficult relations with the Georgians. The Georgians started going around saying we Siberians were murderers and unjust people. We knew we were in the right and that the situation had been resolved in our favour; the rest didn't bother us very much.

We drove to a joint in the Caucasus district called 'The Maze'. It was a kind of bar-cum-restaurant, with a room where you could play billiards and cards.

Begunok had been very specific: he had said the people who had told him the story about the phone boxes were the sons of the owner of that restaurant. And they were Georgians.

We arrived at the Maze at about two in the morning; there were lots of cars outside and the shouts of the gamblers could be heard outside. They were shouts in Georgian, interspersed with a lot of Russian swear-words with Georgian endings.

We got out of the cars – our drivers said they would keep the engines running just in case – and entered all together.

When I think about it now it makes my hair stand on end: a bunch of juveniles – snotty-nosed kids – not just boldly walking around in a district full of people who want them dead, but actually entering a bar packed with real criminals who were far more dangerous than them. And yet at the time we weren't in the least afraid because we had a job to do.

As soon as we entered the Maze the owner's eldest son, a boy named Mino, came over to us. I knew him by sight; I had heard he was a quiet guy who minded his own business. He greeted us, shaking us by the hand, then invited us to sit down at a table. We did so and he asked a girl to bring wine and Georgian bread – it was on the house. Without our even asking him, he started telling us what he had seen in Centre.

He had been with some friends, including three Armenian boys, one of whom ran a flower stall in the market, not far from there. They had been standing near the phone boxes – where people often arrange to meet – when they had seen about ten youngsters, drunk or high on drugs, pestering a girl, trying to pick a quarrel in a rough and threatening way. One of the Armenians had asked them to stop it and leave her alone, but they had insulted him, and one had even shown him his gun, telling him to get lost.

'At that point,' said Mino, 'we decided to back off. It's true, we left the girl in the hands of those thugs, but only because we weren't sure who they were. We were worried they might turn out to have links with the people of Centre, and you never know, they might have closed down my friend's flower stall . . .'

Judging from Mino's description, though, the girl didn't sound like our Ksyusha.

Meanwhile the waitress had brought to our table some Georgian wine with some of their traditional bread, which is baked in a special way, spread on the walls of the oven. It was delicious, and we drank and ate with relish, together with Mino, talking about all sorts of things. Including our relationship with the Georgians.

He said we were right, and that his fellow-countrymen had behaved shamefully, like traitors.

'Besides, we're all Christians, aren't we?' he said. 'We all believe in Jesus Christ. We're all criminals, too, and the criminal law applies to everyone – Georgians, Siberians and Armenians . . .'

He told us the Georgian community had recently split in two. One part supported a rich young Georgian of noble blood who liked to be called 'the Count'. This Count spread a hatred of the Russians and forbade Georgians to marry Russians and Armenians, to preserve the purity of the race. Mino called him 'Hitler', and was very angry with him; he said he had weakened the whole community. The rest of the Georgians supported an old criminal whom we also knew, because he often came to Low River: Grandfather Vanò. He was a wise man; he had spent a long time in prison in Siberia and was highly respected by the criminal community. It was mainly the old folk who liked him. He wasn't so popular among the young because he stopped them living a life of pleasure and opposed nationalism, which the boys didn't like at all.

From Mino's account we understood that the situation was more difficult than it might seem at first sight, because the division cut across families, and many sons, brothers and fathers had lined up on opposite sides of the barricade. A war in those conditions was impossible, so everything was in a state of suspense, which according to Mino was even more dangerous than open warfare.

At a certain point five people came into the restaurant. They were young – no more than twenty-five years old – and they spoke to Mino in Georgian. He got up at once and went over to them.

They seemed pretty angry, and a couple of times I saw them point at us. At first they all talked at once, then their leader started speaking, a thin boy with eyes that popped out of their orbits whenever he raised his voice.

Mino, however, was calm; he leaned against the counter with a glass of wine in his hand and listened to them, looking at the floor with an indifferent expression.

The leader suddenly stopped talking, and all five of them left. Then Mino hurried over to our table and explained to us in an agitated voice that they were young members of the Count's gang:

'They said if you don't leave the district at once they'll come back in numbers and kill you.'

After Mino's warm welcome this threat seemed unreal.

Before getting up from the table, Speechless, one of our group, said:

'I'd be prepared to bet my right hand they've set an ambush for us outside.'

Speechless was so nicknamed because he hardly ever spoke, but when he did speak he always said true things. Once I spent three days fishing with him, and in three days he didn't utter a sound, I swear it, not one.

Gagarin gave the signal to get ready to leave the bar. Everyone put their hands under the table and there was a sound of pistols being cocked one after the other.

We took our leave of Mino. He begged us to use the security exit, but we went through the front door, the way we'd come in.

In the square outside the bar there were about fifteen people waiting for us, gathered under the street light.

Mel and Gagarin stepped forward; I walked behind them with Speechless, then came the others. I saw Mel pull out his Tokarev and at the same time Gagarin hide the hand holding his Makarov behind his back. I was clutching Grandfather Kuzya's Nagant in my jacket pocket.

They were blocking our way towards the cars. Our drivers had got out and were smoking casually, sitting on the bonnets.

We stopped a few metres short of the Georgians.

The thin boy, their leader, came forward to challenge us:

'You're finished. There's no escape for you.'

He spoke with great confidence. In his hands I saw a pistol, and behind him there was another guy with a double-barrelled shotgun.

'If you don't want any trouble, you only have one chance: lay down your arms and surrender.'

Then he started joking:

'Aren't you a bit young to be playing with guns?'

Quite unperturbed, Gagarin explained to him the reason for our visit, and stressed that it had nothing to do with relations between the Georgians and the Siberians.

'And anyway,' Gagarin reminded him, 'according to the criminal law, in cases like this even wars are suspended.'

He recalled a case in St Petersburg, where because of a hunt for a paedophile who was raping and killing young children a bloody war between two gangs – from the district of Ligovka and the island of Vasilev – had stopped, and the two sides had joined forces to search for the maniac.

The Georgians were rather confused now.

I noticed that while Gagarin was talking to their leader many of them had lowered their weapons, and their expressions had become rather pensive.

The Georgian, however, didn't give up.

'Well, in that case,' he asked suddenly, 'why didn't you speak to our Guardian? Why did you come here in secret, like snakes?'

On the one hand he was right: we should have gone to see their Guardian, because making inquiries behind his back was against the criminal regulations. But he was overlooking two things.

First, we were juveniles, and according to the law nothing could be 'asked' of us: only other juveniles could 'ask' us, adults had no power over us. Out of respect and for our personal pleasure we could choose to obey the rules and the criminal law of the adults, but until we came of age we would not be part of the criminal community. If a Guardian had reported our case to an old Authority, the latter would have laughed in his face: in cases like this the Siberians usually say:

'Boys are like cats – they go wherever they want.'

The second mistake the Georgian had made was much more serious, and showed that he was inexperienced in negotiations and quite incapable of using criminal diplomacy. He had insulted us.

An insult is regarded by all communities as an error typical of people who are weak and unintelligent, lacking in criminal dignity. To us Siberians, any kind of insult is a crime; in other communities some distinctions can be made, but in general an insult is the quickest route to the blade of a knife.

An insult to an individual may be 'approved': that is to say, if I have insulted someone and they take me before an old Authority, I will have to explain to him the reason why I did it, and he will decide how I will be punished. Punishment is inflicted in any case, but if the insult is approved, they don't kill me or 'lower' me; I remain myself and get off with a warning. An insult is approved if you utter it for personal reasons and in a non-serious form: for example, if you call someone who has damaged your property an 'arsehole'. If, however, you offend the name of his mother, they are quite likely to kill you.

Insults are forgiven if they are uttered in a state of rage or desperation, when a person is blinded by deep grief – for example, if his mother or father or a close friend dies. In such cases the question of justice is not even mentioned; he is judged to have been 'beside himself', and there the matter ends.

Insults are not approved, however, in a quarrel that arises from gambling or criminal activities, or in matters of the heart, or in relations between friends: in all these cases the use of swear-words and offensive phrases usually means certain death.

But the most serious insult of all is that known as *baklanka*, when a group or a whole community is insulted. No explanations are accepted: you deserve either death or 'lowering' – a permanent transfer to the community of the lowered, the tainted, like the people who lived in the district of Bam.

So from childhood onwards we learned to 'filter words', and always to keep a check on what came out of our mouths, so as not to make a mistake, even unwittingly. For according to the Siberian rule, a word that has flown can never return.

The insult the Georgian had thrown at us was quite a serious one: he had said 'you have come like snakes', so he had offended us all.

So we performed the typical scene known in slang as 'purchase'. This is one of the many tricks that are used among criminals to conclude a negotiation favourably; we

Siberians are adept at these tricks. The principle of the 'purchase' is that of convincing your adversary that he is in the wrong and making him yield little by little, until you utterly terrorize him and take complete control of the situation, which in slang is termed 'purchasing'.

Our whole gang, following Gagarin's example, turned their backs on the Georgians. This gesture rendered them powerless, because it meant we had deprived them of all rights of criminal communication, even that of starting a fight.

It is normal to turn your back on people who are described as 'garbage', policemen or informers – those you despise so much you think they don't even deserve a bullet. But if you turn your back on another criminal, it's a different matter. You're sending a definite signal. You're telling him his behaviour has cost him his criminal dignity.

On the other hand, turning your back is always a risk. A true criminal will never attack someone who has his back to him, but if the person is not familiar with criminal relations, or if he's treacherous, you might get a bullet in the back.

As we stood there with our backs turned, Gagarin explained to the Georgians that they had committed a serious error of conduct: they had insulted the juveniles of another district while they were carrying out a task that their community regarded as sacred, a task that must be respected by every criminal community.

'I renounce the responsibility of holding negotiations with you,' he added. 'If you want to shoot us in the back, go ahead. Otherwise, withdraw. In the next few days we'll present the question to the Authorities of Low River and ask for justice.'

Gagarin concluded with a master-stroke: he asked what their names were. In so doing he underlined another error committed by the Georgians, which was less serious but quite significant. Dignified criminals introduce themselves, exchange greetings and wish each other every blessing even before they start killing each other.

The Georgian spokesman didn't reply at once: it was clear that the purchase was working. Then he introduced himself as the brother of another man, a young criminal very close to the Count, and said:

'I'll let you go this time, but only because I don't want to complicate relations between our communities, which are already difficult enough.'

'Well,' Gagarin rebuked him sardonically, 'I think you've already done enough to worsen the situation – for yourself and for your superiors.'

Without saying goodbye to them we walked towards our cars.

When we left they were still there under the street lamp, talking among themselves. Evidently they still couldn't understand what had happened.

But it would all become clear very soon.

Three days later, to be precise, when Gagarin, Mel, Speechless and I made a formal 'request' to Grandfather Kuzya for the insult to the group and the threats.

After diplomatic negotiations with the criminals of various areas of the town, those louts were punished by the Georgians themselves, who were tired of the burden of being boycotted by the communities of other districts.

I know for a fact that some people of Centre threatened to close all the shops the Georgians owned in their area.

The thin boy who had spoken to us vanished into thin air. Some said he had been buried in a double grave: that was how troublesome corpses were hidden, by putting them in the same grave with another person. It was a certain way of making people disappear. The grave of one ordinary old man might contain several people who had been given up for lost by their community.

Leaving Caucasus, we headed for Centre, where we wanted to get some more information about the strangers who had been seen by Mino and his friends. We needed to find out if they had anything to do with our own sad case.

The road from Caucasus to the heart of Bender passed through a district called Balka, which in Russian simply means 'wooden beam', but in criminal slang means 'graveyard'. It had earned that name because it was the former site of the old cemetery of the Polish Jews. The Jewish quarter, my grandfather told me, had grown up around the cemetery and then expanded, from the 1930s onwards.

I could never go through Balka without remembering a beautiful and terrible story which my grandfather used to tell me. And which I will now tell you.

* * *

The spiritual leader of the Jewish community of Balka was an old man called Moisha. According to the legend he was the first Jew to arrive in Transnistria, and through his character and his strong personality he had earned everyone's respect. He had three sons and one daughter, who was, as we say, 'preparing for marriage' – that is, she was a young woman who had no other social task than that of looking after the house and learning how to obey her future husband, bring up his children and, as we say, 'cough into her fist' – that is, show total submission.

The rabbi's daughter was called Zilya, and she was a really beautiful girl, with big blue eyes. She helped her mother run a draper's shop in Centre, and many a customer would enter simply for the joy of spending a few moments in her company. Numerous Jewish families had asked the rabbi to give her in marriage to their sons, but he wouldn't accept any of them, because many years earlier, when Zilya was only a baby, he had promised her hand to a young man of Odessa, the son of a friend of his.

It was customary among Jews to make arranged marriages, on the initiative of the fathers of families that were interested in uniting their stock; on these sad occasions the bride and bridegroom knew nothing of each other, and they rarely agreed with their parents' choice, but they didn't dare to contradict them, and above all they didn't dare to break the traditions: for anyone who did so would be permanently expelled from the community. So they accepted their destiny with heavy hearts, and their whole life would become an eternal tragedy. It was such a well-known custom that even we Siberians used to joke among ourselves about the unhappiness of Jewish women, calling any hopeless and sad situation a 'Jewish wife'.

Zilya already seemed completely convinced. Like a good Jewish girl she accepted, without rebelling against her father, the idea of marriage to a man twenty years older than her and – to judge from what people said – one with many faults.

Then one day into the shop came Svyatoslav, a young Siberian criminal who had just arrived in Transnistria. He belonged to the gang of a famous criminal called 'Angel', who had terrorized the communists for more than ten years, robbing trains in Siberia. Svyatoslav had been wounded in a gun battle, and his friends had sent him to Transnistria to convalesce. They had given him some money to give to the community of the Siberians, who had welcomed him without any problems. Svyatoslav had no family; his parents were dead. To cut a long story short, Svyatoslav fell in love with Zilya, and she fell in love with him.

As etiquette required, he went to Rabbi Moisha's house and asked him for his daughter's hand, but the rabbi dismissed him scornfully, thinking he was a pauper because his appearance was modest and, in accordance with Siberian law, he didn't flaunt his wealth.

After suffering this humiliation, Svyatoslav appealed to the Guardian of Low River, who at that time was a criminal by the name of Sidor, nicknamed 'Lynx's Paw', an old Siberian Urka. After listening to his account of the matter, Lynx's Paw thought the Jew might have reacted like that because he had doubts about Svyatoslav's financial position, so he advised him not to despair, but to go back to the rabbi with some jewels to offer as a gift to his daughter.

Siberian custom requires that the bridegroom himself make a proposal of marriage, but that he be accompanied by a member of his family, or in extreme cases by an old friend. So, in order to respect the law, Lynx's Paw suggested that he himself should accompany Svyatoslav on his second attempt. They arrived at the rabbi's house with many precious jewels, and again presented his suit, but again the rabbi dismissed them scornfully, even daring to insult them. Putting the jewels in his hand, he pretended that his palm had been burnt and dropped them on the floor, and when his guests asked him what had burnt him, he replied:

'The human blood they are covered with.'

The two Siberians went away, already knowing what they had to do. Lynx's Paw gave Svyatoslav permission to take the rabbi's daughter to live in the Siberian quarter, if she agreed.

The beautiful Zilya ran away from home that very same night. Under Siberian law she could not take any possession from her father's house except herself, so Svyatoslav had even brought her some clothes for her elopement.

Next day the rabbi sent some Jewish criminals to negotiate with the Siberians. Lynx's Paw explained to these men that according to our law any person who reaches the age of eighteen is free to do what they want, and it is a great sin to oppose this, especially when it is a question of forming a new family and of love, which are two God-willed things. The Jews showed their arrogance and threatened Lynx's Paw with death. At that point he lost his temper and killed three of them instantly with a wooden chair; the fourth one he struck on the arm, breaking it, and sent him to Rabbi Moisha with these words:

'He who names death doesn't know that it is closest to him.'

At this all hell broke loose. Moisha, finding himself up against Siberians, about whom he knew nothing except that they were murderers and robbers who always stuck together, couldn't challenge them on their own territory, so he asked the Jews of Odessa to help him.

The leaders of the Jewish community of Odessa, who were very rich and powerful, organized a meeting to discover where the truth lay, and how justice could be done. Everyone attended, including Svyatoslav, Zilya and Moisha.

After listening to both sides, the Jews tried to blame Svyatoslav, accusing him of kidnapping Moisha's daughter, but the Siberians replied that according to Siberian law she had not been kidnapped, because she had left of her own free will, and this was proved by the fact that she had left in her father's house everything that linked her with that place.

Moisha retorted that there was one thing she had taken away: a coloured ribbon with which she bound up her hair. It was true – Zilya had forgotten to take it off, and Moisha's wife had noticed it.

Such a tiny detail was enough to turn the situation against the Siberians. According to our rules, now the girl would have to be returned to her father. But there was one objection.

Zilya, the Siberians said, had already married Svyatoslav, and in order to do so she had converted to the Orthodox faith and had been baptized with the Siberian Cross: therefore, according to our laws, the powers of the parents could no longer extend over her, since they were of a faith different from hers. However, if Moisha, too, converted to the Orthodox faith, his word would carry a different weight . . .

In a fury, Moisha tried to stab Svyatoslav with a knife, and wounded him.

And thereby he made a serious mistake: he violated the peace in a criminal meeting, a crime that must be punished by immediate hanging.

To take his own life, Moisha decided to use that ribbon of cloth that his daughter wore in her hair. He died cursing Zilya and her husband, wishing every evil on their children, on their children's children and on all those who loved them.

Soon afterwards Zilya fell ill. Her condition deteriorated, and no medicine could cure her. So Svyatoslav took her to Siberia, to see an old shaman of the tribe of the Nency, a native Siberian people who had always had very close ties with the Siberian criminals, the Urkas.

The shaman said the girl was suffering because an evil spirit always kept her in the chill of death, removing the warmth of life from her. To stop the spirit it was necessary to burn the place that still tied him to this world. So returning to Transnistria, Svyatoslav, with the help of other Siberians, set fire to Rabbi Moisha's house, and later to the synagogue too.

Zilya recovered, and the two of them continued to live in our district for a long time. They had six sons: two of them murdered policemen and died young in prison; one went to live in Odessa, and in time set up a flourishing trade in clothes with fake brand-names (he was the most successful of all the brothers); and the other three lived in our district and carried out robberies; the youngest of them, Zhora, belonged to the gang led by my father.

In their old age Svyatoslav and Zilya went to end their lives in the Tayga, as they had always wanted to do.

After the synagogue was burned down by the Siberians many Jews left the area. The last of them were deported by the Nazis during the Second World War, and all that remains of that community now is the old cemetery.

Abandoned for years, it became a desolate place, where rubbish was dumped and kids went to fight. The graves were looted by some members of the Moldovan community, who committed this outrage against the dead simply to get stone ornaments that they could use as decorations for the gates outside their houses: this custom was the origin of a very offensive proverb: 'A Moldovan's soul is as beautiful as his garden gate.'

In the 1970s the Ukrainians started building houses in the old Jewish quarter. A lot of promiscuous girls lived there, and we often had parties with them. All you had to do to pull a Balka girl was buy her a drink, because not having a strict upbringing like the girls of Low River they saw sex as just fun; but as often happens in these cases, their over-lax behaviour became a kind of malaise, and many of them remained trapped in their own sexual freedom. They usually started having sex at the age of fourteen, or even earlier. By the time they were eighteen each one of them was already known to the whole town; it was convenient for the men to have women who were always ready to sleep with them without asking for anything in exchange. It was a game, which lasted until the man got fed up with one and moved on to another.

When they grew to adulthood, many Balka girls became aware of their situation and felt a great emptiness; they too wanted to have a family, find a husband and be like other women, but that was no longer possible: the community had permanently branded them, and no worthy man would ever be able to marry them.

Those poor souls, realizing they could no longer enjoy the positive emotions that are given by a simple life, committed suicide in appalling numbers. This phenomenon of girls killing themselves was rather shocking for our town, and many men, when they realized the origin of their despair, refused to have sex with them, so as not to participate in the destruction of their lives.

I knew an old criminal from Centre called Vitya, who was nicknamed 'Kangaroo', because in his youth he had been wounded in the legs in a gunfight and ever since then had had a strange, hopping kind of gait. He was the owner of a number of nightclubs in various towns in Russia, and had always had a weakness for the girls of Balka. After the first cases of suicide Kangaroo was the first to guess the true extent of the problem, and vowed in front of a lot of people that he would no longer seek their

company, and suggested the matter be discussed openly
with the girls' families. But the Ukrainians had a strange
sense of dignity: they let their daughters put themselves
in compromising situations, but then pretended they
didn't know anything about it and were furious if anyone
spoke the truth. Consequently many of them were
hostile to Kangaroo's initiative, saying it was a plot to
bring dishonour into their district. Later there were very
unpleasant developments: some fathers actually killed
their daughters with their own hands just to show others
they didn't accept any kind of interference.

The situation deteriorated partly because of the
incredible consumption of alcohol by the people of that
district. The Ukrainians drank a lot, a habit they shared
with the rest of the Soviet population, certainly, but they
did so in a particularly unrestrained manner, without the
filter of tradition and without a trace of morality. In Siberia
alcohol is drunk in obedience to certain reasonable rules,
so as not to cause irreparable damage to one's health:
accordingly, Siberian vodka is made exclusively of wheat,
and is purified with milk, which removes the residue of
the manufacturing process, so that the final product has a
perfect purity. Moreover, vodka must only be drunk with
food (in Siberia people eat a lot, and dishes are very rich,
because you burn off a large amount of fat in resisting
the cold and preserving vitamins in winter): if you eat
the right dishes, it is possible to drink as much as a litre
of vodka per person without any problem. In Ukraine,
however, they drink vodka of various kinds: they extract
the alcohol from potatoes or pumpkins, and the sugary
substances make you drunk at once. The Siberians never

get too drunk, don't pass out and don't vomit, but the Ukrainians drink themselves unconscious, and it can take them as long as two days to work off the hangover.

So life in Balka, formerly the Jewish and later the Ukrainian quarter, was like one long party, but a party with a sad atmosphere, with a nostalgia for something simple and human which those people could no longer have.

My grandfather always used to say that this happens when men are forgotten by God: they remain alive, but are no longer really alive. My own opinion was that it was an extreme form of social degradation affecting the whole community, perhaps because the young people who had come to live in our town had broken violently away from their parents and had been left to themselves, and without any form of control they had burned themselves up, indulging in all kinds of vice. And, in turn, without the support of their old folk they brought up their own children badly.

The Ukrainians' sons were notorious as mothers' boys, and as people incapable of doing anything useful either for themselves or for others. In Bender nobody trusted them because they were always telling lies to make themselves seem important, but they did it so clumsily that no one could possibly have believed them: we just treated them as poor idiots. Some of them even tried to make money by inventing non-existent laws: for example, that a brother could force his sister to prostitute herself. The exploitation of prostitution had always been considered an offence unworthy of a criminal: men convicted of that kind of crime were liable to be killed in jail; it could happen outside as well, to tell the truth, but it was rare for them to get out of prison alive. The Ukrainians simply didn't understand this; they would wander around the districts of the town, trying in vain to get into the bars and nightclubs. All doors were always closed to them, since the money they wanted to spend had been earned in an unworthy manner. They went on without stopping to wonder why, creating an increasingly deep rift between their community and the rest of the town.

There was only one road through the district of Balka, and by the side of it there was a kiosk run by an old Ukrainian criminal by the name of Stepan, who sold cigarettes, drinks, and now and then drugs, usually the kind you smoke. He would also sell you weapons and ammunitions from the Ukrainian military bases, which he obtained with the help of his elder brother, a career soldier.

Stepan was partially paralysed, because he had once drunk some alcohol intended for scientific use. When he told the story of that terrible day he always made a joke of it: as soon as he realized that the left side of his body was on the point of losing all feeling, he said, in the nick of time he'd flipped his 'honourable member' over to the right-hand side and thereby saved it.

I often stopped to chat with him, because I loved to see his spirit and his good humour even in his pretty desperate situation. He would sit all day in his wheelchair under a big umbrella, talking to the people who passed by. He had a daughter, perhaps the only respectable girl in the whole district, who looked after him and was studying to be an architect. His wife had left him shortly before he was paralysed; she had run off with her lover, a young male nurse. I respected Stepan because he had succeeded in bringing up his daughter while remaining exactly what he was, a simple, uneducated person, but to judge from the results also a good one, capable of transmitting his natural affability to others.

His kiosk was always open. By day he ran it himself, sometimes with his daughter's help, and at night it was run by his trusty assistant, a boy by the name of Kiril, whom everybody called 'Nixon' because he was obsessed with American presidents. A lot of people said he was retarded, but I think he just liked to take things slowly. Stepan used to pay him in food and cigarettes. Nixon smoked, and did so in a very theatrical manner: he seemed like an actor. He also had a dog, a small, ugly and very nasty mongrel, who with the most humble and amiable of expressions on its face would bite your ankles when you were least expecting it. Nixon used to call him 'my secretary', or sometimes *dorogoy gospodin*, 'my dear sir'. The dog had no other name.

If you got into conversation with Nixon he would start criticizing the communists, saying they wanted to destroy his country and calling them 'dirty terrorists'. He said he didn't trust anyone except his 'secretary', who would then demonstrate his devotion by knocking his disgustingly mangy little tail against his master's leg.

'The Arabs have pissed me off,' he said, 'and Fidel Castro should be killed, but that's impossible. And do you know why? Because he's hiding in Siberia, where he's protected by the communists. They've replaced him in Cuba with a double who doesn't even look like him: his beard is obviously false, and he smokes cigars without inhaling.'

That was the way Nixon was. 'And do you know what the American flag represents?' he would ask. 'I'll tell you: a dead communist. The stars are his brain, which was blown to smithereens when he was shot in the head, and the red and white stripes are his blood-spattered skin.'

He hated blacks – he said their presence had stopped the progress of democracy – and he got Martin Luther King mixed up with Michael Jackson, saying that 'he was a good nigger, he liked dancing and singing', but that some other niggers had killed him just because one day he had decided to become a white.

When we approached the kiosk we found Nixon sitting on his presidential chair as usual, playing Tetris. I was the first to get out of the car, and when he saw me he ran over to to greet me, as he always did with people he liked. I gave him a hug and asked him to wake Stepan because it was urgent. He immediately rushed off to his house, which was only a few dozen metres away.

Nixon couldn't stand having my friend Mel around: for some unknown reason he was convinced he was a spy; once he had even given him a couple of blows with an iron bar because he was so scared of him. Because of this I had told Mel to stay in the car and not show himself, so as not to stir up a quarrel in the middle of the night. However, when Nixon had gone to call Stepan, Mel had got out of the car to relieve himself in the nearby bushes. And while Mel peed, making a noise like a waterfall, Nixon arrived, pushing a wheelchair with a still half-asleep Stepan on it.

Since I knew Stepan better than the others did, I stayed to talk to him, with Speechless; the others either waited in the cars or drank beer by the kiosk.

Stepan must have guessed that something important was at stake, because he didn't joke as he usually did. I apologized for waking him at that time of night and told him our sad story. As I talked I saw the living side of his face become a kind of mask, like the ones the Japanese use to represent their demons.

He was angry. When I mentioned the reward he made a contemptuous gesture with his hand and said he had something to give us. He called Nixon and gave him an order: the boy disappeared and returned after a few minutes with a cardboard box in his hands. Stepan gave it to me, saying he was a humble and poor person and couldn't give us anything more, but in its own small way this was the most beautiful and useful thing he had.

He opened the box: inside was a Stechkin with silencer and stabilizer, and six magazines full of ammunition. A splendid and pretty expensive weapon: the only pistol made in the USSR that could fire a continuous burst, with twenty shots in the magazine.

I thanked him and said that if it was all right with him I would gladly pay for it, but Stepan refused, saying it was okay, all he asked was that I tell our elders about his gesture. He promised me he would keep his ears open, and that if he heard anything interesting he would let me know at once. Before leaving I tried at least to pay for what the boys had consumed at his kiosk – a few beers, cigarettes and some food – but again he wouldn't hear of it. So I slipped a little money into the pocket of Nixon, who waved to us delightedly, like a little child, as we got into the cars.

Two hundred metres further on Mel was waiting for us: to avoid a clash with Nixon he had gone through the bushes, and he was angry, because in the darkness he'd got scratched all over his face.

Nobody wanted to take Stepan's gun, because – it emerged – they all had at least two on them already. So I took it myself.

We were approaching Centre, and the dark of the night was becoming ever more transparent: day was breaking, the second day of our search.

In the car I slept for a while, without dreaming about anything in particular, as if I'd fallen into a void. When I woke up we were already in Centre and the cars had stopped in the yard of a house. Except for me and Mel, who was still asleep, the boys were all outside, talking to two guys by a door.

I got out of the car and went over to the others. I asked Grave what was happening and he replied that the two people Gagarin was talking to were assistants of the Guardian of Centre.

'What have they been saying?'

'That they don't know anything about what happened by the phone boxes. And they haven't heard anything about strangers pestering a girl in their district.'

Shortly afterwards the two guys went away.

'Well?' I asked Gagarin.

'It's a challenge for them now: admitting they know nothing about it is like admitting they're out of the loop. It might land them in serious trouble, if that really is the case. Anyway, they've asked us to give them time to check all the facts. And not to tell the Guardian, for the time being. They've assured us of their complete cooperation. We've arranged to meet again at noon under the old bridge.'

So we got back into the car and decided to go and have breakfast in a place called Blinnaya, which means 'The Pancake Parlour', in the district called The Bank.

The Bank was situated in the most attractive part of the town, where there was a big park on the river with beaches and places where you could relax and pass the time pleasurably. The most expensive restaurants, bars and night clubs were all there. There was also a clandestine gambling den, where admission was strictly by invitation.

The district was run by various Bender criminals, and was a kind of tourist attraction: a lot of people came from Odessa – rich Jews and merchants of various kinds – because it was highly fashionable to breathe in the air of exotic criminality. But the real criminals of the town were forbidden to settle their personal scores in the Bank; if some people created a few problems or got a bit rowdy it was only an act put on specially for the guests, to make them believe they'd come to a disreputable area: a way of making them feel a bit threatened, to raise their adrenaline. In reality no one ever committed any serious crimes in that district.

The Blinnaya made the best pancakes in the whole town. In Russia pancakes are called *bliny*, and everyone has their own way of cooking them: the best ones are those made by the Cossacks of the Don, who add yeast to the mixture, which they then quickly scorch on red-hot pans smeared with butter, so that the *bliny* turn out thick and very greasy, crisp and with an unforgettable flavour.

There at the Blinnaya people ate them in the Siberian manner, with sour cream mixed with honey, drinking black tea with lemon.

We were pretty tired. There were quite a few people in the restaurant. We ordered fifty *bliny*, just to start with (on average a Russian will eat at least fifteen *bliny* at a time, and guys like Mel and Gagarin as many as three times that number). In three minutes the plate was empty. We ordered several more helpings. We took the tea straight from the samovar that stood on the table; every now and then the waiter came to add more water to it. That's normal in my country: in many restaurants you can drink as much tea as you like; every person, however much food he orders, can drink all the tea he can get inside him, and it's free.

As we ate and drank we discussed the situation. The morale of the group was fairly high, as was our anger and our desire for justice.

'I can't wait to break the back of the bastard who raped her,' said Speechless.

I thought our situation must be really exceptional, seeing as that was the second time Speechless had spoken in two days.

Then I thought we were really a strange group. I thought about the lives each of us had led. Gigit and Besa, in particular.

Gigit was the son of a Siberian criminal; his mother was an Armenian woman who had died when he was six, murdered by one of her brothers because by marrying a Siberian criminal she had insulted the name of the family.

He was a bright boy, with a strong sense of justice: in fights he was always one of the first to enter the fray, so he had a lot of scars. A couple of times he had been wounded quite seriously, and on one of those occasions I had given him my blood, which is compatible with all groups. Since then he had been convinced that we had become blood brothers; he tried to watch my back in every situation, and would always be there when I needed him. We were friends; we understood each other almost without speaking. He was a quiet person; he liked reading, and I could talk to him about literature. Quiet up to a point, though: he had beaten a Centre boy to death with a hammer for trying to humiliate him in the eyes of a girl he wanted to impress – a girl Gigit had gone out with for a while and remained good friends with afterwards.

Besa was a real tough guy. He was a year younger than me, but looked much older, because he already had a lot of white hairs. He wasn't born in our area; he came from Siberia. His mother, Aunt Svetlana, was the leader of a small gang of robbers, with whom she carried out *turne*, literally 'tours', series of robberies carried out from town to town. They used to rob rich people – local politicians, but especially the so-called 'hidden industrialists', people involved in illegal manufacturing and trade, who had links with the managers of the big factories. The phenomenon of a woman leading a gang was quite common in Siberia: women with a criminal role are affectionately called 'mama', 'mama cat' or 'mama thief', and are always listened to; their opinion is considered to be a perfect solution, a kind of pure criminal wisdom.

Besa's mother had been in prison several times, and he had been born in the special-regime women's prison of Magadan, in Siberia. Born in jail, he had experienced freedom for the first time at the age of eight. His prison upbringing was very obvious, and had left an indelible mark: an immense anger, above all.

Besa had never known his father. His mother said she had spent one night, out of pity, with a man who had been condemned to death, after being moved by train to the prison of Kurgan. She was put in a special block, and as soon as she arrived in her cell she received a letter from the next cell: a young boy nicknamed 'Besa', which means 'little devil', asked her to spend the night with him. Out of compassion and a sort of criminal solidarity she agreed to the condemned man's request, and after paying the guards she was taken to his cell. She became pregnant.

A few months later she learned through the prisoners' secret mail system that the biological father of the son she was carrying in her womb had been executed a week after their meeting. So she decided to give the baby his name. All she knew about the man was that he had been a killer of policemen, that he had been good-looking and that he'd had a lot of white hairs; and Besa must have inherited them, because, as his mother used to say, he was as close a likeness to his father as Adam was to God the creator.

Ever since I'd known him Besa had had an obsession. In the prison where he had grown up he had heard from another child the story of the Kremlin star, the one on top of the main tower, where the gigantic clock is. According to the story, the star weighed five hundred kilos and was made of solid gold, but had been covered with red paint out of prudence. Many similar stories circulate among the children of criminals, especially in the juvenile prisons: they always concern a fabulous treasure hidden in some well-known place in full view of everyone and yet very hard to steal; but if you succeed in stealing it, it will set you up for life. One such story concerns the diamonds that Tsarina Catherine II is said to have hidden in the Bridge of Hope in Moscow, together with the body of her housekeeper, whom she is supposed to have killed with her own hands for trying to steal them. Another concerns the golden armour of the knight Elya of Murom, which is reputed to be buried under the monument of Tsar Alexander III in a monastery near Moscow.

All these stories were told in order to pass the time and create a mystery, but the mystery was always connected with criminal activity, so no one could say when you got to the end of the story that it had been a waste of time. After two hours of intrigue among the bourgeoisie, of descriptions of life in the Tsar's palace, of wars, heroes, knights, ghosts, mysterious thieves, and murders committed with sophisticated techniques, there was always a treasure to be stolen: a treasure that was just waiting for someone to go and get it.

After such a story, nine times out of ten the listeners would ask:

'Well, since you know the secret, why don't you make use of it? Why don't you get your hands on that treasure?'

The most effective answer was usually:

'I'm an honest criminal; all I ask is that you give me a little cigarette money for telling you this story.'

Everyone would give a contribution and then they would start planning how to recover the treasure by destroying the national monuments. Besa was no exception: he, too, had worked out a plan for getting the star down from the Kremlin tower. Periodically he would go back to the plan to improve on it a little: for example, at first he didn't know you couldn't just walk into the Kremlin, and when he did find this out (thanks to me), he decided to fake some guards' identity papers, kidnap five of them on their way to work and then enter the Kremlin disguised as guards. Initially he thought of lifting the star down with a crane, which he intended to steal from a building site. Then he decided on a more risky course: he would saw it off manually, after first securing it with ropes, then drop it down to the ground (after all, we didn't care about its condition – we were going to break it up into pieces afterwards anyway, to extract the gold), and finally pick it up and put it into a car to carry it out of the Kremlin. To prevent the star making too much noise when it hit the ground it would be necessary, according to Besa's plan, to cover it with rags.

Besa never stopped planning this crime of the century, and we had the honour of being included in his plan as assistants. He talked about it seriously, and given the vagaries of his fiery personality none of us dared to contradict him.

Meanwhile we continued our humble criminal activities without carrying out any crimes of the century. For the moment we were happy to participate in some black marketeering and try to keep Besa in the creative phase of his plan, so that he never reached the decisive phase, let alone the executive one. But lately he had grown rather restive – I think because he was beginning to realize that we weren't particularly interested in stealing the Kremlin star.

Outside the Blinnaya, our stomachs full, we decided to split up. Gagarin would drive around the bars with Grave, Cat and Gigit, talking to the criminals of the district, while Mel, Speechless, Besa and I would go and see an old friend of my father's, Uncle Fedya, who owned a mega-disco on the other side of town and knew everything about everybody, and could even recount events that hadn't yet happened, using his criminal sensibility and his knowledge of human nature.

Uncle Fedya was what in the criminal community is called a 'Saint'. This is a term of the highest respect. A Saint is a person who lives according to very strict rules of self-control and tries in every sphere of his life to be a perfect example of the criminal ideal. The Saint lives in isolation from everyone, like a kind of hermit, and like the old Authorities he possesses nothing of his own; even the clothes he wears are not his, but gifts from other criminals. But unlike the Authorities he has no real power over other criminals, simply living his life as an example to them.

The Saint sends all his earnings into prison. Often the administrator of the *obshchak* – the criminals' common fund – finds it difficult to satisfy everyone, especially in large prisons, where there are more than thirty thousand people and the structure is divided into hundreds of blocks. And often the assistants cannot agree among themselves how to divide up the funds. At that point it is always the Saint who supports them, because with his earnings he can get round any kind of internal conflict.

The Saint has no right to judge other criminals, and must remain neutral in all conflicts, but he may help to resolve them by communicating with all parties without getting personally involved. However, unlike the old Authorities he is allowed to touch money and commit crimes himself.

No one can become a Saint through his own wishes: it is a role that, like all roles in the criminal community, is given to you on the basis of your abilities and your particular talents.

The position of Saint is the rarest of all in the criminal community: in practice it is these men who administer the circulation of funds. It is they who collect the money from all the communities and send it to the prisons, either as cash or in the form of material aid. Consequently, Saints are closely protected.

In the whole of Bender there had only ever been three Saints. The first, Grandfather Dimyan, known as 'Fur Hat', died of old age in the late 1980s, and was a Siberian of our district. The second, Uncle Kostya, known as 'Wood', also from our district, was killed in a gun battle with the police in St Petersburg in the early 1990s. The third was Uncle Fedya, the last Saint of Bender.

He was a cheerful and very optimistic person; he seemed more like a monk than a criminal. In his youth he had killed three policemen and been condemned to death, but later the sentence had been reduced to life imprisonment. After he had spent thirty years inside a special-regime prison they had released him, judging him to be an 'individual suitable for reintroduction into society'. He was over fifty by then. Soon he became a Saint. He organized various black market operations with a group of loyal Siberian criminals, and ran a bar. They lived together in the same house, without families: they were completely at the service of the criminal world; they helped people in prison and those who had just been released, and they supported the families of deceased criminals and elderly ones.

If anything happened in town you could be sure Uncle Fedya's men would know about it. They were also in contact with prisoners held in even the most distant jails, as far away as Siberia, and could get any information they needed extremely quickly.

In view of their position in our society I thought it was very important to tell them what had happened. Even if it didn't produce any positive leads for our inquiries, it would be a sign of respect on our part, and might win us some secondary assistance in gathering information.

We reached the Saint's house. It was a kind of tenement block, with a yard and a fine garden full of small tables and benches. In accordance with the old tradition, the front door had been taken off its hinges and thrown on the ground, as a sign that the house was open to all, and indeed there were always guests; people came from all over the USSR to visit the Saint and his friends.

I too had often been a guest in that house, because my father was a good friend of Uncle Fedya's. They had done business together and shared a passion for pigeons. My father used to give him pigeons because he couldn't buy anything for himself: the Saint would keep them but say they were my father's, and if in conversation I should let slip a compliment to one of 'his' pigeons, Uncle Fedya would always correct me, saying that those pigeons weren't his, and that he only kept them because there was no room at our house.

As usual, Uncle Fedya was on the roof, where he kept 'my father's pigeons' in a special shed. He saw me and beckoned to me to come up; I pointed to my companions and he repeated the gesture, inviting us all up. We went indoors and walked up three flights of stairs, greeting everyone we met, until we came to the door that led up to the roof. Before opening it we took off the weapons we were carrying, leaving them on a shelf on which there was a bucket of food for the pigeons. According to the rules, no one may appear before a Saint armed. You can't even carry a knife, and that should be stressed, because usually the knife is regarded as a cult object, like the cross, which you must always have on you. Even the knife must be laid aside when you meet a Saint, to emphasize each criminal's position with respect to his power, which is greater than that of force and of money.

While we were leaving our guns and knives, Mel saw me putting Grandfather Kuzya's Nagant on the shelf. He looked amazed and asked me where I'd got it.

'I'll tell you later,' I said. 'It's a long story.'

I opened the little door and at last we went up the narrow stairway that led to the roof. Uncle Fedya was standing there among the pigeons, which were pecking at grains of wheat; he had a pair of pigeons in his hand. I noticed that they were of the Baku breed, so they would be good at flying and especially at 'hitting' – that's what we call the way the males of some breeds have of displaying their agility to attract the attention of the females.

We greeted Uncle Fedya, and my friends introduced themselves. As tradition requires, first I had to talk for a while about matters which had nothing to do with our visit: this is not just a formal rule; it is done to enable you to assess the other person's state of mind and to judge whether that is the right moment for discussing the matter that is your main concern. So I asked him about his health and made some small talk about pigeons, until he asked me what brought me there.

'I came for "a bit of a chat",' I replied.

In conversation, especially with important figures in the criminal world, it is usual to talk ironically about the problems you need their help in solving. In the same way the Authorities themselves never begin discussions about their life or about some personal question as if they were matters of the greatest importance: they speak of themselves with lightness and humility. For example, if you ask a criminal how his affairs are going, he will answer ironically that his affairs are all under investigation by the Public Prosecutor's office, and that he is only occupying himself with bagatelles, trifles, matters of no importance.

That is why I was obliged to present our problem rather nonchalantly, saying that I'd come for a 'bit of a chat', something of no great consequence.

He smiled and said he already knew what had happened. He asked me to tell him how our inquiries were going. Briefly, and without going into too much detail, I explained the situation to him; he listened calmly and patiently, but now and then he sighed heavily.

When I had finished he stood motionless for a while, thinking it over; then suddenly he said it would be better if we went downstairs and sat at the table and drank some chifir, because 'it's hard to find the truth standing up'.

We went downstairs with him. There were already two old criminals sitting at the table, whom Uncle Fedya at once introduced to us. They were guests of his who had come from a little Siberian village on the River Amur.

The tea ceremony began.

Uncle Fedya prepared the chifir himself. All his teeth were dark, almost black: an unmistakable sign of the habitual chifir drinker. After heating the water on the wood stove, he took the *chifirbak* off the fire, put it on the table and poured a whole packet of Irkutsk tea into it.

As we waited for the chifir to brew, Uncle Fedya recounted our story to his guests, who listened to him sadly. One of the two, a big, strong man with a tattooed face, crossed himself every time Ksyusha's name was mentioned.

Uncle Fedya poured the chifir into the mug, took three long swigs and passed it on to me. It was strong and boiling hot and 'caught' well: that's what we say when the chifir has an immediate effect, giving a slight sensation of light-headedness. We passed the chifir round three times; Mel took the last swig, then washed the mug, as tradition prescribes.

Finally Uncle Fedya put on the table a dish of sweets, perfect for tempering the strong taste of chifir that remained in the mouth. My favourites were those that had the flavour of *klyuchva*, a very sour berry that grows on small bushes in northern Russia, in marshy areas. As we ate the sweets we started talking again.

Uncle Fedya said that the people who ran his clubs already knew the whole story, and that if any interesting news had been reported at 'The Cage' – the largest and most spectacular disco in town, where large numbers of people went – they would certainly have passed it on to him at once.

Then he laid on the table his financial contribution to the cause. One of the guests immediately imitated him, producing a pack of dollars – no less than ten thousand; and finally, without a word, the Siberian giant with the tattooed face, who was known as 'Cripple', added another five thousand.

Uncle Fedya also gave us a couple of tips: he advised us to go back to the district of Bam.

'It's hard to have an honest conversation with those people; terror tactics are better,' he said, winking at me. 'If you fire a few shots and someone gets killed, it won't matter; they'd kill each other anyway, sooner or later. If you scare them they'll actually start doing something, and who knows, in the midst of all the trash that lives there perhaps they'll find your man.'

He also advised us to put more pressure on the people of Centre; after all, it was partly their fault if the girl had been raped in their territory. In his opinion – and people like the Saint were rarely mistaken – all the leaders of Centre might as well 'write letters home' – that is, prepare for a violent clash with the unknown.

Uncle Fedya didn't approve of Gagarin's generous decision to give the Centre boys half a day to gather information without the Guardian's knowledge.

'For the love of Jesus Christ,' he said, 'what do we care if the Guardian is angry with them? He'd be perfectly right to be angry, because they're a bunch of incompetent fools. These people of Centre only think about womanizing and playing cards; they look like gipsies with all the gold they wear, and then, when something happens in their area, they're left with the shit between their legs, stinking in front of the whole town . . . No, you go straight to the Guardian now, and tell him that if he doesn't bring you by this evening the idiots who've been causing trouble in his area while he and his men were sleeping, you'll tell all the Authorities about the matter . . . They'll bring them to you on a blue-edged salver, you'll see . . .'

While he was saying all this, I was already imagining the scene. We wouldn't even be allowed to see the Guardian of Centre, let alone rebuke him and threaten him. However, as my late lamented uncle used to say: 'A person who takes no risks drinks no champagne.'

Thanking Uncle Fedya for his hospitality, his excellent advice and the money for increasing the reward, we went to join the rest of our group so that we could plan our rendezvous with the Centre guys.

We had arranged to meet the others at a bar owned by old Plum, a criminal who hadn't participated in any criminal activities for a long time and just ran his bar, or rather, sat at a table drinking or eating, while two young girls, his granddaughters, did all the work.

Plum was well known in the town for the life of hardship and suffering that he had led. He wasn't born into a criminal family: his parents were educated people, intellectuals – his father was a scientist, and his mother taught literature at the University of Moscow. In the late 1930s, when Stalin's regime unleashed a wave of terror, his parents were arrested and declared enemies of the people. His father was accused of having links with American and British spies, his mother of anti-Soviet propaganda. The whole family, including the two children – Plum, who was twelve at that time, and his sister Lesya, who was only three – were deported to the gulag of Vorkuta.

There the communist comrades, patriots and builders of peace throughout the land, subjected political prisoners to the most inhuman tortures. Plum's father, who was physically very weak, died in the train from the beatings he had taken, and a bad attack of pneumonia. When they arrived in Vorkuta, the mother and the two children were not separated, but only because the children's block had not been built yet. They lived in Vorkuta for a long time, seeing many people die around them of cold, disease, parasites, mistreatment and malnutrition.

Plum told how one day he, his sister and his mother had been taken to a place where the so-called 'special squad of internal investigators' operated: a gang of butchers who tortured condemned people – not in order to obtain information, but for 're-educational' reasons. The mother was made to strip and to undress her children in front of the guards, after which they had started to beat her, standing the children in a corner and forcing them to watch their mother being tortured. Then those animals took Plum and invented a game: they told him that if his mother didn't break his sister's little finger with her own hands, they would break all his fingers, one by one. In a long and terrible process of torture, they broke six of his fingers in front of his mother. He said he had been terrified and kept screaming that he couldn't stand any more, and eventually his mother, in a fit of madness and desperation, took little Lesya, whom she was holding in her arms, and dashed her head against the wall. Then she tried to kill him too, but the cops managed to stop her and beat her savagely. She was never to leave that block alive.

Plum was thrown outside on the snow to die of cold, with his fingers broken, and half-dead. He said the only thing he had hoped for was to die as soon as possible, so he had started to eat the snow, in order to freeze more quickly. At that time a group of ordinary prisoners were working nearby, cutting wood to build the huts that were needed for the enlargement of the gulag. When they saw the little boy in the snow they picked him up and took him under their protection. The guards turned a blind eye because in the gulags the ordinary prisoners – at least at the beginning, before the Soviet penitentiary system became a kind of perfect mechanism, a production line – were treated differently from the political ones. They were criminals and the administration feared them because they were united and very well organized, and if they wanted to they could start a real rebellion.

So Plum went to live with them in the huts. One of them healed his broken fingers by putting sticks of soft wood along them and carefully binding them on. From that day onwards the criminals looked after him and brought him up. They called him 'Plum' because of the colour of his face, which was always blue because he was always cold.

At the age of sixteen Plum became the 'executor' of the gang that had found him and taken him in. A war had broken out among the criminals in the camp, between those who supported the old Authorities – who included Plum's friends – and those who proclaimed themselves to be new Authorities, proposing new rules. The latter were in the majority; they came from the lowest social classes and belonged to the generation of war orphans;

394 · NICOLAI LILIN

they represented a criminal reality which had never been seen before, there or anywhere else in Russia, where characteristics such as ignorance, ferocity and the absence of moral laws were respected. One night Plum and his friends entered the huts of the *shigany* – the young, unscrupulous criminals – and stabbed them to death as they slept. Before the victims even realized what was happening half the hut had been killed.

Plum killed enormous numbers of people; I may be mistaken, but I suspect that is why he survived. Perhaps he managed to stay sane, despite the terrible trauma of his childhood, by giving vent to his anger in this way.

Plum endured many prisons and also lived a long time as a free man, always acting as a criminal executor. He married a good woman and had three sons and two daughters. On his right hand, where they had broken his fingers, he had a tattoo of a skull with a policeman's hat. On its forehead was written: '*Az vozdam*', which in the old Russian language means 'I will avenge myself'.

I don't know if he did avenge himself, but he was constantly killing policemen. He had a huge collection of badges of the police officers and members of the security forces he had killed during his career. He kept them on a large dresser in the red corner of his house, under the icons, where there was also a photograph of his family with a candle always burning in front of it.

I saw the collection with my own eyes. It was staggering. Dozens of badges of all periods, from the Fifties to the mid-Eighties – some blood-stained, others with bullet-holes in them. They were all there: policemen from the forces of towns all over Russia, members of special units formed to combat organized crime, KGB agents, prison guards, agents of the Public Prosecutor's office.

Plum said there were more than twelve thousand of them, but that he hadn't been able to recover the badges in every case. He remembered everything about each man with total precision: how and when he'd killed him. As I gazed at them, he kept repeating to me:

'Take a good look at them, son, these murderers' faces . . . Human tears never fall on the ground: the Lord catches them first.'

He said he had told his daughters to send those badges after his death to the Ministry of the Interior in Moscow, accompanied by a letter which he had been writing and rewriting all his life.

He showed me the letter. It wasn't so much a letter as an entire notebook in which he explained almost everything: the story of his life, the reasons for his anger, his view of the world. At the end he revealed the places where he had hidden the bodies of some policemen, and wrote that he was performing a generous act, because this would make it possible for the dead to have their graves, and even though many years had passed their families would know where to go and mourn them, whereas he had not been given the chance to weep on the graves of his father, his mother and his sister.

One section of that notebook contained his poems, which were very simple, naive, even coarse, in a sense, if you didn't consider the story that lay behind them. I remember one addressed to his little sister Lesya, perhaps the longest of all. He called her 'innocent angel of Our sweet Lord', and said that she smiled as 'the sky smiles after the rain', that her hair 'shone like the sun' and had the colour of 'a field of wheat that asks to be harvested'. He told her in simple and affectionate words, with no attempt at rhyme, how much he loved her; and he asked her to forgive him for not being able to hold out when the policemen were breaking his fingers, because he was 'small, only a child who was afraid of pain, like all children'. He told her that their mother's action, in dashing her head against the wall, had been 'the generous gesture of an affectionate mother who is driven to desperation; I know that you understand her and that now the two of you are together in Heaven with Our Lord'.

You could tell from the poem how simple and in many respects primitive, and yet how beautiful and generous Plum's soul was.

Now that he was old and his wife was dead, Plum was lonely. He always sought the company of the others in the bar, telling them stories about his life and showing them the life-size portrait of his family that he kept there.

I enjoyed talking to him; he was always ready to share his wisdom and teach me something.

It was thanks to him that I had learned to fire a pistol properly; my father, my uncle and my grandfather had taught me before, but I was too weak, and my hands were small and delicate, so when I fired I couldn't control the weapon very well – I gripped it too tightly. He took me down to the river, where you could shoot freely into the water without having to worry about hurting anyone, and said to me:

'Relax your hand, lad.'

We used the Tokarev 7.62, a quite large and powerful but well-balanced gun which didn't have much kick in the hand. Later he also taught me to shoot with two guns at the same time. This was called the Macedonian method because the ancient Macedonians fought with a sword in each hand.

So I often went to see him. Apart from anything else, one of his granddaughters was a good friend of mine, and made the best apple cakes in the whole town.

When we reached Plum's bar our friends hadn't arrived yet. He was at his table, as usual; he was having tea with cake and reading a book of poems. As soon as he saw me he put it down, came to meet me and gave me a hug:

'How are you, son? Have you caught him yet?'

He knew everything already, and I was relieved about that: at least I wouldn't have to retell that story, which I found very painful to put into words.

I told him we were still looking for the culprit, and he immediately offered me help, money and weapons.

I replied that we had already collected more than enough money, and probably more than enough guns. But, as they say in Siberia, 'so as not to offend the deaf old tiger, you must make a bit of noise when you walk', so I added:

'However, if you spread the word round among your customers and keep your ears open, it might be useful. And some of your granddaughter's cake with a cup of tea would be a great comfort.'

Soon afterwards we were all sitting round a table eating cake and drinking tea with lemon, which was just what we needed after Uncle Fedya's chifir. And that cake – as soon as you bit it, it melted in your mouth.

We discussed the advice that Uncle Fedya had given us. We all agreed with his words, and we realized that if we'd gone to see him earlier we would have saved ourselves a lot of time.

In the meantime the others arrived: they seemed tired – exhausted, in fact; Grave seemed even deader than usual, and when I looked at him I noticed that he had a faint bruise under his left eye. They were clearly excited.

'What's happened?' I asked.

Gagarin told us that while they were doing the rounds of the bars they had walked straight into the louts Mino had told us about. There were seven of them, in a black four-by-four with a Ukrainian numberplate. 'We asked them if we could speak to them,' he said, 'but instead of replying they started shooting at us. And one them hit Grave in the face with a Japanese thing.'

'With a what?' asked Besa.

'A kind of combat stick. You know, those things you see in martial arts films, the ones they whirl around really fast in their hands . . . When they drove off we tried to stop them – we fired at their car – but it was no good . . .'

'I hit one of them in the head, though, I could swear it,' added Gigit.

'The Wheel arrived with the car, but it was too late – the four-by-four had already gone,' said Gagarin. 'So I stopped at a phone box and called home to ask our elders to have road-blocks set up in all districts, to stop the car before it leaves town.'

As I looked at Grave's sad face, battered by a weapon straight out of a Japanese–American action film, and listened to that tale of gun fights and car chases, for a moment I thought we were all going mad. Then suddenly I felt an urge to do something, to move, to act. But, as my late uncle used to say, 'the mother cat doesn't give birth when she wants to, but when her time comes'.

I told Gagarin what Uncle Fedya had said.

'When I was talking to those two I did have my suspicions,' he said. 'They seemed to be hiding something. They wanted to get rid of us; they needed to gain time so they could do something . . . But what?'

We decided to go to the meeting-place anyway, under the old bridge.

'But to be on the safe side, Gagarin,' I said, 'maybe it's better if we don't all go. A group of three would be best, don't you think? And we'd better go on foot, so we can split up if there's any trouble . . .'

Gagarin agreed:

'Okay, but one of those three has to be me.'

'Better not,' said Mel. 'You were appointed by the elders; you're the leader of the mission. If anything happens to you the situation will only get worse.'

After a brief discussion we decided that Mel, Besa and I would go, and the others would wait nearby, ready to spring into action if necessary.

While we were in the car we made a plan: I would walk to the middle of the meeting place, under the old bridge, and watch the area in front and to the left, Mel would walk on the right and look to that side (after all, he only had a right eye), and Besa would bring up the rear and bend down occasionally to do up his shoelaces, to check the situation behind us.

We parked in a narrow street near the bridge; the others stayed in the car to wait for us. We spread out as we had agreed and walked slowly down towards the bridge, pretending to be just out for a stroll.

We had deliberately arrived ten minutes late, to keep the guys who were waiting for us guessing.

But when we reached the bridge there was no one there. We walked around the area, then went back to the cars.

Now we really would have to go and see the Guardian of Centre and say the things Uncle Fedya had recommended we say. It was obvious that his two assistants had done something really stupid, and that that was why they had played this trick on us.

We were flying towards Centre like a squadron of bombers. Furious and grim-faced, we already imagined the trouble there would be in town when our mission was completed. Mel and I even discussed the destiny of the Guardian, as if it were in our hands.

'They'll kill him for sure,' said Mel. 'He can't go unpunished after this demonstration of weakness. Being tricked by your assistants is worse than being a rat yourself.'

'I reckon they'll only lower him,' I said. 'They'll make him move to Bam, where he'll rot until the day some bastard kills him for his golden chain.'

It's not very normal for two teenagers to speculate about the future of an experienced Authority.

In the criminal world it's preferable to avoid getting into this kind of situation; even if everything around you is wrong and you're sure you're right, before turning your decisions into actions it's as well to 'cross yourself thirty times', as my grandfather used to say.

To be sitting on the crest of the highest wave in the sea is very nice, but how long can such a wave last? And what happens when that brute you're riding smashes you like a tiny parasite?

I always ask myself questions like that when I feel the need to jump on a large and violent wave.

Some criminals, when they sense that the ground is crumbling beneath their feet, forget all the splendid, equitable laws of nature, and then the lead starts to fly and you can't be sure of anything.

I warned the others that we were going into an area controlled by a man who didn't have the slightest respect for us, since according to his rules under-age teenagers counted for nothing. What might happen if those same teenagers caused him to lose his power? He wouldn't just let us go home in peace after humiliating him. He might declare an all-out war, turning us from hunters into quarry. We might seem – and even be – as tough as we liked, but if the ten of us had to fight a whole district whose Guardian had gone crazy and hated us, we'd be slaughtered like pigs on New Year's Day.

When we reached Centre, we found an enormous number of cars parked outside the bar we had visited at the start of our tour. So they were all there, perhaps waiting for us, perhaps discussing the situation. I sensed from the way the wind was blowing, from the breeze in our faces, that we were already riding the wave.

I looked at Gagarin as I climbed out of the car. I was worried about his state of mind, since he was going to have to talk on our behalf, and it was on his word, and the way he said it, that our future depended.

He seemed relaxed, and his sly smile told me he had a plan.

We didn't say anything to each other, so as not to seem indecisive in front of the others, who were now looking at us as we entered the bar.

All the people of Centre were sitting round a table eating and drinking, with Pavel the Guardian in the middle. He had a furious expression on his face, and was violently attacking a pork chop, spraying fat all over the place. Next to him was the troublemaker who had insulted us on our previous visit. As soon as he saw us he got up and started shouting wildly: 'What the hell do you want?', and hurling various insults at us.

We stood still, and the thug came towards us; now and then he turned back towards the table to see his master's face, to assess whether he approved of his behaviour. Pavel seemed indifferent; he went on eating, as if we didn't exist.

When the guy reached Gagarin and started shouting right in his face, Gagarin's left hand shot out and grabbed him by the neck – which was long and thin, like a turkey's – while his right hand slowly extracted his Tokarev from his pocket.

With one hand round the neck of this guy – who was trying to punch him but couldn't reach him and looked like a insect impaled on a needle – and the other holding his gun, Gagarin didn't take his eyes off Pavel. Then he raised his right hand and held it in that position for a moment: the fool started squealing like a wounded animal, trying to turn his face as far away as possible from the probable trajectory of Gagarin's right hand. But in vain. Suddenly that hand started hitting him in the face with the gun with terrible force and speed. The blows rained down.

The guy's face became one big wound. He passed out and his legs fell limp, but Gagarin still held him up by the neck and kept hitting him over and over again in the same place. Then, as suddenly as he had started, he stopped hitting him and dropped him on the floor like a sack. Ten seconds later he started kicking him. It was a massacre.

When Gagarin had finished, he went over to the table where Pavel was sitting, with a face like thunder. At this point, I realized that we all had our guns in our hands.

Gagarin hooked a seat towards himself with his foot, sat down on it, and without giving the people of Centre time to get over their confusion at his mauling of the thug, started insulting Pavel. He used very offensive words. He spoke to him as you speak to a person whose fate is sealed.

It was very risky, but if the terror tactics worked, if we succeeded in creating a division among Pavel's people, we would be all right. No self-respecting criminal will support a Guardian who because of his own mistakes is on the brink of ruin, so we were deliberately separating him from his people.

The decision Gagarin had taken was an extreme one, and it was a good thing he hadn't told us about it in advance, because we would certainly have opposed it. But now that he'd started we were going to have to give him our full support, or we'd be in a real mess.

The essence of what Gagarin was saying to Pavel was simple: he was rebuking him for incompetence, but above all he was insulting him, to humiliate him in the eyes of his companions.

His approach was working: the expression on Pavel's face had changed, he had gone very pale and his posture had altered too: he had been sitting with his shoulders erect and his chest puffed out, but now his shoulders had fallen, his chest had caved in and his whole body seemed shrunken. Only his eyes continued to glare with the same anger and contempt as before.

Gagarin told him he had been rude to us from the outset simply because we weren't adults, ignoring the fact that we had come as representatives of our district and of the entire Siberian community, and ignoring the fact that we were on a mission to resolve a situation which all the communities worthy to be called criminal considered extremely serious.

He said he had told our elders what had happened that morning – that Pavel had refused to talk to us and had sent us two of his assistants, who had proved untrustworthy, since they had made an appointment with us which they had failed to keep. This called into question his very authority, because it was clear that either he was a Guardian who had no control over affairs in his district, or – even worse – he was trying to conceal important information from us.

'The only thing we're interested in is in carrying out our mission,' said Gagarin to everyone present. 'It's not our responsibility to deal with everything else. The Authorities have been informed and will take their decisions: that's the important thing.'

While Gagarin was speaking Pavel glared at him scornfully, then suddenly he exploded in a fit of rage. He threw a dirty handkerchief at him, hitting him full in the face, then stood up and repeated the act he had performed on our previous visit: he ripped open his shirt, displaying his chest covered with old tattoos and with golden chains that hung down to his navel, and shouting a torrent of words in criminal slang the gist of which, leaving aside the profanities and insults, was:

'Since when have little boys been allowed to argue with adult criminals?'

Then he kept repeating the same phrase over and over again:

'Do you want to shoot an Authority? Well, shoot me, then!'

Gagarin stood motionless; I couldn't tell what he was thinking.

I noticed that Pavel's people were planning something; one had left the table and gone towards the kitchen.

Meanwhile Pavel came over to us and went along the line, shouting in each of our faces, asking if we still wanted to kill him.

Mel and the others kept still and silent; it was very clear that they didn't want to make a false move and were waiting for an order or a signal from Gagarin, who sat motionless at the table, with his back turned.

When Pavel came to me and I smelled his breath, reeking of wine and onions, coming out of his disgusting mouth together with the same words as before, I pulled Grandfather Kuzya's Nagant out of my pocket. Putting it against the brute's fat cheek and pressing so hard that the end of the barrel sunk into the skin of his face, which was distorted with surprise, I said:

'Grandfather Kuzya loaded this for me, do you understand? He said I could kill anyone who stops me catching the person who raped our sister. Even an Authority, if necessary.'

He stood rooted to the spot and glared at me with eyes full of anger, but also of sadness. Gagarin got up from the table and announced to all present that we were going to leave the district and that we would take Pavel with us, to make sure no one took a shot at us as we left.

A man stood up. His face was disfigured by a long scar which started from his forehead, ran across his right eye and nose and ended on his neck. Very calmly he said to us:

'No one will hurt you; we had already agreed on that before you came. We were intending to report Pavel to the Authorities.'

Little by little it emerged from his explanation that Pavel, with the help of some people who had already been locked up in a safe place, had planned a series of murders and other violent acts to provoke a war among the various communities. His aim was to gain control of the trafficking of alcohol, which was in the hands of a group of old criminals from various districts.

While the man with the scar was talking Pavel had turned pale, and with my pistol stuck into his cheek I could feel through the steel how much he was trembling. It was the end for him, and he knew it.

The man introduced himself as 'Paunch'. I had never heard of him. From his way of talking and standing, with his back bent and his head leaning forward, I realized that he had recently come out of prison. He confirmed this shortly afterwards: he had been released less than a month earlier, he said; and he added that when he was inside many had complained about the way Pavel supported the prison. He only sent aid to people he had chosen himself, he had never visited anyone and he had actually encouraged some internal wars, which had proved devastating. So on instructions from some elderly criminals Paunch had infiltrated Pavel's gang to check up on it and report back.

In other words we were talking to a *voydot*, a criminal executor and investigator who answered only to the old Authorities, and whose task it was to uncover injustices committed by the young Authorities and the Guardians.

It was the first time in my life I'd seen a person on such an assignment; usually they kept their identity secret, though of course Paunch might not have been his real name.

Paunch went on with his story: he said Pavel had hired a group of young Ukrainians to stir up trouble. During the past month they had killed two people, and no one had been able to trace them because everything had been organized to make it seem like an attack carried out by another district – a declaration of war. These were the same methods the police had used years before.

I couldn't believe my ears; the situation seemed surreal.

'What about Ksyusha? Why did they rape her?' I asked.

'Just for fun. Because they were out of their minds. There was no other reason,' replied Paunch. 'But it roused your community, so Pavel tried to keep them hidden, but they went on causing trouble all over the place.'

Everyone had seen them; they'd left traces everywhere. Gagarin and the others had clashed with them, and after the shoot-out they had tried to get out of town, taking the road through Balka. Stepan too had reported their presence in that district; they had taken cigarettes and beers from his kiosk without paying and beaten up Nixon, but he had managed to hurt one of them with his iron bar – which was quite an achievement for a disabled man. But a group of Armenians had been waiting for them at the entrance into Caucasus. They had tried to drive their four-by-four through an orchard, and had knocked down one Armenian, but then they had crashed into a little river that ran between Caucasus and Balka.

All this had happened in the space of two hours, and now these thugs were in the hands of the Armenians, who Paunch said were waiting for us.

Paunch said we would have to go there together, because he needed them to confirm in the presence of three witnesses that they had been paid by Pavel: only then could he take him before the old Authorities for judgement.

'You keep Pavel until you're sure what he's told you is true,' he concluded.

One of us, therefore, would have to give up his place to Pavel and go in another car with Paunch. Without giving the others time to make up their minds, I volunteered.

We went in a car driven by a boy from Centre.

'Are you really so keen to kill those people?' Paunch asked me when we had set off.

I thought this over for a moment before replying:

'I'm not a murderer; I get no pleasure out of killing. I just want justice to be done.'

Paunch didn't reply; he just nodded and turned towards the window. He remained like that, still and silent, until we reached Caucasus. He seemed struck by what I had said, but I wasn't sure whether he agreed or not.

When we arrived in Caucasus we drove to the house of an old Armenian called Frunzich. I knew him; he was a good friend of my grandfather's; he had been one of the organizers of the armed revolt of the prisoners in the Siberian gulags in 1953. He'd had a very sad life, but had never lost his cheerful disposition: even a short conversation with him left you feeling full of energy.

Frunzich was waiting for us in a car outside the front door of his house, with three other Armenians – young guys; one was only a teenager. When he saw us coming he switched on the ignition and drove off in front of us, to lead the way.

He took us to an old military warehouse on the outskirts of the district, where fields and patches of woodland began. It had been built by the Germans in the Second World War and had a number of basements which were often used by various criminals for dirty business, when it was necessary to shed a bit of blood.

In the yard there were about twenty Armenians, men and boys, all armed with rifles or Kalashnikovs. They were standing around a very battered four-by-four; its windscreen was smashed and a door on the right-hand side was missing. Inside the four-by-four sat five men. They looked terrified, and for some reason were stark naked.

Their clothes were piled up in front of the car near two bodies. One had a still bleeding wound in its neck, the other a hole in its head, from which the blood had stopped flowing.

I got out of the car after Paunch and went over to stand beside my friends, who were looking with interest at the faces of those five still alive animals.

'They're all ours. But first it's Paunch's turn,' said Gagarin.

Before I had time to wonder how Paunch was going to make them talk I saw Pavel collapse on the ground, felled by a very hard kick.

Lying there on the ground Pavel cut a pitiful figure. He reminded me of a fat little boy who had once lived in our district: this kid was clumsy in his movements, not so much because of his weight but because of the weakness of his character. He was convinced that he was practically disabled and was always falling over, sometimes deliberately, so he could attract the attention of others and cry and moan about his physical state. A few years later this pathetic great lump discovered that nature had endowed him with an artillery piece as long and powerful as the Dragunov precision rifle, and he abandoned his childish weaknesses. Especially with girls, whom he changed as frequently as a gentleman who is fastidious about personal hygiene changes his socks.

I always used to laugh when I thought about that boy, but now the association aroused a strange feeling of anger in me. Yes, I was angry. I had suddenly realized that although we were only one step away from completing our mission I felt no particular emotion, nothing. My only feelings were anger and weariness, two almost primitive, very animal sensations. I felt no higher human emotions at all.

There was Pavel, curled up on the ground, being beaten by the others. I looked at him and reflected that there was nothing certain and definite in life; this piece of human garbage, which now looked like a piece of meat being pounded into a steak, had only a short time before been full of its own importance and held real power in its hands.

When they had finished beating him up they loaded him into the boot of the car, as the rule requires because, since he was now tainted, he could no longer share the same space with honest criminals.

I don't think those five thugs sitting naked in the off-roader knew what was about to happen to them. I don't know what was going through their heads, but I looked at them and they seemed unconscious, as if they were under the effect of some drug.

I was sorry. I had thought so much of that moment. I had imagined the fear in their eyes, the words with which they would beg us to spare their lives, 'We don't want to die, have mercy . . .', and the words I would say in reply, constructing an elaborate speech that would make them realize the enormity of the crime they had committed and ensure that they spent their last moments in pure terror, feeling something resembling what Ksyusha had felt. But I only saw indifferent faces, which seemed to be urging us to get on with what we had come to do. Perhaps it was only my impression, because my friends seemed happy enough. They approached the four-by-four smiling with anticipation and pulled out their guns demonstratively. They loaded them so slowly you could hear the bullets slip out of the magazines and enter the barrels, clicking into place.

I looked at Mel: he was walking behind Gagarin. He had two pistols in his hand and his ugly face was twisted into a cruel scowl.

I grasped Grandfather Kuzya's Nagant and cocked it with my thumb. The drum turned and stopped with a loud click. I felt the trigger rise under my index finger: it was ready, taut.

In the other hand I had the Stechkin. Using the reloading technique I had been taught by Grandfather Plum I gripped it, released the safety catch with my index finger, pushed the rear sight against the edge of my belt and heard the mechanism move, driving the fixed part forward and loading the bullet into the barrel.

As I concentrated on the four-by-four, trying to decide which bastard to shoot first, Gagarin, without any concluding speech or warning, opened fire with both his guns. Immediately – almost simultaneously – the others fired, and I realized that I was firing too.

Grave fired with his eyes closed, and very fast. He emptied the magazines of his Makarovs before anyone else and stood there motionless, still holding the two pistols raised in the direction of the car, watching how those five guys were taking all our anger as it hit them in the form of lead.

Gagarin, by contrast, fired relaxedly, calmly, letting his bullets find their own route, without aiming carefully.

Mel fired, as he always did, chaotically, trying to reproduce the effect of a burst of machinegun fire with his pistol and sending lead in all directions. As a result no one ever dared to stand in front of him during a gunfight, except Gagarin, because he had a natural trust in Mel which was like a sixth sense.

Cat fired with such dedication and concentration he didn't realize his tongue was sticking out; he was trying his best, putting everything into it.

Gigit fired well, with absolute precision, without hurrying; he would take aim carefully, fire two or three shots, pause, then calmly take aim again.

Besa fired like the gunfighters of the Wild West, holding his guns at hip level and shooting with the regularity of a clock; he didn't hit very much but he looked impressive.

I fired without thinking too much about it, adopting my usual Macedonian technique. I didn't take aim, I fired at where I knew the guys were, and watched their dying convulsions.

Suddenly one of them opened a door and started running desperately towards the warehouse, then dashed down a corrugated iron tunnel, a narrow passage through which the daylight filtered, a kind of lighted street in the darkness. He ran with such energy that we stopped, rooted to the spot.

Mel fired a few shots after him but didn't hit him. Then Gagarin went over to an Armenian boy, a teenager, who was holding a Kalashnikov in his hands, and asked him if he could borrow his rifle 'for a second'. The boy, clearly shocked by what he had seen, passed him his Kalashnikov, and I noticed his hand was shaking.

Gagarin put the rifle to his shoulder and fired a long burst in the direction of the fugitive. The guy had already covered some thirty metres when the bullets hit him. Then Gagarin set off towards him, walking as if he were out for a stroll in the park. When he got close he fired another burst at the body lying on its back on the ground, which gave another twitch and then lay still.

Gagarin grabbed him by one foot and dragged him over to the car, putting him next to the other two bodies which had been there since the beginning of the massacre.

In the car there were four corpses disfigured by wounds. The four-by-four was riddled with holes and the air was slowly hissing out of one tyre. There was blood everywhere: splashes, pools spreading out on the ground to a radius of five metres, drips that fell from the car onto the floor, mingling with the petrol and becoming rivulets which ran towards us, under our feet.

There was total silence; none of those present said anything; everyone stood motionless, looking at what was left of those men.

We left the four-by-four and the bodies in the place where we had performed that act of justice.

Afterwards we went to old Frunzich's house. Paunch had to leave, but before going he said goodbye to us warmly and respectfully, saying we had done something that needed to be done.

Frunzich said the corpses would be disposed of by Armenians belonging to the family of the man who had been hurt in the attempt to stop the car; it would be a kind of personal satisfaction for them, and he assured us that 'there won't be so much as a cross over those dogs'.

Frunzich wasn't his usual humorous, cheerful self. He was serious, but in a positive way, as if he wanted to show us that he supported us. He didn't talk much; he brought us some bottles of excellent Armenian cognac.

We drank in silence; I was beginning to feel a heavy, overwhelming weariness.

Gagarin took out the bag with the money and told Frunzich he deserved the reward. Frunzich got up from the table, disappeared into another room and came back clutching a wad of money – five thousand dollars. He put it in the bag with the rest of the money, saying:

'I can't give any more because I'm a humble old man. Please, Gagarin, take it all to Aunt Anfisa and ask her to forgive us all; we're sinners, wicked people.'

We finished the third bottle in silence, and by the time we left Caucasus it was already dark; I almost fell asleep in the car. A lot of things were spinning round in my head, a mixture of memories and unpleasant sensations, as if I had left behind something unfinished, or poorly executed. It was a sad moment for me; I felt no satisfaction. I couldn't stop thinking about what had happened to Ksyusha. It was impossible to feel at peace.

Some time later I discussed this with Grandfather Kuzya.

'It was right to punish them for what they did,' I said, 'but by punishing them we haven't helped Ksyusha. What still tortures me is her pain, against which all our justice has been useless.'

He listened to me attentively, then smiled at me and said I should retrace the path of my grandfather's elder brother, go and live on my own in the woods, in the midst of nature; because I was too human to live among men.

I handed the Nagant back to him, but he wouldn't take it; he gave it to me.

A month or so later we heard that Pavel had been killed, along with three of his men who had participated in the plot against the criminal community. Their executioners had tied them to trees in the park, opposite Tiraspol police station, and hammered nails into their heads.

It was rumoured that the plot had in fact been hatched by the police, in an attempt to weaken the criminal community of our town.

They finally succeeded in doing this five years later, when they set many young criminals against the old ones and sparked off a bloody war. That was the beginning of the end of our community, which no longer exists as it did at the time of this story.

Grandfather Kuzya died of old age three years later, and his death – in addition to other events – caused an upheaval in the Siberian community. Many criminals of the old faith, unhappy with the military and police regime that had been established in our country, left Transnistria and returned to Siberia, or emigrated to far-off lands.

My father went to live in Greece, where he spent five years in prison. He still lives in Athens today.

Old Plum is still alive and still lives in his bar; he has gone deaf, so he shouts when he talks. His granddaughter, the one who made the best apple cakes in town and who was a good friend of mine, married a nice guy who sells accessories for personal computers, and together they went to live in Volgograd.

Uncle Fedya was strongly opposed to the advent of the government regime in Transnistria: he put up a stubborn resistance, trying as hard as he could to persuade the criminals to fight, but eventually he gave up and went to live in Siberia, in a small village on the River Lena, where he continues to perform his role as a Saint.

Barbos, meanwhile, has become a very important person in the criminal community: he made a deal with the police and now holds enormous power in our town.

In fact, Black Seed is the only caste that is protected by the police. They are hated by everyone else, but no one can do anything about it. They are in charge now; they control all the prisons and all criminal activities.

In the Georgian community there has been a bloody war with the Armenians, which brought the young to power. They are still at war with them now. Mino was killed in the course of the fighting. He arrived with a gunshot wound at the hospital where his wife had just given birth to a son. He never got to see his baby.

Grandfather Frunzich decided to leave Bender, also because of the war between the Georgians and the Armenians. Like many old men of both those communities, he went to live in his homeland, where now he does some small-scale alcohol trafficking.

Stepan still runs his street kiosk, but no longer sells weapons; the criminals of Black Seed have stopped him, so he now makes his living by selling cigarettes and the occasional batch of counterfeit vodka. His daughter has finished her studies and found a job in an architects' studio in Moscow. Nixon helps Stepan as loyally as ever; he still hates communists and blacks but has finally made friends with Mel, although to achieve this Mel had to sacrifice his Game Boy.

Mel says, though, that Nixon has grown a lot more white hairs lately and is ageing too quickly.

Gagarin only lived for three years after this story: he was killed in St Petersburg because he had got involved in business with some people who enjoyed the protection of the police and the former KGB. We didn't hear about his death until later, when a girlfriend of Gagarin's contacted his parents to tell them he was buried in the cemetery of Ligovo.

Cat moved to southern Russia, where for a while he belonged to the gang of a Siberian criminal who robbed HGVs en route from the Asiatic countries. Then he met a girl from Rostov, a land of Cossacks, and went to live with her in the countryside by the River Don. Officially he is no longer involved in criminal activities; he has three children, two boys and a girl, and goes hunting and does carpentry jobs with his wife's father and brothers. Mel has been to visit him several times, and on those occasions Cat unsuccessfully tried to persuade Mel to marry his wife's younger sister.

Grave was arrested in Moscow during the attempted robbery of an armoured van, and sentenced to sixteen years in prison. In jail he killed two people, so he was sentenced to life and transferred to the special prison of Ust-Ilimsk, where he still is. It's impossible to contact him because of the strict regime at the prison.

Gigit and Besa robbed a number of banks together, then the anti-robbery squad managed to track them down and kept them under surveillance for a while. At that point they fell into an elaborate trap. Acting on information provided by an informer who was being manipulated by the police, Gigit and Besa robbed a certain bank: that same evening, however, they were killed in their room in the Inturist Hotel of the town of Tver by the police, who walked off with the loot. Mel went on his own to bring their bodies home, and buried them in the old cemetery of Bender; hardly any of us went to the funeral – only Mel and a few relatives.

Mel still lives in Transnistria, close to his parents. We chat on the phone now and then. He no longer carries out any criminal activities, because he has no one to work with and can't manage on his own. For a while he worked as a bodyguard for an Authority from the new generation, but he tired of that. After doing a course, he tried teaching aikido to a group of children, but that came to nothing because he always turned up for lessons drunk. Now he doesn't do anything; he spends all his time playing on his PlayStation, goes out with the occasional girl and now and then helps someone collect their debts.

Ksyusha never got over it. From the day of the rape she didn't communicate with anyone; she was always silent, with downcast eyes, and hardly ever went out. Sometimes I managed to coax her out and took her for boat trips on the river, but it was like lugging a sack around with you. Previously she had loved going out in a boat: she would constantly change position, lie down in the bows and trail her hands in the water, lark about, get tangled up in the fishing nets, play with the fish we had just caught, talk to them and give them names.

After the rape she was motionless, limp; the most she would do was stretch out a finger to touch the water. Then she would leave it there and sit watching her hand immersed in the water, until I picked her up in my arms to lift her on to the bank.

For a while I thought she would gradually recover, but she got worse and worse, until she stopped eating. Aunt Anfisa was always crying; she tried taking her to different hospitals, to various specialists, but they all said the same thing: this behaviour was due to her old mental disturbance, and there was nothing to be done about it. At the worst moments Aunt Anfisa gave her vitamin injections and put her on a drip feed to keep her alive.

The day I left the country, Ksyusha was sitting on the bench outside the front door of her house. She was holding her game, the woollen flower, which in Siberia is used as a decorative detail on pullovers.

Six years after this sad story, one night I received a phone call from Mel: Ksyusha had died. 'She hadn't moved for a long time,' he told me. 'She let herself die, little by little.' After her death, Aunt Anfisa went to live in the house of a neighbour, who needed someone to help his wife with their children.

I left my country; I've been through many different experiences and stories, and I've tried to do what I thought was right with my life, but I'm still unsure about many things that make this world go round. Above all, the more I go on, the more convinced I am that justice as a concept is wrong – at least human justice.

Two weeks after we had handed out our own kind of justice, a stranger arrived at our house; he said he was a friend of Paunch's. He explained to me that Paunch had gone away somewhere and would not be coming back, but before leaving he had asked him to give me something. He handed me a little parcel; I took it without opening it, and out of politeness I asked him in and introduced my grandfather to him.

He stayed in our house until the next day. He ate and drank with my grandfather, talking about various criminal questions: ethics, the lack of education among the young, how the criminal communities had changed over the years, and above all the influence of the European and American countries, which was destroying the young generation of Russian criminals.

I sat near them all the time, and when they emptied the bottle I would hurry down to the cellar to refill it from the barrel.

After our guest had gone I opened Paunch's parcel. Inside it I found a knife called *finka*, which means 'Finnish', the typical weapon of the criminals of St Petersburg and north-western Russia. It was a used – or, as we say in Russian, 'worldly-wise' – weapon, with a beautiful haft made of white bone. There was also a sheet of paper, on which Paunch had written in pencil:

'Human justice is horrible and wrong, and therefore only God can judge. Unfortunately, in some cases we're obliged to overrule his decisions.'

FREE FALL

On my eighteenth birthday I was abroad. I was studying physical education in a sports school, trying to build myself a different future, outside the criminal community.

It was a very strange time for me: I read widely, met more and more new people and was beginning to understand that the path of crime, which I had previously seen as good and honest, was an extreme one, which society saw as 'abnormal'. But 'normal' society didn't impress me greatly either; people seemed blind and deaf to the problems of others, and even to their own problems. I couldn't understand the mechanisms that propelled the 'normal' world, where ultimately people were divided, had nothing in common and were unable to feel the pleasure of sharing things. I found the standard Russian morality annoying: everyone was ready to judge you, to criticize your life, but then they'd spend their evenings in front of the television, they'd fill the fridge with good cheap food, get drunk together at family parties, envy their neighbours and try to be envied in their turn. Flashy cars, preferably foreign, identical clothes, to be like everyone else, Saturday evening in the village bar showing off, drinking a can of Turkish-made beer and telling others that everything was fine, that 'business' was going well, even though you were only a humble exploited worker and couldn't see the true reality of your life.

Post-Soviet consumerism was an appalling thing to someone like me. People wallowed in branded detergents and toothpastes, no one would drink anything unless it was imported and women smeared themselves with industrial quantities of French face-creams they saw advertised every day on television, believing they'd make them look like the models in the commercials.

I was tired and disorientated; I didn't think that I'd ever succeed in fulfilling myself in some honest and useful way.

However, I had never stopped attending the sports club in my town. I did yoga: I was slim and supple, I could do the exercises well and everyone was pleased with me. One of my wrestling coaches had advised me to attend the yoga lessons given by a teacher in Ukraine, a man who had studied for many years in India. So I often went to Ukraine for advanced courses, and every year, with a group from my sports club, I spent a month and a half in India.

By the age of eighteen I was about to take my diploma as a yoga instructor, but I didn't like the way things were run at my school; I often quarrelled with the teacher, who told me I was a rebel and only let me stay on because many of the other boys were on my side.

The teacher exploited a lot of his students. He would get them to do his accounts, paying them a pittance, and then justify his behaviour with strange arguments connected to yoga philosophy, but which in my view were simply opportunistic. The only reason I put up with all this was that I needed to get that diploma, which would enable me to continue my studies at any state university, and so avoid compulsory military service. I dreamed of opening a sports school of my own and teaching yoga to the people of my town.

But it was to remain just a dream. Because just before the end of the course something very unpleasant happened: one of the boys in our yoga class died of a heart attack.

Many people who do yoga believe in things that are remote from everyday experience. This teacher always used to tell us about people who after years of exercises had been able to fly, or turn into various life forms, and other such claptrap; I never listened to him, but there were others in my group who believed those things. Among these people was Sergey. He had had heart problems since birth, and he needed regular medical treatment and supervision from doctors, but our teacher had led him to believe that the problem could be resolved with the help of exercises. Sergey really believed his weak heart could be cured in that way. I often tried to explain to him that yoga couldn't treat serious illnesses, but he wouldn't listen to me; he always said it was just a matter of exercise.

One day Sergey went to a big gathering of the schools of yoga in Hungary, and on the way back, in the train, he had a heart attack and died. I was upset, nothing more than that; I wasn't particularly close to him and we weren't great friends, but to my mind his death was entirely on the conscience of our teacher.

The upshot was that I told the teacher exactly what I thought, and we quarrelled. He expelled me from the school, so I didn't get my diploma; instead they gave me a kind of certificate of participation which entitled me to perform some disciplines in public. A complete farce, in other words.

All this happened in the spring, when Transnistria was blooming like a bride dressed in white, full of scents and refreshing breezes.

I did nothing for a while, except think about what had happened; then I went to stay with my Grandfather Nikolay in the Tayga. We hunted together, made nets and traps for catching fish in the river, took saunas and talked a lot about life.

Grandfather Nikolay had lived alone in the woods since the age of twenty-four, and had a wisdom all of his own. It was good for me to be with him during that period.

* * *

When I returned to Transnistria I organized a big party on the river with my friends to celebrate my birthday, which was already a few months past. We took ten boats, filled them with bottles of wine, some of the bread that Mel's grandmother made and our fishing equipment, and set off upstream for a place called 'The Big Drip'.

The spot was renowned for its beauty and tranquillity, and was situated about fifty kilometres from the town. At this point the river widened out and here and there formed clusters of little interlinked pools, where the water was warm and still. The current hardly ever reached there, except when the river was high in March and early April, the period of the floods. Many fish, especially the wels catfish, would stop there, and we used to go and catch them. We would set out at night in our boats, turn on a big torch, and shine it down into the water: attracted by the light, the fish would come up to the surface, and then we'd kill them with a sort of long-handled wooden mallet specially made for that kind of fishing. One person would hold the torch while another stood ready to strike with the mallet; everything had to be done in silence, because the slightest noise or movement would frighten the fish, and then it would be at least another couple of hours before you could entice them back up to the surface.

I used to team up with Mel, because nobody else would fish with him, as he would never keep quiet at the crucial moment. He was also a menace with the mallet: once he had missed the wels but hit his fishing partner, our friend Besa, breaking his arm. Since then, whenever he asked anyone if he could go with them they would make excuses, claiming they'd already agreed to go with someone else. As a result he often got left on the bank, but sometimes I relented and took him along; unlike the others, I could usually get him to behave at the critical moment.

We had a pleasant trip upriver to the Big Drip; the weather was beautiful and the water seemed blessed by the Lord – it offered no resistance, even though we were going upstream. My boat's motor worked very well that day and didn't stall even once. In short, everything was perfect, like on a picture postcard.

When we arrived we had lunch, and I overdid the wine a bit, which made me too good-humoured – unusually so – and as a result for the umpteenth time I agreed to team up with Mel, who was delighted we weren't going to leave him ashore.

I was feeling so relaxed I allowed him to hold the mallet. Well, 'allowed' isn't really the right word; he just sat down in my boat and, without asking, picked up the mallet, with a nonchalant glance at me. I said nothing; I just showed him my fist to indicate that if he made a mistake he was in serious trouble.

We set off for our pool. Each boat entered a different one: you had to be absolutely alone, because if everyone had hunted in the same pool, at the noise of the first blow the fish would have hidden on the bottom and the other boats wouldn't have caught anything.

The night was beautiful; there were lots of stars in the sky and in the middle a faint tinge of white which gleamed and shimmered – it seemed like magic. In the distance you could hear the sound of the wind blowing over the fields, and sometimes its long, thin whistle came close, as though passing between us. The scent of the fields mingled with that of the woods and was constantly changing – you seemed to catch the smell of acacia and lime leaves, separately, and then that of the moss on the river bank. The frogs sang their serenades in chorus; now and then a fish would come up to the surface and make a pleasant sound, a kind of plash, in the water. At one point three roe deer came out of the wood to quench their thirst: they made a lapping noise with their tongues and afterwards sneezed, as horses do.

I was carried away by the enchantment of it. If someone had asked me what heaven was I might well have said it was this moment prolonged for all eternity.

The only thing that stopped me rising towards heaven was the presence of Mel: as soon as I looked at him I was filled with a heavy sense of reality, and I realized that as long as that person – like a penance which I was destined to endure – continued to be at my side, I would never be able to free myself completely from my coarse human frame.

'Keep your mouth shut, Mel, or I'll crown you with that mallet,' I said, starting to row slowly, so as not to make too much noise.

Mel was in a state of absolute concentration. He sat in the middle of the boat, gripping the mallet with both hands, as if he were afraid it would try to get away.

When we got to the middle of the pool I took out an old underwater torch. I turned it on and gradually lowered it, leaning out over the edge of the boat. The light under the water created a beautiful effect – it shone down to a depth of ten metres, where you could see lots of little details – tiny fish circling round the torch in a kind of lap of honour.

Mel stood over me, ready with the mallet, awaiting my signal.

Usually the arrival of the catfish was marked by a large black shadow rising up from the bottom and advancing towards the light. As soon as you saw the shadow it was essential to move the torch at once: to bring it up slowly, without making a noise, so that the fish would follow it, but without ever quite reaching it. When the lamp reached the surface and came out of the water it was the climactic moment: the person with the mallet had to bring it down with all his strength on the spot where an instant before the lamp had been, and hit the fish. If you hesitated a moment and the fish managed to touch the lamp, it would immediately dive down again, because catfish are very cowardly creatures and are frightened of any contact with objects they don't know. So to catch the fish with this technique it was important to move in perfect harmony.

I peered into the water, and suddenly I saw a shadow rise from the bottom, so I started to lift the torch by slowly pulling the string. Mel, behind me, raised the mallet, ready to strike.

I had no doubts: it was clearly a catfish and it was coming up very quickly. I just had to recover the torch in time.

When I had nearly pulled it right up and only a small part of it remained in the water, Mel brought down the mallet with such violence I heard it whistle through the air, as if a bullet had passed close to my ears.

'Christ!' I shouted, and just managed to take my hands off the torch before Mel's mallet struck it with brutal force. The torch smashed and the light went out instantly. In the darkness I heard a faint sigh from Mel:

'Shit! What a stupid fish, I thought it was coming up faster . . .'

He was still standing over me, mallet in hand. I got to my feet, picked up an oar and without a word hit him on the back.

'Why?' he asked me, alarmed, retreating towards the bow of the boat.

'For Christ's sake, Mel, you're a fool! What the hell did you hit the torch for?'

I heard the voices of Gagarin, Gigit and Besa on the bank.

'What's happening? Have you two gone crazy?' asked Gagarin.

'Ah, nothing's happening! It's just that the fish is so big they can't get it onto the boat,' said Gigit sarcastically, knowing perfectly well that that bonehead Mel must have ruined the fishing as usual.

'Hey, Kolima!' shouted Besa. 'You can go ahead and kill him, don't worry. None of us saw a thing. We'll say he went swimming on his own and was drowned.'

I was angry, but at the same time the situation made me laugh.

'Switch on that motor. Let's get back to the bank,' I said to Mel gruffly.

'Don't you want to have another go?' he asked me, sounding rather crestfallen.

I looked at him. His face in the darkness seemed to belong to a demon. I said to him with a smile:

'Another go? And what torch are we going to do it with?'

On the bank everyone laughed.

When we reached the bank, Besa, who was always joking, looked into the boat and confirmed:

'Just as I thought, brothers! These two have eaten all the fish themselves! And they were so desperate not to share it with us they've eaten it raw!'

And they all roared with laughter. Mel laughed too.

I alone was a bit sad. I had a feeling something new was about to happen in my life; I sensed an air of change around me.

We had a fantastic party. The others had caught some big wels catfish; we cleaned and prepared them for cooking in the earth. Everyone seemed a bit withdrawn, though, as if they were aware that we were about to go through a significant period of change. We talked about things of the past; each boy told stories about his childhood, and the others laughed or sat in silence, respecting the atmosphere that was created by the narrative.

We sat around the fire all night, until dawn, watching the sparks and the pieces of ash that had turned to dust rise up into the air, mingling with the faint gleams of the morning which was bringing a new day.

I too laughed and told a few stories, but I was filled with a new emotion, a kind of sad nostalgia. I felt that I was standing in front of a great void towards which I had to take the first step, and this was my last chance to look back and fix in my memory all the beautiful and important things I was about to leave behind me.

After drinking wine and eating and talking until dawn, I went away to sleep in the woods. I took a blanket from my boat, wrapped it around me and walked towards the bushes, where there was a freshness in the air that brought relief. My friends were scattered around; some were asleep in front of the nearly dead embers. Mel was lying in the middle of the track that led to the pool where we had left the boat: it was a very muddy path, but he was sound asleep, with his arms round an oar. Besa was wandering around with an empty bottle, asking the boys if anyone knew where the supplies were. Nobody answered him – not because they didn't know where the things were, but because they were all in a total stupor.

As I walked along, wrapped up in my blanket, I felt a sense of disgust; I remember that although I was drunk and couldn't even walk straight, I thought with absolute lucidity that we were a bunch of pathetic drunkards who were only capable of getting into trouble and making a mess of our lives.

As soon as I lay down on the ground, I fell asleep. By the time I woke up it was already evening and darkness was beginning to fall. My friends were calling my name. I opened my eyes and lay there, not moving; I felt even more strongly than the night before that something was really about to happen in my life. I didn't want to get up; I wanted to stay in the bushes.

When we got home I took a sauna. I lit the stove and burned some wood, then I prepared the dry oak branches and put them in the warm water so I could use them later for the massage. I mixed some pine extract with some lime essence and put it by the stove, to infuse the air that I would breathe. I made myself two litres of a tisane of dog rose, lime, mint and cherry blossom. I spent the day relaxing in the sauna, lying naked on the wooden benches which slowly cooked me. Now and then, as I lay surrounded by that aromatized steam, I drank the hot tisane in big gulps, without noticing how much it scalded my throat.

That night I slept flat out, as if I had fallen into a void. The next day I woke up and went out of the house. I opened the mail box to see if anything was there and found a small piece of white paper with a red line across it from one corner to the other. It said that the military office of the Russian Federation asked me to present myself for verification, bringing my personal documents. It added that this instruction was being sent for the third and last time, and that if I didn't present myself within three days I would receive a criminal conviction for 'refusal to pay my debt to the nation in the form of military service'.

I thought the note was a trifle, a mere formality. I went back indoors, fetched my documents and, without even changing my clothes, set off in my flip-flops towards the address indicated, a place on the other side of town, where there was an old Russian military base.

At the entrance I showed the note to the guards and they opened the door, without a word.

'Where do I have to go?' I asked one of them.

'Go straight on. It's all the same anyway . . .' a soldier replied, without enthusiasm and with obvious irritation.

'Bloody idiot,' I thought, and I headed for a large office where there was a notice saying: 'Military service and new arrivals section.'

The office was dark; I could hardly see a thing. At the back there was a little window in the wall, out of which there came a dismal, faint, yellow light.

There was the sound of someone tapping on a typewriter. I approached and saw a young woman, in military uniform, sitting at a small desk, typing with one hand and clutching a mug of tea in the other. She took little sips and kept blowing into the mug to cool it.

I leaned on the counter and craned my neck: I saw that on her knees, under the desk, the woman had an open newspaper. There was an article about Russian pop stars, with a photo of a singer wearing a crown decorated with peacock feathers. I felt even sadder.

'Hello. Excuse me, ma'am, I've received this,' I said, holding out the note.

The woman turned towards me and for a second looked at me as if she couldn't understand where she was and what was happening. It was clear that I had interrupted a train of thoughts and personal dreams. With a quick movement she picked up the newspaper that lay at her knees and put it upside down behind the typewriter, so that I couldn't see it. Then she put down her mug of tea and, without getting up or saying anything, and with an indifferent expression on her face, she took the white sheet of paper with the red line from my hands. She glanced at it for a moment and then asked, in a voice that sounded to me as if it belonged to a ghost:

'Documents?'

'Which documents, mine?' I asked awkwardly, taking my passport and all the other things out of my trouser pocket.

She eyed me rather scornfully and said through clenched teeth:

'Well, certainly not mine.'

She took my documents and put them in a safe. Then she took a form from a shelf and started filling it in. She asked me my first name, surname, date and place of birth, and home address. Then she went on to more personal information. After asking me for my parents' details, she said:

'Have you ever been arrested? Have you had any problems with the law?'

'I've never had any problems with the law, but the law seems to have problems with me now and them . . . I've been arrested dozens of times, I can't remember how many. And I've done two stretches in juvenile prison.'

At this her expression changed. She tore up the form she had been filling in and took another, larger one, with a line running from one corner to the other, like that on the postal note.

We started afresh; once again, all my personal details, including, this time, those of my convictions: the article numbers, and the dates. Then my health: diseases, vaccinations; she even asked me if I consumed alcohol or drugs, if I smoked cigarettes. And so it went on for an hour . . . I couldn't remember the exact dates of my convictions, so I made them up on the spur of the moment, trying at least to get the right time of year, and if possible the right month.

When we had finished I tried to explain to her that there must be some mistake, that I couldn't do military service, that I had asked for and been granted a postponement of six months, promising that in the meantime I would finish a course of study and then go to university. If everything went according to plan, I added, I was going to open a school of physical education for children, there in Bender.

She listened to me – but without looking me in the eye, which worried me. Then she gave me a sheet of paper: it said that from that moment onwards I was the property of the Russian government and my life was protected by the law.

I couldn't understand what all this meant in practical terms.

'It means that if you try to escape, self-harm or commit suicide, you'll be prosecuted for damaging government property,' she informed me coldly.

I suddenly felt trapped. Everything around me began to seem much more ominous and sinister than before.

'Listen,' I snapped, 'I couldn't give a shit about your law. I'm a criminal, period. If I have to go to jail I'll go, but I'll never pick up the weapons of your fucking government . . .'

I was furious, and when I started to talk like that I immediately felt strong, even stronger than that absurd situation. I was sure, absolutely sure, that I would succeed in changing this machine that was supposed to regulate my life.

'Where are the fucking generals, or whatever you call your authorities? I want to see one and talk to him, since I can't make you understand!' I raised my voice, and she looked at me with the same indifferent expression as before.

'If you want to speak to the Colonel, he's here, but I don't think it'll get you anywhere . . . In fact, I advise you to keep calm. Don't make things worse for yourself . . .'

It was good advice, if I think about it now. She was telling me something important, I'm sure of it; she was trying to show me a better way, but at the time I was blinded.

I felt sick. How can this be, I said to myself. Only this morning I was free, I had my plans for the day, for my future, for the rest of my life, and now, because of a piece of paper, I was losing my freedom. I wanted to shout and argue with someone, show them how angry I was. I needed it. I interrupted her, shouting in her face:

'Jesus, Blessed Lord on the cross! If I want to speak to someone, I speak to him, and that's that! Where is this fucking commandant, general, or whatever he's called?'

She got up from her chair and asked me to calm down and wait for ten minutes, on the bench. I looked around but couldn't see any bench. 'Oh for Christ's sake, what is this place? Everyone's crazy here,' I thought, as I waited in the dark.

Suddenly a door opened and a soldier, a middle-aged man, called me by my first name:

'Come with me, Nikolay. The Colonel's expecting you!'

I jumped up like a spring and hurried towards him, eager to get out of that dingy little office as quickly as possible.

We went out onto a small square surrounded by buildings all painted white, with propaganda drawings and posters with pictures of the exercises the soldiers had to do to learn how to march in a group. We crossed the square and entered a room full of light, with large windows and lots of flowers in pots. Among the flowers was a bench, and beside the bench a large ashtray.

'Wait here. The Colonel will call you from this door. You can smoke if you like . . .'

The soldier was kind; he talked to me in a very friendly tone. I had calmed down and felt more confident; it seemed that my situation was at last going to be cleared up and my voice heard.

'Thank you, sir, but I don't smoke. Thank you very much for your kindness.'

I tried to be as polite as possible myself, to create a good impression.

The soldier took his leave and left me alone. I sat there on the bench, listening to the sounds made by the soldiers, who had gone out onto the square for their drill. I watched from a window.

'Left, left, one, two, three!' came the desperate shouts of the instructor, a young man in an immaculate military uniform, marching with a platoon of men who didn't seem very keen on drilling.

'Nikolay! You can come in, son!' a very rough male voice called me. Despite its kind, almost gentle tone, there was something false about it, an unpleasant tune in the background.

I approached the door, knocked and asked for permission to enter.

'Come in, son, come in!' said a big strong man sitting behind an enormous desk, his voice still amiable and kindly.

I entered, closed the door and took a few steps towards him, then stopped abruptly.

The Colonel was about fifty years old and very stocky. His head, which was shaven, was marked by two long scars. His green uniform was too small for him; his neck was so wide the collar of his jacket was stretched tight and seemed on the point of tearing. His hands were so fat you could hardly see his fingernails, so deep did they sink into the flesh. One split ear was a sure sign of an experienced wrestler. His face might have been copied from the Soviet military propaganda posters of the Second World War: coarse features, straight thick nose, large resolute eyes. On the left side of his chest, a dozen medals hung in a row.

'Jesus be with me, this guy's worse than a cop . . .' I was already imagining how our meeting might end. I didn't know where to start; I felt incapable of expressing what I wanted to say in front of someone like him.

Suddenly, interrupting my thoughts, he started the conversation. He was looking at a folder which resembled those in which the police keep classified information about criminals.

'I'm reading your story, my dear Nikolay, and I like you more and more. You didn't do too well at school – in fact you hardly ever attended – but you belonged to four different sports clubs . . . Excellent! I did a lot of sport myself when I was young. Studying is for eggheads; real men do sport and train to become fighters . . . You did wrestling, swimming, long-distance running and shooting . . . Excellent! You're a well-qualified young man; I think you've got a great future in the army . . . There's only one blemish. Tell me, how did you get two convictions? Did you steal?'

He looked me straight in the eye, and if he could have done he would have looked into my brain.

'No, I didn't steal anything. I don't steal . . . I hit some guys on two different occasions. I was charged with "attempted murder with serious consequences".'

'Never mind, don't worry . . . I used to get into fights when I was young; I quite understand! Men need to carve out their own space in the world, to define themselves, and the best way of doing that is to fight. That's where you find out who's worth something and who's not worth a spit . . .'

He was talking to me as if he were about to give me a prize. I hesitated; I didn't know what to say now, and above all I didn't know how I was going to explain to him that I had no intention of doing military service.

'Listen, son, I couldn't care less about your past in prison, the criminal prosecutions and all the rest of it; as far as I'm concerned you're a good lad, may Christ bless you, and I'm going to give you a hand because I like you. I've got your whole life in writing here, since your first day at school . . .' He laid the file on the desk and closed it, tying up the two ribbons at the side. 'I'll give you two choices, something I only do in exceptional cases, for people I think very highly of. I can put you in the border guard, on the frontier with Tajikistan: you'll have a good career, and if you like climbing mountains that's the place for you. Alternatively I can put you in the parachute regiment, a school for professionals: you'll become a sergeant after six months and you'll have a good career there too; and in time you'll be able to join the special forces, despite your past. The army will give you everything: a salary, a home, friends and an occupation suited to your abilities. Well, what do you say? Which do you prefer?'

It was like listening to the monologue of a madman. He was saying things that were complete nonsense to me. The army giving me everything I had already! How could I explain to him that I didn't need an occupation suited to my abilities, or friends, or a salary, or a home . . .

I felt like you do when you get on the wrong train and suddenly realize there's no way of making it go back.

I took a bit of air into my lungs and blurted out my reply:

'To be honest, sir, I want to go home!'

He changed in a second. His face went red, as if an invisible man was strangling him. His hands closed into fists and his eyes took on a strange tinge, something that might have had a distant resemblance to the sky before a storm.

He picked up my personal file and threw it in my face. I just managed to put my hands up in time to parry the blow. The file hit my hands and came open, and the papers scattered all over the room, on the desk, on the windowsill, on the floor.

I stood as stiff and motionless as a statue. He continued to glare at me with hatred. Then he suddenly started shouting in a terrible voice, which immediately sounded to me like his real voice:

'You wretch! So you want to wallow in shit? All right, I'll make you wallow in shit! I'll send you where you won't even have time to pull down your trousers, you'll be shitting yourself so much, and every time it happens you'll remember me, you ungrateful little upstart! You want to go home? All right, from today your home will be the brigade of saboteurs! They'll teach you what life's really like!'

He was shouting at me, and I stood there as stiff as a ramrod, not moving, while inside I was completely empty.

It was better getting beaten up by the cops; at least there I knew how it would end, whereas here everything was unknown to me. I felt a tremendous anxiety, because I didn't know anything about soldiers, I didn't understand why I should shit myself and above all I couldn't remember who the saboteurs were . . .

'Out! Get out!' he pointed to the door.

Without a word I turned round and went out of his office.

Outside, a soldier was waiting for me. He saluted.

'Sergeant Glazunov! Follow me, comrade!' he said in a voice which sounded like the piston of a Kalashnikov when it sends the cartridge into the barrel.

'A flea-bitten dog is your comrade,' I thought, but said in a humble tone:

'Excuse me, Sergeant, sir, may I use the toilet?'

He looked at me in a strange way, but didn't say no.

'Of course. Down to the end of the corridor and turn left!'

I walked down the corridor; he followed me, and when I went into the toilet he stood outside waiting for me.

Inside the toilet I climbed up to the window at the top and since it didn't have any bars I jumped down without any problem. Outside, in the garden behind the office, there was no one around.

'To hell with this madhouse, I'm going home . . .'

With this and other similar thoughts in my head I started walking towards the exit of the base. There the guard stopped me. He was a young soldier, about the same age as me, very thin and with a slight squint in one eye.

'Documents!'

'I haven't got them with me. I came to visit a friend . . .'

The soldier looked at me suspiciously.

'Show me your permit to leave the base!'

At these words my heart sank into my boots. I decided to act stupid:

'What do you mean, permit? What are you talking about? Open that door! I want to get out . . .' I walked towards the door, going past the soldier, but he pointed his assault rifle at me, shouting:

'Stop or I'll shoot!'

'Ah get out of the way!' I replied, grabbing his gun by the barrel and tearing it out of his hands.

The soldier tried to punch me in the face, but I defended myself with the butt of the gun. Suddenly someone dealt me a hard blow on the head from behind. I felt my legs go limp and my mouth dry. I took two deep breaths, and at the third I passed out.

I woke up a few minutes later. I was lying on the ground, surrounded by soldiers. The sergeant who should have been accompanying me was also there; he looked anxious, and was walking around saying to everyone in a conspiratorial tone:

'Nothing's happened, everything's okay. Remember, nobody saw anything. I'll take care of him.'

It was clear he was worried he might be punished for his carelessness.

He came over to me and gave me a kick in the ribs.

'Do that again, you bastard, and I'll personally kill you!'

He gave me a couple more kicks, then held out his hand and helped me to my feet. He took me to a kind of house with barred windows and a steel-clad door. It looked just like a prison.

We went in. There wasn't much light and everything seemed dirty and grey, neglected, abandoned. There was a long narrow corridor, with three more steel-clad doors. At the end of the corridor a soldier appeared, a lad of about twenty, quite thin but with a kindly face. He was holding a big bunch of keys of different sizes and kept moving them, making a strange noise, which in that situation almost made me burst into tears of sadness and despair. With one of the keys the young soldier opened a door, and the sergeant ushered me into a very small, narrow room, with a tiny barred window. There was a wooden bunk against the wall.

I looked at the place and I couldn't believe it. Just like that, simply, suddenly, I had ended up in a cell.

The sergeant said in a very authoritarian tone to the soldier, who was clearly some kind of guard:

'Feed him at suppertime like all the others, but be careful: he's violent . . . Don't take him to the bathroom on your own; wake up your partner and both of you go together. He's dangerous; he attacked the guard at the gate and tried to steal his submachinegun . . .'

The soldier with the keys looked at me in alarm: it was obvious he couldn't wait to lock me up.

The sergeant looked me in the eye and said:

'Stay here and wait!'

I, too, looked him straight in the eye, making no attempt to conceal my hatred. 'What the hell am I supposed to wait for? What's all this about?'

'Wait for the end of the world, you arsehole! If I tell you to wait, wait and don't ask any questions. I'll decide what you have to wait for!'

The sergeant motioned to the soldier to shut the door and went out triumphantly.

Before locking me in, the soldier came towards me and asked me a question:

'What's your name, boy?'

His voice seemed calm and not aggressive.

'Nikolay,' I replied quietly.

'Don't worry, Nikolay, you're safer here than you would be with them . . . Have a good rest, because in a couple of days they'll be taking you to the train that will carry you to Russia, to the brigade you've been assigned to . . . Have they told you where they're sending you yet?'

'The Colonel said they're putting me in the saboteurs . . .' I replied in an exhausted voice.

He paused, then asked me in alarm:

'The saboteurs? Holy Christ, what's he got against you? What have you done to deserve this?'

'I've received a Siberian education,' I replied, as he closed the door.

FREE FALL
A SNIPER'S STORY FROM CHECHNYA
NICOLAI LILIN

A unique and remarkable memoir of the war in Chechnya by the internationally acclaimed author of *Siberian Education*.

Free Fall is a brutal but engrossing memoir of the Second Chechen War, told through the eyes of a young Russian soldier. Nicolai Lilin was conscripted and then trained as a sniper in an unorthodox Russian Special Forces regiment called the Saboteurs. Together, this elite band of men, which operated outside the purview of traditional military codes, fought their way through multiple assignments, including guerilla warfare in inhospitable mountainous terrain and intense hand-to-hand fighting in urban areas. Along the way, they faced mercenary fighters, anti-personnel mines and torture of the most extreme kind.

Both an immediate sequel to the author's previous book, *Siberian Education*, and a remarkable stand-alone memoir in its own right, *Free Fall* offers a unique perspective on one of the most controversial wars in living memory. Lilin writes with honesty and extreme cynicism, and with a sharp eye for the banality of evil. It is an unflinching, unforgiving and unputdownable read.

£12.99

978 184767 971 0

Available as an
e eBook

978 085786 131 3

www.canongate.tv